John Christian

Behar Proverbs

Classified and Arranged According to their Subject-Matter

John Christian

Behar Proverbs
Classified and Arranged According to their Subject-Matter

ISBN/EAN: 9783337180423

Printed in Europe, USA, Canada, Australia, Japan

Cover: Foto ©Paul-Georg Meister /pixelio.de

More available books at **www.hansebooks.com**

TRÜBNER'S
ORIENTAL SERIES.

BEHAR PROVERBS

CLASSIFIED AND ARRANGED

ACCORDING TO THEIR SUBJECT-MATTER, AND TRANSLATED INTO
ENGLISH WITH NOTES, ILLUSTRATING THE SOCIAL CUSTOM,
POPULAR SUPERSTITION, AND EVERY-DAY LIFE OF
THE PEOPLE, AND GIVING THE TALES
AND FOLK-LORE ON WHICH
THEY ARE FOUNDED

WITH AN

APPENDIX AND TWO INDEXES

*GIVING THE SUBJECT OF EACH PROVERB IN ENGLISH AND THE
IMPORTANT WORDS IN HINDI*

BY

JOHN CHRISTIAN.

" Proverbs are the genius, wit, and spirit of a nation."—BACON

LONDON
KEGAN PAUL, TRENCH, TRÜBNER & Co., LIMITED
57 AND 59 LUDGATE HILL

1891

HERTFORD:
PRINTED BY STEPHEN AUSTIN AND SONS.

DEDICATED

TO

G. A. GRIERSON, ESQ., B.A.

B.C.S., M.A.S.B., M.R.A.S.

IN GRATEFUL ACKNOWLEDGMENT OF

EVER FRIENDLY ENCOURAGEMENT AND KINDLY HELP

BY

THE AUTHOR.

INTRODUCTION.

1. *Proverbs in General.*

It is no less a true than a terse Arabic saying, "That a Proverb is to speech what salt is to food." It aptly describes the office of proverbs, and puts in a practical though homely form the part played by them in a language. It is quite possible to derive nourishment and sustenance from food without salt; but if we want to enjoy our meals, we must have salt in them. Just so with Proverbs. Language would be tolerable without spicy, epigrammatic sayings, and life could no doubt be carried on by means of plain language wholly bereft of ornament. But if we wish to relish language, if we wish to give it point and piquancy, and if we want to drive home a truth, to whip up the flagging attention of our listener, to point a moral or adorn a tale, we must flavour our speech with proverbs. There is no language in the world, however poor, that has not its proverbs, its pithy and pointed sayings, and its witty epigrams, "the wisdom of many and the wit of one"—some one who has treasured up and kept ready for use in a concentrated and palatable form the essence of practical wisdom, by availing ourselves

b

of which we become possessed of a clear sight and take a ready view of intricate matters, to unravel which for ourselves would require a disproportionate expenditure of time and mental labour. "Proverbs," says Archbishop Whately, "are somewhat analogous to those medical formulas which, being in frequent use, are kept ready made up, in the chemist's shop, and which often save the framing of a distinct prescription."

2. *Proverbs of a people are the index of their lives.*

Every nation has its peculiar form of expressing its ideas, its special shades of thought. The idea may be the same, but different people will employ different figures of speech and modes of expression to convey it. These may seem quaint, perhaps crude, and even grotesque to others; but they are the appropriate vehicles of thought of the people, and suited to their circumstances in life. "Proverbs, however quaintly expressed, contain the essence of some moral truth or practical lesson; they are drawn from real life, and are generally the fruit of philosophy grafted on the stem of experience." Carlyle says, "That a man's religion is the chief fact with regard to him: a man's or a nation of men's." If the proverbs of a people are not the chief facts with regard to them, they are at any rate a safe index of their lives, their mode of living, their current thoughts, their intellectual and social status, their surroundings, and in fact everything else that goes to make up social life.

3. *Use of Proverbs : they help us to see the people as they are, and understand them better.*

To know a people thoroughly we must accompany them in their homes, find them in their daily occupations and amusements, see them as they are,—not with behaviours and manners assumed for the occasion, but in their natural and every-day habit, just as they appear to their own friends and families. In this unsophisticated state we see them in the natural utterances that form the proverbs and sayings of the people. In them they give vent to their genuine thoughts freely and without constraint. We see them as they are seen in their own circles, in their domestic relations (when human nature unbends itself), in their jovial moods, and in the various phases of social life. It is impossible to understand a people when they are acting a part, when they are playing an artificial *rôle* as it were ; and this is what most natives do when they appear in the presence of a European. It is therefore no exaggeration to say that an illiterate native seldom appears to a European in his true light.

The *rôle* he unfortunately assumes is the one least calculated to produce a favourable impression. He speaks in hyperboles, as language more comprehensible to a European ; he agrees to everything the *Sáhib* advances ; he cringes ; he does not even mind stretching a point ; if questioned about anything which in his opinion would act prejudicially towards his interest, he at once avows ignorance, thinking that the safest way out of the difficulty ; he makes desperate attempts to speak a gibberish made up of Hindi, Urdu, and his own *Ganwári*,

—all this, as he imagines, to acquit himself well and to be in the European's good books. This counterfeit form he always dons when he appears before a foreigner, not because this is his usual manner with his own people, or that he is habitually given to exaggeration or being imaginative, but because he thinks this is the behaviour best calculated to please a European. Thus, with the best of intentions, and with no little trouble to himself, he manages to convey a wrong impression about himself. And the consequence is, that he appears blacker than he really is. This is no doubt an error of judgment based on an inordinate desire to please at any cost: the foundation of this frame of mind probably going down deeper, and resting on a moral nature differently constituted. This view will not be disputed if it is remembered that natives who have long been in contact with Europeans usually behave more straightforwardly, as they know from experience that this is the safest course to pursue to gain the desired end. Another unfortunate fact against the Bihāri peasant is that his European critic does not always approach him prepared to make the largest possible allowance for his failings, drawbacks, and surrounding circumstances. He is too ready to judge him by his own standard of merit and demerit; and as he falls so lamentably short of it, to give him up as past redemption. And this he does, not from any uncharitableness, but solely from want of a thorough acquaintance with his real character. The proverbs, therefore, as helping us to pierce through this assumed veil, and enabling us to see the people in their genuine state, and thus helping us to understand them better, are a useful study. If we knew that the people had some good points, and were not so wholly bad or corrupt, that when moving in their own circle their chief characteristics and prominent features were not exactly those by which they are known to outsiders, we would perhaps be more inclined to view them leniently and give them a helping hand to ameliorate their condition. The writer made it a point, when either his work or excursions into the country brought him into contact with the peasants, never to be overbearing or in a hurry, but always to listen attentively and sympathetically to them, and then, surely as they went on, they gradually " doffed " this mannerism and assumed their natural style. Thus by exercising a little patience he was enabled to see the " real " Bihāri peasant; and would recommend this plan to every one who would care to hear him talk not artificially but naturally. He will find them more truthful, and certainly far more interesting.

4. *Bihār Proverbs : their language.*

By " Bihār Proverbs " is meant those sayings in use among the people of Bihār. They include not only epigrams and pithy utterances containing practical truths, wholesome rebukes or salutary advice, but also nursery rhymes, proverbial figures of speech, short fables and lampoons (some transgressing the conventional brevity of proverbs), which are current among the people and are often quoted by them. "They walk upon men's tongues, dance in their fancies, are carried about in their memories, and are reserved for graces of their discourses, when they desire to appear in their festival habits and holiday behaviour." These are principally of Hindi origin,

and in one of the several vernacular dialects in use in the
province. A proverb couched in the Shāhabad dialect,
for example, would be readily understood by a native of
Champāran, but he would in using it himself employ the
patois of his district. It is difficult for a foreigner,
unless thoroughly conversant with all the provincial
shades of speech, to detect the nice geographical
distinctions of dialect. It would require long familiarity
to do this readily. But, nevertheless, these fine shades of
distinction exist, and Mr. Grierson, in his admirable work
on the Bihār Peasants, has pointed them out to a nicety.
Many of the proverbs in vogue are thus local, and
variations occur frequently. The same ideas are repeated
in different forms. No collection of proverbs therefore
can be comprehensive enough to include all the variations
prevalent in different parts of a province that is larger
than England. The following proverb shows that
variety of speech may sometimes lead to unpleasantness.
What is the usual and polite language of one part
may be regarded as vulgar and even rude in another :—

*Maggah des kanchna pūri
Des bhala pai bhākha buri,
Rahlūñ Maggah kahlūñ re,
Tekra la ka mārbe re ?*

i.e. "Maggah is a rich (golden) country; the place is
good, but the language vile. I lived there, and said in
consequence *re*. Will you therefore beat me?" Where
one who has lived in Maggah, and has acquired the habit
of using *re*, is thus taken to task. It will be noted that
though a quarrel has been picked up with him for using
re, yet he cannot desist from the habit of using it. This

is, of course, aimed at the people of Maggah, who invariably use the interrogative terminal *re* in addressing people — a term considered especially vulgar in polite language. Many Hindi and Sanskrit words are corrupted (either in pronunciation or etymology) beyond recognition, or have come to acquire meanings altogether different from their originals, and in no way traceable, at least immediately, to the primary ones. In such cases the word is written as pronounced in Bihar, and translated in the accepted sense which prevails among the people. Such corruptions are unavoidable in an uncultivated and unwritten language. A purist may object to this style as perpetuating errors. But there can be no doubt that the right way to transliterate words used by the peasants is to write them exactly as they are pronounced in ordinary familiar talk. This may not be etymologically correct, but it is so colloquially, and the only form in which they would be recognized by the mass. Surely the so-called "right" method would be pedantic without any purpose or good being served in a work like this. A few Urdu proverbs that have gained currency, and are freely used by the people of Bihār, have been included in this collection. These have been naturalized and are familiar to the people in their Hindi form. But Arabic, Persian, and Urdu words are treated with scant courtesy in the mouths of the Bihāris; they give them "their own intonation." As Mr. Grierson says, "All the dots in the world will not make a Bihāri pronounce a *Z* as other than *J*, or a *Sād* as other than *S*." But his liking for these foreign words, and his tendency to use them in season and out of season, is none the less very pronounced. Every one

acquainted with the Bihāri rustic has noticed that
shortly after he comes into town, or into better society, he
attempts a refinement of speech by interlarding it with
Urdu phrases and words. He does this perhaps as much
with the object of making himself intelligible (as he
thinks) to the townsfolk, as to air his familiarity with
polite parlance. His ludicrous failure is pathetic at
times, and provokes the good-natured laugh of the
citizen. The writer was once very much puzzled by
the frequent use a respectable villager made of two
words which he, for the life of him, could not make out.
They were "*hama*," "*soma*" (*sic*). At last, after
much patience (for interruption and questioning would
have hopelessly lost the words), he discovered that they
were هما and شما (Persian "I" and "you"),[1] which
he irrelevantly and persistently kept on thrusting
between his sentences, quite to his own satisfaction.

5. *Some peculiarities of these Proverbs. They chiefly bear the country stamp.*

It would be perhaps just as well to note briefly here
a few of the characteristic features of the Bihār Proverbs
—some peculiarities that distinguish them. Regarded
generally, the proverbs in common use among the people
are of a rural and agricultural nature; that is, the images
they call to mind are connected with husbandry, and the
associations they awaken are chiefly such as surround
country domestic life. A little reflection will show that
this is but natural; our ideas and thoughts naturally run
in the grooves of our occupations and daily lives; and we

---

[1] An idiomatic Persian expression meaning "Such as you and I."

readily draw our illustrations, comparisons, and similes, from images familiar to us, and ever present in our thoughts. Hence it is that people whose chief concern in life is with the soil and the country, draw on rustic objects, agricultural implements, and domestic animals to illustrate, emphasize, and explain their thoughts. Thus, when a Bihār rustic wishes to express his sense of the unfitness of things, the unseasonableness of a remark, or the inappropriateness of an act, he puts into requisition the implements of agriculture with which he is familiar, and conveys his sense of incongruity by the proverb: *Hansuwa ke biyāh khurpa ke gīt* (Proverb 202), "In the wedding of the sickle, the song of the hoe!" that is, in the wedding of the sickle, the song should of course be about the sickle. It is therefore singularly out of place to sing on such an occasion in praise of the hoe. This is not merely a figure of speech, but is literally true, however quaint and far-fetched it may appear to us, and points to a time when it was really the custom to hold marriage ceremonies of these agricultural implements. This custom of wedding inanimate objects is still extant in regard to groves, tanks, wells, etc., which are formally married on being opened.[1] Even now artisans and peasants worship their tools and implements with deep feelings of veneration, and the Kāyath (the writer class) has his ink-pot festival (*dawāt pūja*), when he washes his reed pen and ink-bottle clean, and worships them with offerings, and nothing will induce him to write on that day. Similarly,

---

[1] No doubt the underlying idea in these marriages, for instance of a *kudār* (spade) to an untilled field, of a sickle to a field of corn, etc., was the fertility and productiveness supposed to result from the unions.

when a rustic wants to express to you his feeling of uncertainty, the evanescence of anything, or the fleeting nature of an advantage, and desires to warn you against placing too much reliance on an ephemeral object, what better simile can he call to his aid than " the shadow of the palm tree," which he has so often watched! The comparison is picturesque in its simplicity, and quite familiar to him. Changing almost every minute as the sun moves along his orbit, the shadow of the toddy palm cannot be relied on to shelter you for any length of time. If you, therefore, put too much trust on wealth or rely on your post, which you may hold to-day and lose to-morrow, the peasant tells you : *"Daulat tār gāchh ke chhāya"* or *"Naukri tār gāchh ke chhāya."* "Wealth or post is uncertain and transitory like the shadow of a palm tree."

Then again if he wants to express his surprise at the unexpected impudence or pugnacity of any one who suddenly assumes the *rôle* of a bully, but who is naturally expected to be humble and meek, he quotes the following hyperbole : *Jolha ke chher markhāh!* " The goat of a weaver, and given to viciousness!" (*lit.* butting). The quiet, humble, forbearing weaver, the butt of all, and the typical fool of Indian society, is the most inoffensive of human beings; therefore, from a parity of reasoning (helped by imagination), his goat, of all creatures in the world, ought to be the most inoffensive! Then, goats are not usually vicious, and much less the goat of a weaver. It is therefore singularly inconsistent with its nature if it takes to pugnacious ways, and wonder is expressed at this unexpected transformation.

If, again, one of his fellow-villagers, after a short absence, returns home and decks himself out in gay colours and costumes, not usually seen among the homely-dressed peasants, and otherwise gives himself airs (a very common weakness), he laughs at him in the proverb: *Chāre din ke gaile murga mor hoke aile!* "The cock went away for four days only from his home, and returned a peacock!" which is analogous to the story of the jackdaw who arrayed himself in the plumes of a peacock, and suffered an ignominious humiliation at the hands of his former indignant companions.

Thus dozens of proverbs may be quoted to show that they are essentially rustic in their nature. The similes and metaphors are drawn from rustic objects, familiar to the every-day life of the Bihār peasant, and an odour of homely village life pervades them.

6. *The morale of the Proverbs: their tone more practical than moral.*

But it is necessary to examine these proverbs from a higher standpoint of view, to see if they are anything more than a collection of railleries, banters, and jokes, now treating in a spirit of pleasantry certain personal failings, foibles, and vices, and now deriding and taunting in a severe, perhaps cynical, tone the misfortunes and weaknesses of our fellow-mortals. As a very comprehensive division these proverbs, for our purpose, may be classed under two broad heads: those of a *practical* or *worldly* nature, and those of a *moral* and *didactic* nature. The former would lay down rules useful to be observed in our worldly dealings; the latter would embody principles of conduct (whether the result of experience or deduced from religious belief) which are generally accepted as right in our relations to our fellow-mortals, and to a future world. Regarded from this point of view, the proverbs in most common use among the people are decidedly of a very practical nature. They relate more to worldly wisdom than to high principles of rectitude; they tell us oftener what is expedient and useful than what is right and what ought to be our unswerving line of conduct; their teachings would help us rather to meet and combat the acuteness and cunning which pass for wisdom in the world than to shun them as low artifices unworthy of us; they are more selfish and less self-denying. There is a general absence in them of an elevating tone, a want of high ideal, such as one would expect to find in the sayings of wisdom left by the sages of old. There is no ethical principle or choice moral maxim conveyed in them; they rather incline to selfishness and cynicism. Self-interest is their key-note and worldliness their one tune. Perhaps this is the natural outcome of a religion dissevered from morality and ages of grovelling subjection.

7. *Ridicule and Derision their chief aim.*

Ridicule is their chief aim, and persiflage their usual style. Their tone is sometimes bitterly sarcastic and a light vein of satire runs through them all. Ridicule, sarcasm, and derision are the chief weapons in the armoury of these proverbs, and they are often wielded with merciless severity. They are rather the cuts of a blunt, heavy sword than the sharp, clean thrusts of a rapier; very often the jokes are coarse to a degree, and are levelled almost ruthlessly regardless of the feelings of the person aimed at. It is no wonder then that these heavy weapons often leave a deep wound behind. For we all know, if from nothing else, from the fable of the stone-throwing boys and the frogs, that a missile hurled in fun may leave an effect the reverse of funny. One of the commonest methods of ridicule in these proverbs is to put the satire into the mouth of the person to be ridiculed, and to make it appear as if it comes from the person himself. This is no doubt a most effective way of caricaturing, as the extravagant utterances sound much more ludicrous in the mouth of the "subject" (who is thus unconsciously developing his oddities) than in that of the "operator." For example, in Proverb 391, "The misfortunes of a husband who has a shrew at home," the scold is pitilessly held up to laughter, when she is represented uttering the lampoon in which she is so mercilessly satirized. The barber's wife, again, who is represented as lamenting the death of her beloved husband (Proverb 107), because "Who is there now left to shave the town?" is caricaturing in her own person one who is so self-opinionated as to think fondly either herself, or some one dear to her indispensable.

In the same way the witch who is represented (in Proverb 11) as making a grim boast of her infant-devouring powers, is only caricaturing in herself those who take a delight in boasting of their evil deeds. She says: "*Larika khāit khāit būrhi bhelīñ; log kahe bak-dāin,*" "I have grown old in the habit of feasting on infants; yet people have the impertinence to say I am only a novice in the practice" (literally "only half a witch"), which is only meant as a heavy thrust at those perverse natures we occasionally meet who are for ever making a boast of what they ought really to be ashamed of. Similarly, the proverb (No. 112) in which the jackal pup who, being born only in August, has the impudence to speak of a flood that took place in the following month as "such a heavy one that he never saw the like of it in his life," is pleasant irony with humour, and takes off beautifully the presumption of the raw youth who talks as one ripe in experience and knowing everything. Another very common mode of ridiculing adopted in these proverbs is by exaggeration. This puts in the most ludicrous form the object to be ridiculed and provokes the laugh of the hearers, which, in most cases, is all that is aimed at. It is, besides, a form that commends itself most to the taste and calibre of the rustic.

8. *Humour.*

Speaking of humour, it would perhaps be useful here to point out that these proverbs are not wholly destitute of it, at least, as understood by the Bihāri rustic. The peasant has his style of humour, as he has his style of talk. It may be rough and ready, but it is genuine. Like the coarse salt he uses, it lacks refinement, but it helps to flavour his language. We can only afford space for a few examples chosen at random. There is no doubt genuine humour when a despicable effort made to effect a gigantic purpose is likened to the presumption of the seagull in the fable who slept with her tiny feet held upwards, lest the sky should fall (Proverb 108). Again, the man who is foolish enough to confide in a notorious swindler, and to trust him with his money,

is aptly compared to the stupid creature who entrusted
a jackal with a piece of meat to be kept for him till
he wanted it! (Proverb 161). The occasional visit of
an acquaintance is welcome; but if he should take to
the habit of coming frequently, and "sponging" on
you for long periods, his visits become anything but
pleasant. Such a behaviour is satirized in the following humorous simile (perhaps too grotesque in its grim
humour of treating so lightly such a serious subject as
death) : *Būrh ke marle na derāīñ jam ke parikle derāīñ;*
i.e. "The occasional incursion of the 'angel of death'
(*jam*) to seize an old victim is not by any means to be
feared (for that is to be expected), but his getting
accustomed to making frequent raids!" (Proverb 314).
Few who have had experience of camping life in Bihār
will fail to recall a village quarrel into which the women
enter with so much gusto as an indispensable part of
their daily business. The termagants ranged on opposite
sides, brawling, gesticulating, and screaming with all
their might like so many cockatoos, the men going about
their business as usual and quite unconcernedly as if this
periodical outburst was a necessary part of the day's
proceedings, the children and the village pariahs adding
their chorus. On such an occasion we can imagine a
wag, who has been watching the fun with the relish
of a by-stander who is not mixed up in it, turning away
from it, just when the quarrel is raging at its highest,
and the warmed combatants are becoming a bit unmindful
of modesty in their language and gestures, with the
humorous advice thrown in, more in jest than in earnest,
" *Lar parosin did rakh,*" "Yes, go at it, you neighbours!
but please preserve a little shame in your modest eyes "

(Proverb 389).   Of course, the word "neighbours" is not used without a touch of irony.   Those who are quarrelling now so vehemently (in such unneighbourly fashion) will not long after be the best of friends, as neighbours ought to be.   It is only a daily "constitutional."

Akin to humour is drollery and burlesque.   In essence they are a coarse form of humour, where effect is sought by sportive tricks, buffoonery, ludicrous or unnatural representation and exaggerated parody.   These predominate in the proverbs that are descriptive of the peculiar traits characteristic of certain castes and classes, where the prominent failings are laid hold of and are mercilessly gibbeted and parodied in a fashion which, to those unused to this style, would almost seem inhuman. The oddities, for example, of the *Jolha* (the Mussalman weaver, the proverbial fool of Indian society) are travestied in a melodramatic style in the sarcastic lines describing his encounter with the frog, where, after being defeated by that mighty creature, he recounts his adventure (not without a tone of vaunting) to his admiring wife, and winds up with the bathos, "Now, whatever happens, whether I live or die, I am off to the battle of the frogs!"—intended not only to excite his wife's wonder at his prowess, but her commiseration (Proverb 313).   The *Kanaujia* Brahmin, than whom there is not a greater stickler in regard to caste rules, is similarly ridiculed in the over-drawn picture of "three Brahmins and thirteen separate cooking places" (Proverb 259).   And the "poor" *kāyath* is with great art ludicrously represented as "picking" up the bits that drop when two *laddus* (sweetmeat balls meant figuratively for "rich fools") fight: *Laddu lare jhilli jhare kāyath bechāre ka pet bhare*, "When *laddus* fight bits drop out; the poor *kāyath* gets his living" (Proverb 280). But though somewhat exaggerated, a better portrait could not be given than in the description of him when taking anything on "tick" and when paying cash. *Nagad kāyath bhūt udhār kāyath deota*, "A *kāyath* when paying cash is the very devil (in exacting a bargain); but when taking a loan he is as meek as an angel!" When a perverse nature, that cannot under any circumstances behave straightforwardly, is satirized in the saying, "If he is very straight, he is like a sickle" (Proverb 230), or when one, whose acrid nature is increased in acerbity by outward circumstances, is likened to "the bitter *karela* creeper climbing the still more bitter *nīm*," the images called forth are eminently calculated to provoke a laugh by their extravagance (Proverb 143).

9. *Nature of some of the Proverbs: simile half expressed.*

In these proverbs as it will be readily noticed the simile is usually only half expressed. The incident or object to be compared is not mentioned, but only the image is quoted to illustrate it. The former is always taken for granted as being present; the latter only is brought into prominence. The particle or word indicating comparison is seldom expressed; but the things are placed side by side and the hearer is left to draw his inference. In fact, the primary meaning of the Arabic word *mashl*[1] is likeness, and probably the office of proverbs

---

[1] "The title of the 'Book of Proverbs' in Hebrew is *Mishle-Māshāl*, rendered in the Arabic version 'by-word,' 'parable,' 'proverb.' It is derived from a root *māshāl* 'to be like,' and the primary idea involved in it is that of likeness, comparison. Probably all proverbial sayings

was originally, as has been conjectured, to furnish comparisons only.

10. *Oftener concrete than abstract in their form.*

And this brings us to the consideration of one marked feature of these proverbs, being as they are the rude primitive utterances of illiterate minds. They are oftener concrete than abstract in the forms in which they appear. For, as is well known, abstraction and generalization are habits acquired after long civilization and training. The form of expression which readily commends itself to the uncultivated mind is the concrete form. A truth or a fact is expressed by the uncivilized in a tangible shape, associated with images familiar to him. The same idea is made of general application by the trained mind in an abstract expression. The notion is the same, but the form different. Many instances of this will readily occur to all who have had experience of the illiterate Bihār peasant. The images, illustrations, and expressions they employ are almost always material. For example, the idea expressed by us in the abstract and generalized form, " He laughs best who laughs last," is comically illustrated in the story of the potter and the greengrocer, who jointly hired a camel to convey their respective articles of trade. The potter filled his side of the pack with earthen pots and chatties, and the greengrocer did likewise with greens and vegetables. As they proceeded on their journey, the camel frequently helped himself to the greens from the greengrocer's bag. This

were at first of the nature of similes. From this stage of its application it passed to that of sententious maxims generally, many of which, however still involve comparison."—*Dr. Chambers.*

excited the potter's laugh, who thought he had the best of the bargain, and quizzed his friend on his bad luck. To this he retorted by saying, "We shall see, my friend, on what side the camel sits." Presently they had occasion to stop on the road, and the camel was made to sit. He naturally sat on the heavier side of the potter's package, and also, probably, with an eye to having occasional mouthfuls from the green-grocer's bag. This caused all the pots to smash, and then of course the greengrocer had the laugh all on his side. Hence the saying: " *Kauna kare to ūnt baithela*," "Let's see on what side the camel sits" (Proverb 194). "Ingratitude" is illustrated by the common story of the young cuckoo remaining after all a cuckoo, and causing disappointment and shame to its foster-mother, the crow, who, under a delusion, was led to hatch the eggs of a cuckoo (Proverb 50). "Inattention" is cari-catured in the person who, having sat through the whole epic of the *Rāmāyan*, inquires innocently at the end, " Whose wife is Sīta?" (Proverb 65). "Presumption" is similarly illustrated in the story of the donkey who attempted to ford a stream in which huge animals, like the camel, were drowned, and paid with his life for his audacity (Proverb 98). Extreme feminine vanity is similarly travestied in the " blind woman " keeping three collyrium boxes to beautify her eyelashes (Proverb 84), and so on.

11. *Some Proverbs convey their meaning by suggestion rather than expression.*

Some proverbs convey their meaning, more by sugges-tion than expression; they refer to some folklore or to an analogous case which brings out the point to be illustrated, or the absurdity of the situation prominently. It is vain to endeavour to find in them a parallel idea corresponding to every word used: the result would be nonsense. You have to infer the comparison as a whole from the parallel instance put forward. The implied metaphor, from its very incompleteness as it were, strikes you forcibly. The parallel is not complete, but ends half-way, and suggests the corresponding idea and simile, more by implication than expression. Instances of this occur in every language, *e.g.* "Money makes the mare to go," "Blood is thicker than water," etc. Of this nature are proverbs,

> *Gāi gāi ka hokhah bāur,*
> *Bhūsa kutale niksi chāur ?* (Proverb 160).

Said when one is advised not to waste his breath in trying to convince a man who will not be convinced. The process is similar to extracting rice by pounding husk : *E, gūr khāyeñ, kān chhedāyeñ* (Proverb 159). Said when one is bound to do a thing *nolens volens*, however much he may object to it at first. This proverb refers to the practice of giving a piece of sugar (jaggery) to a child whose ears are to be bored ; while she is thus engaged her ears, or rather the cartilages of her ears, are pierced, etc.

12. *Rhyming Proverbs.*

Often a telling effect is obtained by a casual rhyme of words of widely different import, e.g. *Chor jaisne hīra ke, waisne khīra ke,* "A thief is a thief whether he steals a diamond or a cucumber;" or *Jekra hāth meñ doi, tekra hāth meñ sab koi,* "He who holds the helping spoon commands everybody" (Proverb 175); or *Kām piyāra chām nahi piyāra,* "Handsome is that handsome does" (*lit.* "Work is loveable, not the skin"). But oftener the rhyme is there, but not the reason.

13. *Feminine Proverbs.*

There are some proverbs and expressions especially in use among the women; they are peculiar to females, and applicable to them only. They are seldom used by men, unless by those despicable creatures called *Maūgrās,* or a class of effeminate men who affect the ways of women. They talk and behave like them, assume a feminine gait and tone, clothe themselves like women, and pretend in all respects to have feminine tastes. They prefer women's company to men's, sing feminine songs in feigned voices, and are looked upon as buffoons. It is strange to notice the freedom with which they are allowed to mix with women—a liberty not usually permitted to men in native society.

The writer can only afford space to direct the attention of the reader to a few of the Proverbs (out of a great many) that are used in reference to the women only: they are for instance Proverbs 82, 87, 103, 104, 318, 368, 401, etc.

It will be noticed that the feminine gender is denoted by the terminal "o," and that a wife never speaks of her husband by his name, but simply by the personal pronoun "he," and its cases. Among other curious domestic customs, in connection with the wife, may be

noticed the extreme reserve which she is supposed to
exercise towards her husband's father and elder brother,
at all times. Her person is sacred to them, it is therefore considered a pollution to be touched by them. She
will never speak to them, or if she can help it, be seen
by them. She will hide herself on their approach, or
if she is obliged to serve them she will draw her *sári*
cloth over her head. The following warning thrown in
by the wife, who was serving out dinner to her father-
in-law, in the form of a riddle, is interesting as illustrating
that direct speech on the part of the daughter-in-law,
under any circumstances, is considered highly indecent.
While she was engaged one day in helping her father-
in-law to his meal, a drop of milk from her breast fell
in his food. Unable to warn him directly, she repeated
the following lines which conveyed to him the necessary
hint and stopped him in time from making himself " the
son of his daughter-in-law :

> *Kāhat mora lāj lage, sunat par gāri,*
> *Sās ke patoh lāgūñ, sasur ke mahtāri ?*

" I am ashamed to say so, and those who hear me will
take it as an abuse : I am the daughter-in-law of my
mother-in-law and (am I to become) the mother of my
father-in-law ?" These restrictions are not so strictly
observed among the lower classes in Bihār, who, owing
to their circumstances, are often thrown together ; but
there is, notwithstanding, always a reserve between the
father-in-law, the elder brother-in-law, and the wife.
While on the other hand she is allowed the utmost
liberty to joke with her husband's younger brother, who
is a legitimate object of her practical jokes.

Speaking of conundrums and riddles, the writer will just notice in passing that some very witty ones exist in the mouths of the people. They are chiefly characterized by a play of fancy and humour, and by the very good use made of familiar domestic objects to amplify and clothe the metaphors and give a quaint turn to common expressions so as to conceal the real meaning. They are replete with "quips and cranks" and happy twists, which sometimes recoil on the head of the solver of these riddles himself. A spirit of hilarity breathes through them and a "*double entente*" is often used with telling effect.

14. *Sources of these Proverbs.*

It is impossible now to trace the history of most of the proverbs, to say who were their authors, or how they originated and became current among the people. A few are no doubt of classical origin, and are traceable to well-known Hindi works, such as the great Epics, the Rāmāyan, the Mahābhārata, etc. Others are the remarkable sayings of local poets, seers, and astrologers. For example, a great many of the clever sayings regarding agriculture, seasons, and pastoral subjects in general, are attributed to the two brothers Ghāg Rāe and Bhāg Rāe, who, it is said, were natives of Bhojpur. To Bhaddar,[1] also supposed to be a native of the Shāhabad district, are ascribed, on the other hand, many of the remarkable utterances relating to the science of *jotish* or astrology, by which an undertaking is ascertained to be auspicious or inauspicious. These are *formulæ* and *dicta*

---

[1] See a note on Bhaddar under Proverb 437.

based on astrology, and are quoted to recommend or
dissuade any one from taking an impending step, such
as starting on a journey, building a house, undertaking
a heavy responsibility, etc., and have the greatest hold
on the imagination and belief of the people. Others,
again, are no doubt the sayings of clever villagers, being
the outcome of experience or of popular superstition.
The Proverbs relating to agriculture, seasons, and purchase of cattle, are especially useful as rules of guidance
for all agriculturists and farmers, who want to keep on
the right track, and profit by the experience of others.

15. *Classification and Arrangement of the Proverbs; their Transliteration and Translation.*

In concluding this rambling and discursive notice of
the Proverbs the writer would wish to make a few remarks on their classification and arrangement. That
this is a difficult task will be readily acknowledged by
all who have taken the subject into their consideration ;
but the peculiar difficulties besetting one who attempts
to translate proverbs into a foreign language, and then
to reduce them into certain order, are perhaps greater.
Perhaps, no attempt to classify the proverbs and group
them under definite heads can be perfect and give universal satisfaction. The same proverbs may be viewed
from different standpoints by different individuals, and
each would naturally class it under the head which
appeared to him the fittest. It is, therefore, almost a
trite saying that there are as many ways of looking at
a proverb as there are dispositions and temperaments.
The following will show that proverbs may reasonably

be classed under any out of the several general heads adopted in this compilation. For instance (Proverb 496) :

Kāniñ gaiya ke alge bathān,

" A blind cow requires a separate house " (cattle yard).

(*a*) Can be taken as referring to cattle and put under class vi.

(*b*) Can be considered as aimed at a foible (a crotchet or queer whim, which is really the object of the proverb) and classed under class i.

(*c*) Can be taken as a saying of worldly wisdom and put under class ii.

(*d*) May be taken as a social proverb and classed under class iv.

Similarly proverb 325.

Nanado ke nanad hola,

" A sister-in-law has a sister-in-law too " (to tyrannise over her). May be taken either as a piece of consoling advice to those who are tyrannised over (class ii.); or may be classified according to the particular foible aimed at, *i.e.* home oppression (class i.); or may be regarded as a scene out of native domestic life in which the sisters-in-law figure (class iv.). It will thus be noticed that the classification in each case would be right, according to the point of view from which the proverb was regarded. Another difficulty of reducing the proverbs under general heads is the variety of subjects they treat of. A generic head does not take in the various shades of difference, and is thus to some extent deceptive. This difficulty increases considerably when the attempt is made to arrange them under sub-heads.

In the early history of this compilation, shortly after the work was undertaken, the writer in submitting a few specimen sheets to Mr. G. A. Grierson, C.S., for his opinion, had applied to him for his suggestions as to the lines on which it would be advisable to classify and group the proverbs. He was kind enough to give them freely. Indeed, without his kind encouragement and advice, given from time to time, and given so gracefully, the work would never have been persevered with. He was then good enough to direct the compiler's attention to the following methods. (As these are clearly and concisely laid down by him in his letter the compiler will give Mr. Grierson's own words):—

"There are many principles to choose from. The simplest and easiest is that of Fallon in his 'Dictionary of Proverbs.' He arranges them alphabetically according to the first word of each. But as the same proverb varies greatly in different people's mouths it is not a good arrangement. It is better to arrange them either according to subjects or according to objects. In the first method you group all proverbs about, say, birds, then all those about plants, and so on. In the second method you arrange them according to the particular vices or foibles aimed at, *e.g.* those aimed at gluttony, then those at parsimony. Both these methods are difficult to carry out. The best way I think is to class them, as far as possible, according to subjects and to add a complete index giving every important word which occurs. No collection of proverbs can be satisfactory without such an index, for such a collection is a work of reference, and unless proverbs can be found easily, they may just as well remain in the brains of the natives as in a printed labyrinth without a clue."

Now, each of these methods has its advantages and its disadvantages, its recommendations and its drawbacks. The alphabetical system, besides the important reason given by Mr. Grierson, could not be adopted, as it was unsuited to the original plan of this work, which is not a dictionary of proverbs, but a compilation with notes on the context, in which it was essential to follow some principle of grouping the proverbs under certain "heads." Moreover, if a dictionary of proverbs were needed, there is Dr. Fallon's excellent work, which perhaps some may think renders this compilation unnecessary. To such I would say in the words of George Elliot (slightly altered), "One could not carry on life comfortably, without a little blindness to the fact, that everything has been done better than we could do it ourselves." But, as a matter of fact, this compilation is altogether different from Dr. Fallon's important work, as will be seen at a glance.

The next method of grouping them according to the subject, *i.e.* the images employed to illustrate, exemplify, or emphasize the idea, would be certainly easier and perhaps complete, and less open to questioning. But notwithstanding these recommendations, the principle can hardly be pronounced to be satisfactory. The simile or metaphor employed, is, after all, the mere husk, the outward form and accidental. Birds, plants, animals, various rustic tools, implements, etc., are put into requisition simply to act as illustrations to the prominent idea involved. Thus the tusk of an elephant is in one proverb (Proverb 246) made to symbolise straightforwardness and in another (Proverb 3) exactly the opposite quality.

When the *parās* tree is spoken of as having but three leaves, this incidental natural fact is seized to emphasize the main idea of the extent of one's power — "thus far thou shalt go and no further." Again: when the delicate *bulbul* is made use of in keen irony to ridicule a rough coarse woman, who pretends to be fine, the prominent idea of the proverb is not the bird, but "affectation." Similarly, when a vain man makes a boast of his short-lived power and is giddy with his slight elevation, he is likened to a "cricket on a bundle of clothes;" the harmless insect is the least part of the proverb, and is simply a casual metaphor employed to laugh at the common human failing, because its chirping, when seated on a slight eminence, is not unlike that of the upstart. And so on, the images are merely the outward integument to enclose and hold the germ of idea involved in the proverb. It would be as reasonable in a classification of English proverbs to class the proverb, "Casting pearls before swine," under the head of "animals" or "precious stones" as to put the last Hindi proverb under the generic head of insects. The classification, to say the least of it, would be misleading.

The third method, no doubt, has the least to be said against it; it is classifying the proverbs according to their subject-matter. This would include the "object" (*i.e.* the particular vices or foibles aimed at) which would, in the case of these proverbs, form their true subject-matter. For example, the proverbs relating to "human failings, foibles, and vices" (class i. in this collection) would be grouped, according to their "objects," *i.e.* the particular vices aimed at, such as "hypocrisy," "parsimony," "gluttony," etc., while proverbs relating to "peculiarities, traits," etc. (class iii.), or those relating to "agriculture" (class v.), would be grouped according to the subject-matter treated of. But this principle of classification has its drawback also. In a few instances, especially in proverbs coming under classes i. ii. and iv., the grouping of the proverbs under the general heads has to be somewhat "forced" — perhaps a distinction has to be made without much of a difference. This is unavoidable from the nature of the cognate subjects treated of in the proverbs, which, viewed from different standpoints, might come just as easily under one head as under another. The proverbs coming under class ii. cannot easily be comprised under definite sub-heads. The variety of subjects are too numerous and diversified to admit of classification. Even cognate ideas are often expressed in a variety of shades that require separate grouping. Thus the sub-heads have a tendency to become as numerous as the proverb heads.

In classifying the proverbs the compiler has followed the last method. He has been principally guided by their subject-matter, their application and use ; their object rather than their subject or form. This system might not be the best, but it seemed to him to be the one which had most reason on its side. It is natural, and has the advantage of easy reference. Of course some of these groupings may appear arbitrary, but this is also unavoidable, so long as a proverb can be viewed from different standpoints. In the index the object has been to give the subject-matter (substance) of the proverbs in their own words, expressed as concisely as possible. This, it was thought, would have the advantage of directing attention to the proverb when it was heard or a reference was made to it, and would also avoid the use of hackneyed phrases. In order, therefore, to have a correct idea, we must turn to the proverbs themselves, as very often the brief index-heads will fail to convey an adequate idea of the proverb. They are expressed so quaintly and in a form so foreign to our notions and ideas of things, though the subject-matter may be familiar enough. The general heads will also be a guide where to look for proverbs of a certain kind.

The system of transliteration adopted is the same as that of the Bihār Peasant Life by Mr. Grierson. It may be briefly described as the Jonesian system, with every possible diacritical mark omitted. In pursuance of this the cerebral letters are given no dots, and, as nearly every final vowel is long, the long mark has been omitted from final vowels. As Mr. Grierson has described this system clearly in the Introduction to his Bihār Peasant Life, I give his own words: " Every native word is written twice over—once with accuracy in the native character for those who are able to read it, and once in the English character for those who are not acquainted with the Indian vernaculars. This transliteration does not pretend to be scientifically accurate. Such a transliteration with its diacritical dots and dashes would only puzzle those for whom it is intended, viz. those who are ignorant of the language. All that has been attempted for them is to give them a general idea of the correct pronunciation of the words, without professing to tell them the exact pronunciation, which they hardly require, and which would be difficult to do. For these persons all that is necessary is, that they should pronounce the vowels as in Italian, and the consonants as in English, and they will then approach sufficiently near to the way in which the natives themselves pronounce the words. For those who are acquainted with the vernacular languages, no instructions for pronouncing the words in their vernacular dress are necessary."

Dark passages the writer has not shunned to the best of his knowledge and light in translating. But he has been careful to avoid holding "a farthing rushlight to the sun." To those familiar with the vernacular of the peasantry nothing would be dark, and to those not so conversant, every expression would need a commentary. Thus to adopt a middle course was by no means such plain sailing as might be imagined at first sight. Then the peculiar difficulty of translating idiomatic, terse, and colloquial expressions, which chiefly make up the language of the proverbs, from one tongue into another, is known to all. To translate these by their literal meanings would, in most cases, be to make great nonsense in another language. Of course the only safe method in such cases is to translate the idiom of one language into the corresponding idiom of the other. But this proposition, which is so easy to state, is most difficult to carry out. Besides requiring a perfect familiarity with the idiom of both languages on which the translator is at work, there are seldom exactly corresponding idiomatic expressions to be found in two languages—expressions which convey exactly the same ideas and no more and no less, and with equal force and terseness. It is truly said, that "metaphor, which is the strength of language, is invariably the stumbling-block of the translator," and a "pun," according to Addison, "can be no more engraven than it can be translated."

My sincere and grateful acknowledgments are due to my friend Mr. H. F. Drummond, of the Opium Department, for his friendly help and kind advice (always freely given, whenever I was in doubt or difficulty) throughout the compilation of this work. To his nice literary judgment and extensive reading I owe many valuable suggestions.

JOHN CHRISTIAN.

HAJIPUR, TIRHUT, BEHAR,
December, 1890.

CLASS I.

Proverbs relating to Human Failings, Foibles, and Vices.

Sub-Class.	No.	Subject of Proverbs.
Affectation, Pretence, Shamming, Dissembling, Hypocrisy, etc.	1.	Cutting off the head and pretending to preserve the hair.
	2.	Father a drunkard, and the son pretending to play the *rôle* of a religious man.
	3.	Like the tusk and teeth of an elephant, one set for show and another for use.
	4.	Pretending to turn over a new leaf.
	5.	Pretending the end of the cucumber is bitter.
	6.	Sinner turned a saint.
	7.	Shamming to shirk.
	8.	She knows nine, but not six.
	9.	She calls herself a *sayad*, but stoops to steal a nose ornament.
	10.	She calls herself a *bulbul*, but swallows a *gular*.
	11.	Old in sin yet a novice.
Avarice, Parsimony, Covetousness, Greed, etc.	12.	A life's hoarding lost at a stroke.
	13.	Almighty dollar.
	14.	The miser's loss is sudden.
	15.	The miser and his wife.
	16.	To take one and give two.
	17.	When gaining he is discontented, when losing contented.
Aping.	18.	Aping—a losing game.
	19.	Aping often causes discomfort.
	20.	Paying dearly for aping.
Bullying, Oppressing, Venting rage, etc.	21.	The weak bullying the weaker.
	22.	The cunning bullying the weak.
	23.	The anvil bears the missing stroke.
	24.	The fallen are trampled.
	25.	Entirely at your mercy.
	26.	Venting one's rage on the innocent.

d

Sub-Class.	No.	Subject of Proverbs.
Bad writing.	27.	Bad hand-writing.
Blabbing.	28.	A blabber dying to blab.
	29.	The tell-tale causes the downfall of a kingdom.
" Counting the chickens before they are hatched," Anticipating, etc.	30.	The son is born before the father.
	31.	The father is still unborn, but the son attends a wedding (safflower).
	32.	Proclaiming before the son is born.
	33.	Crying before he is hurt.
	34.	Anticipating evil.
Conceit.	35.	Conceit about one's wisdom.
Extravagance.	36.	Can't afford rice-gruel, but drinks toddy.
	37.	Expenditure on a thing more than it is worth.
	38.	Cost of the wood is 9 pice, but he spends 90 on it.
	39.	Useless appendage.
	40.	Servant to a servant.
Exaggeration.	41.	Critics say more than the poet.
	42.	Making a mountain of a mole-hill.
	43.	A lakh is on the lips of a brag.
Gluttony.	44.	A greedy daughter-in-law.
	45.	Pretended fasting before her husband.
	46.	Ambition dying for name : greed for belly.
	47.	The greedy advised to eat with eyes closed before children.
	48.	Hunger to be appeased before devotion (a " full belly, then a devout heart ").
	49.	" Enemy to food."
Ingratitude.	50.	The young of a cuckoo will after all be a cuckoo.
	51.	A snake bites its charmer.
	52.	A viper is never grateful.
	53.	Like a horse that grumblingly neighs when given *ghi*.
Ignorance.	54.	Poor attainments taunted.
Improvidence.	55.	An improvident man overtaken by the flood.
Inability to appreciate worth, merit, etc.	56.	Can a low caste appreciate *bará* (a kind of sweetmeat) ?
	57.	Can a monkey appreciate ginger ?
	58.	The hubble-bubble in the hands of a monkey.

Sub-Class.	No.	Subject of Proverbs.
	59.	Music hath no charms for a buffalo.
	60.	Useless to adorn before a blind husband.
	61.	To the blind day and night are the same.
	62.	Worth unappreciated.
	63.	Merit not recognized (illustrated by an allegory).
	64.	Making no distinction.
Inattention.	65.	Enquiring who is the hero after the whole tale is finished.
Love of false display, empty boast, foppishness, etc.	66.	Affecting high-sounding names.
	67.	Foppishness in dress.
	68.	One who asks for alms should not enquire after the rent-roll of a village.
	69.	Dying to eat *pān*.
	70.	A vain woman's love for display.
	71.	False outward display.
	72.	Fashionable father and son, with frogs for kettle-drum.
	73.	One who cannot afford it keeping up a dance at his gate for display.
	74.	Falsely calling himself a " Benares man."
	75.	The cock after four days' absence returns home a peacock.
	76.	Display in borrowed plumes.
	77.	A vain woman thinks of adorning herself only.
	78.	Himself a beggar and a beggar at his door.
	79.	Love of worthless finery.
	80.	When out he wears long *dhotis*; at home he eats *masūr* bread.
	81.	Tall talk when out and *kodo* rice at home.
	82.	Boasting of three-seer anklets.
	83.	Demanding a torch at another's house.
	84.	A blind woman owning three collyrium boxes.
	85.	The needy keeping company with the great.
	86.	Rags to wear and carpets to spread.
	87.	Proud of her *Chundri Sāri*.
	88.	A poor fop.
	89.	The poor man at the prow of the boat.
	90.	Vain boast of learning.

Sub-Class.	No.	Subject of Proverbs.
"Pot calling the kettle black," Alike faulty or defective. Presumption, Audacity, Cheek, Arrogance, Over-confidence, Imprudence, etc.	91.	An upstart affecting gentility.
	92.	Affecting familiarity with the great (a snob).
	93.	The sieve blaming the *sūp*.
	94.	Equally miserable and poor.
	95.	Both alike defective.
	96.	Blind to one's own fault.
	97.	Where giants have failed, the pigmy has come to try his strength.
	98.	Where camels are drowned, the donkey ventures to ford.
	99.	Falsely claiming kinship.
	100.	While the superior spirits are crying from hunger, *Mūa* has the cheek to ask for cakes.
	101.	Breeze of the fan pitted against the hurricane.
	102.	The goat of a *jolhā* (weaver) and addicted to butting !
	103.	Cheek in a young girl.
	104.	Can the dance get on without *gango* ?
	105.	Cricket on a bundle.
	106.	Making free with another's property.
	107.	The barber's wife lamenting the death of her husband.
	108.	Can the sea-gull support the falling skies with its tiny feet ?
	109.	He does not know the charm for scorpions, yet ventures to put his hand in a snake's hole.
	110.	Self-praise is no praise.
	111.	Arrogating superiority over one's teacher.
	112.	Presumption of the inexperienced.
	113.	The young crow wiser than its mother.
	114.	Born but yesterday and to-day a giant.
	115.	An old goat quizzing the wolf.
Recklessness.	116.	Recklessness of those who have nothing to lose.
	117.	One who has nothing to lose can be reckless to any extent.
	118.	Reckless waste of other's property.
Selfishness, Heartlessness,	119.	What is play to one is death to another.
	120.	Dying man asked to sing.

Sub-Class.	No.	Subject of Proverbs.
Obstinacy, Self-willed, having one's own way, etc.	121.	A self-willed man.
	122.	Requiring full weight when the *banyā* does not come to terms.
	123.	The goat has paid with its life, yet its meat is not tasty.
	124.	The poor dog is dying, but the Raja thinks of his sport only.
	125.	The Rani has thoughts of the Raja only.
Vain or impotent desire, Vain expectation, Useless labour, etc.	126.	Vain desire of the handless woman to dance.
	127.	Wife vainly waiting for the collyrium to put in her eyes.
	128.	Fruitless labour in spinning.
	129.	The earless woman wishing for earrings.
	130.	An old cow's desire to take part in the *Sohrāi* festival.

CLASS II.

PROVERBS RELATING TO WORLDLY WISDOM AND MAXIMS, EXPEDIENCY AND CUNNING, AND WARNINGS AND ADVICE.

A new broom.	131.	A circuitous route.
	132.	Absurd sight or situation.
	133.	A new washerwoman applies soap to rags even.
	134.	The barber's wife with a wooden nail-cutter.
	135.	A chip of the old block.
	136.	All that glitters is not gold.
	137.	A good man needs speaking once.
	138.	All in the same plight.
	139.	An old parrot never gets tame.
	140.	After meals wait awhile.
	141.	A dog is brave at his own door.
	142.	Grinding corn on the dead.
	143.	The *Karaila* climbing on the *Nim*.
	144.	A bear, and he with a spade on his shoulders.
	145.	Insulting the dead.
	146.	A demon and a torch in his hand.

Sub-Class.	No.	Subject of Proverbs.

147. A bad workman quarrels with his tools.
148. A barking dog seldom bites.
149. A black goat has no heart.
150. A ludicrous attempt to frighten.
151. A rat's skin is not sufficient to cover a kettle-drum.
152. "A prophet is with honour save in his own country."
153. Among butchers a devout man can never be happy.
154. Annoying an old man.
155. Whatever is in the vessel will come out of the spout.
156. Beneath notice is Bhak Bhaun Puri.
157. Bamboos make the clump.
158. Beating is pleasant, but the consequences!
159. Bound to do it, *nolens volens.*
160. Constant repetition not conducive to conviction.
161. Can meat be kept on trust with a jackal?
162. Drowning the miller.
163. "Diamond cut diamond."
164. Dear at his native place, and cheap at the market.
165. "Do as they do in Rome."
166. Do what he may he is still a beggar.
167. Dictum for preserving health.
168. The *Parás* (tree) has but three leaves.
169. However strong the grain, it cannot break the cooking pot.
170. Follows the rich and "spunges" on the poor.
171. Fate and self-help equally shape our destiny.
172. Can a dead horse eat grass?
173. Can a frog catch cold?
174. Can a goat eat nine maunds of flour?
175. He who holds the spoon commands everybody.
176. He who has suffered can sympathize with those in pain.
177. He thatches his roof whose house leaks.

Sub-Class.	No.	Subject of Proverbs.

Sub-Class.	No.	Subject of Proverbs.
	239.	A needy troupe of dancers use their own oil.
	240.	The meanest can injure.
	241.	The less the grain to be parched the more noise it makes.
	242.	Things to be avoided as leading to danger.
	243.	Things we ought to pray to be saved from.
	244.	Taking a pleasant view of everything.
	245.	The staves of ten men make the load of one.
	246.	The word of a man is like the tusk of an elephant : it cannot be withdrawn.
{	247.	If the *bel* fruit is ripe, it matters little to the crow.
(	248.	If she disappoints, the bed will remain empty.
	249.	Without restraint.
{	250.	What is in a name ?
)	251.	The cunning of the dwarf, the squint-eyed, and the one-eyed compared.
(	252.	Beware of grey eyes.
	253.	Warning against men with certain peculiarities.
	254.	Where there is a will there is a way (mind compared to a blacksmith).
	255.	What houses are on the certain road to ruin (according to Ghāgh the soothsayer).

CLASS III.

Proverbs relating to Peculiarities and Traits Characteristic of Certain Castes and Classes.

Ahīrs or Goālās (milkmen).	256.	An Ahīr knows only how to sing his Lorik ballad.
	257.	Rent receipt given by the cunning Kāeth to the burly Ahīr.
	258.	The young barber practises on the Ahīr's head.
Brāhmans.	259.	Hair splitting about difference of castes. When three Kanaujiya Brāhmans meet, adieu to cooking.

Sub-Class.	No.	Subject of Proverbs.
	260.	The Pāñre does not practise what he preaches.
	261.	A Kāeth wants payment, a Brahmin feeding, and paddy and betel watering, but the low caste only kicks to make them do their work.
Barber.	262.	A barber's wedding.
Baniya.	263.	The owed baniya gives further tick.
Bābhan.	264.	A Bābhan, a dog, and a bhāt are always at variance with their own caste.
	265.	A Bābhan never to be believed.
	266.	One Bhuiñhār is equal to seven Chamārs.
Barhai (carpenter).	267.	A pretentious barhai or carpenter.
Chamārs (cobblers and shoemakers).	268.	When shoemakers quarrel, the king's saddle suffers.
	269.	A shoemaker's daughter with an aristocratic name !
Darji (tailor).	270.	Sticking to his last.
Dhobi (washerman).	271.	The Dhobi and his ass.
	272.	Washermen wash best under competition.
	273.	The washerman never tears his father's clothes.
	274.	The Dhobi, the tailor, and the barber are always careless.
	275.	A Dhobi is likely to starve in the village of the nude.
Kāyath.	276.	A Kāyath essentially a man of figures.
	277.	Sinning in good company is no sin (story of the Kāyaths who ate donkey's meat).
	278.	A Kāyath helpless without pen and paper.
	279.	Kāyaths, crows, and sweepings gather their own kinds.
	280.	A Kāyath when paying cash is the very devil.
	281.	A Kāyath gains when fools quarrel.
	282.	Wherever three Kāyaths gather together, a thunderbolt will fall.
	283.	Comparison of castes.
	284.	The three people who dance in others' houses.
Kurmi.	285.	A Kurmi always untrustworthy.
Kumhār (potter).	286	A Kumhār sleeps secure.

Sub-Class.	No.	Subject of Proverbs.
Musalmān.	287.	A Musalmān, a parrot, and a hare are never grateful.
	288.	To a Musalmān give toddy, to a bullock khensāri.
Mīyānji (or family tutor).	289.	When the Mīyānji is at the door, it is a bad look out for the dog.
	290.	The Mīyānji loses his beard in praise.
	291.	A Mīyānji's run is up to the mosque only.
Noniya.	292.	A Noniya's daughter is born to labour.
Rajpūt.	293.	Thick-headed.
Suthrā fakirs.	294.	Selfishness in Suthrā fakirs.
Sonār (goldsmith).	295.	Hundred strokes of the goldsmith will not equal one of the blacksmith.
Teli (oilman).	296.	A Teli, though possessed of lākhs, cannot equal Rāja Bhoj.
Jolha (weaver).	297.	The weaver bearing the sins of others.
	298.	The weaver as a cultivator.
	299.	The weaver penny wise and pound foolish.
	300.	A whip does not make an equestrian.
	301.	A weaver's daughter aping her betters.
	302.	A weaver becomes proud as a king when he has a gagra-full of rice.
	303.	The avaricious weaver.
	304.	The weaver asks to be let off fasting, but gets saddled with prayers.
	305.	The weaver suffers on leaving his loom.
	306.	Id without weavers.
	307.	A weaver makes a sad hash when required to reap a field.
	308.	The weaver going to cut grass at sunset.
	309.	The weaver tries to swim in a linseed field.
	310.	The weaver's wife.
	311.	Weavers' and shoemakers' promises never to be relied on.
	312.	A weaver as an impressed labourer.
	313.	A fight between a frog and a weaver.

CLASS IV.

Proverbs relating to Social and Moral Subjects, Religious
Customs and Popular Superstitions.

Sub-Class.	No.	Subject of Proverbs.
	314.	Angel of death to be feared.
	315.	As the Debi, so the offering.
	316.	A weak Debi and a strong he-goat for sacrifice.
	317.	A saddening reflection.
	318.	A fast woman of course blames others when she elopes.
	319.	A meddlesome woman.
	320.	A disgraced cat is as humble as a wife of the rat.
	321.	A forward woman.
	322.	Born to labour.
	323.	Bad lineage.
Brother and Sister-in-law.	324.	A weak elder brother-in-law is not respected.
	325.	A sister-in-law has a sister-in-law to annoy her.
Bride and Bridegroom.	326.	The bride gets rice gruel only, and others sweets !
	327.	A foolish bride gets no presents.
	328.	The " face-money " to the bride.
	329.	Crocodile tears of a bride.
Blind and Deaf.	330.	Blind master and deaf pupil.
	331.	Backbiter.
	332.	Charity (sharing the last crust).
	333.	Dying in Benares is going to heaven.
Daughter.	334.	Beware of overpraising your daughter.
	335.	A bad daughter ruins a son-in-law.
	336.	A daughter has three names in succession during her lifetime.
Dependent.	337.	A dependent knows no happiness.
Dancing.	338.	Making absurd conditions for dancing.
	339.	False modesty in dancers.

Sub-Class.	No.	Subject of Proverbs.
Especial haunts or resorts.	340.	The blind man's lodging is at the turner's.
	341.	A loose horse is sure to stand near the chaff-house.
	342.	Faith makes god of a stone.
Fools.	343.	A fool's property the prey of all.
	344.	A fool's property the prey of all.
	345.	A fool thinks of his belly only.
	346.	A fool worries himself with others' concern.
	347.	A fool went to fish, but lost his fishing basket.
	348.	A fool's wife the jest of all.
	349.	A fool unable to distinguish the trunk from the tail of an elephant.
	350.	A simpleton is " checked " by a dog even.
	351.	Who are fools according to Ghágh the poet.
	352.	The three greatest fools in this world.
Guests and hosts.	353.	Unwelcome guests.
	354.	Guests but in name.
	355.	Presuming to play the part of the hostess.
	356.	Assuming a leading part in a marriage ceremony.
	357.	The host, and he to get broken bits of cake.
	358.	Grandfather's funeral ceremony.
Habit second nature and unchangeable (the leopard cannot change his spots).	359.	Notwithstanding all charms and incantations the boy does not change his habit.
	360.	The rope burns, but not the twist.
	361.	A dog's tail can never be straightened.
	362.	Half dead, he still shakes his head.
	363.	Can the crow become white by eating camphor ?
Heart's dearest wish.	364.	What does a blind man want but his two eyes ?
Husband and wife.	365.	The husband claiming unmerited service from the wife.
	366.	The diffidence of the husband in making presents to his wife in his father's house.
	367.	When the cat is away the mice will play.
	368.	Husband unsuited to the wife.
	369.	A greedy wife.
	370.	A would-be paragon of a wife gives a pommelling to her husband.
	371.	Hard won prize.

Sub-Class.	No.	Subject of Proverbs.
Helplessness.	372.	He only "joins" bread who cannot make them.
	373.	If every one takes to becoming pilgrims, who is to do the worldly work ?
	374.	Ignorant villagers are easily duped.
	375.	Ignorant villager mulcted on going to complain.
Jewels.	376.	Ornaments as well as means of livelihood.
	377.	Job's comforter.
	378.	Love defies law.
Mischief makers	379.	Quarrels between relatives are made up ; mischief-makers only return home disappointed.
	380.	He tells the thief to steal and the wealthy to keep awake.
Mother and sister-in-law.	381.	The happiness of one who has neither mother-in-law nor sister-in-law.
	382.	Music is charming at a distance.
One blamed for another's fault, made a scapegoat.	383.	Chamru enjoys, while Deyāl gets whipped for it.
	384.	For the sake of one all are disliked.
	385.	The man with a moustache is blamed for the thieving of the moustacheless.
	386.	She in tatters is blamed for her in ornaments.
	387.	Priest and musician in one.
	388.	Physician prescribing according to the patient's wish.
Quarrelsome women, firebrands, etc.	389.	Quarrelsome women recommended to quarrel with decency.
	390.	A fire-brand, wherever she goes, she sets society by the ear.
	391.	The misfortune of a husband who has a scold of a wife.
	392.	A shrew strikes terror into a demon even.
Quarrels and jokes.	393.	The root of quarrels is practical jokes, as the root of disease is cough.
Sisters.	394.	Envious tears of an elder sister.
Sympathy and want of it.	395.	Pains of a chapped foot.
	396.	Does a barren woman know the pain of childbirth ?
	397.	To cry before a blind man is to waste tears.
	398.	Single-handed.

Sub-Class.	No.	Subject of Proverbs.
Son.	399.	An unworthy son.
	400.	Who avoids the beaten track.
Singing.	401.	Good singers are apt to be bored.
	402.	Social aspirant snubbed.
Troubles increased.	403.	She went to ask for a son, but lost her husband.
	404.	He prayed that his troubles may be lessened, but they were doubled.
	405.	The dead boy had fine eyes.
Tobacco.	406.	The man who offers you tobacco and lime unasked is sure to go to heaven.
	407.	Tobacco is necessary for life.
	408.	The devil even flees from a thrashing.
Thieves.	409.	The thief on the contrary mulcting the police.
	410.	Thick as thieves.
	411.	A thief's heart is in the *kakri* field.
	412.	With a thief he is a thief, to a watchman he is a servant only.
	413.	A thief is a thief, whether he steals a diamond or a cucumber.
	414.	A thief will not stick at a borrowed plate.
	415.	An impudent thief : he warns when he steals.
	416.	A thief with a face bright as the moon.
	417.	Taking tick *sine die*.
	418.	The idler (indolent).
	419.	Uncle and nephew at loggerheads (paying off old scores).
	420.	Vicissitudes of life.
	421.	Waiting for the auspicious time may bring ruin.
	422.	Waverer's repentance.
Widow.	423.	A spinster weeping with a widow.
	424.	Handful of bangles or a widow.
Wedding.	425.	Wedding of a noseless woman and nine hundred obstacles.
	426.	Wedding headdress made of mango leaves even.
	427.	The song ought to be for her whose wedding it is.
Worshipping.	428.	Easy worship of the pīpal-tree.
	429.	Making a virtue of necessity in worshipping.

CLASS V.

Proverbs relating to Agriculture and Seasons.

Sub-Class.	No.	Subject of Proverbs.

430. Distant farming ruinous.
431. The closer the field, the easier its culture.
432. Selling bullocks for seed.
433. A farmer is known when at his field.
434. Anxieties of agriculture unknown to the lazy lubber.
435. If goats and sheep answer for ploughing, why purchase bullocks?
436. Impertinent request to lend a bullock for ploughing.
437. The meaning of a speckled cloud and a widow applying scented oil.
438. The meaning of its beginning to rain on Saturday, Tuesday, Thursday, and Sunday respectively.
439. The meaning of the rainbow at the beginning and end of rain.
440. The meaning of the halo round the moon on Sunday, Tuesday, and Thursday respectively.
441. The rain in the beginning of Aradra and the end of Hathiya.
442. The asterisms of Maggha, Swāti and Hathiya.
443. The effects of the several rains on the different crops.
444. The effect of rain in Baisākh (April–May) on paddy; the yield is doubled.
445. If there is rain in Krittika (middle of May), there will be no rain for the six following asterisms.
446. When to sow *China*.
447. When rice will be plentiful.
448. The rain of Aradra (middle of June) does away with distress.

CLASS VI.

Proverbs relating to Cattle and Animals in General.

APPENDIX.

Popular Superstitions and Errors.

BIHAR PROVERBS.

CLASS I.

PROVERBS RELATING TO HUMAN FAILINGS, FOIBLES, AND VICES.

Affectation, Dissembling, Hypocrisy, Pretence, Shamming, etc.

1. Cutting off the head and pretending to preserve the hair.

९ मूँड़ काटीँ वाल के रच्छा

Muñr katiñ bal ke rachchha.

You make a show of preserving the hair, while you are really cutting off the head (*lit.* cutting off the head and preserving his hair).

It would be applied to one who, while he was secretly trying to do you a serious injury, was all the time pretending to be your friend; one who simulates friendship, but who really is your greatest enemy. E.E. "A wolf in sheep's clothing."

2. Father a drunkard and the son pretending to play the rôle of a religious man.

२ वाप के गले लबनी पूत के गले उदराछ

Bāp ke gale labni, pūt ke gale udrāchh.

The father has a **लबनी** *labni* tied to his neck (his constant companion), while the son wears a necklace of **उदराज** "*udrāj*"! (or **उदराछ** *udrāchh*).

"*Labni*" is a longish earthen pot used for collecting palm juice or "toddy." Smaller ones are also used for drinking. "*Udrāchh*" is the necklace made out of the seeds of the rudrāchh *(Eleocarpus ganitrus)* and worn commonly by devotees or *Bhagats* who eschew worldly ways. Hence the father is a debauchee while the son proclaims himself a religious man, and affects the ways and outward signs of a devotee. Said in sarcasm of a man who ostentatiously parades his horror of vice generally, when it exists in his own family. (There is no reason why one whose father is a confirmed drunkard should not be a virtuous man and lead the pious life of a hermit or an ascetic; but the usual style of sarcasm is to ridicule one by pointing out the failings of his ancestors. The point of sarcasm, it will be noticed, is levelled at the parade the son makes of his virtuous and pure life, knowing his father's failing.)

3. One for show and another for use.

३ हाथी के दाँत खाय के दोसर देखावे के दोसर

Hāthi ke dānt; khāy ke dosar, dekhāwe ke dosar.

Like the tusk and teeth of an elephant; one set for show and another for use (*lit.* to eat with).

Said of a hypocrite; one who plays a double part; one whose outward behaviour is the reverse of his real character. A dissembler. (In proverb 246 this simile is made use of to illustrate exactly the opposite virtue, namely, of keeping to one's word.)

4. Pretending to turn over a new leaf.

४ नव सै चूहा खा के बिल्ली चली हज को

Nao sai chūha kha ke billi chali haj ko.

After eating nine hundred rats the cat is now going on a pilgrimage.

Said of a wicked man who pretends to turn over a new leaf and become virtuous after countless acts of sin. (It is an Urdu proverb. The Hindi form of it from *Sūr Dās* is तप करिबे को चली बिलैया सत्तर चूहा खाय के *Tap karibe ko chali bilaiya sattar chūha khāy ke.*)

5. Pretending the end of the cucumber is bitter.

५ सगरे खीरा खा के भेटी तीत

Sagre khīra kha ke bheti tit.

After eating the whole of the cucumber he says the end of it is bitter!

भेटी "*Bheti*" is the end or part of a fruit attached to the stalk. E.E. "Swallowing a camel and straining at a gnat." It is also called ढेंपी "*dheṅpi.*"

6. Sinner turned a saint.

६ कब की बीबी बाम्हनी

Kab ki bibi bāmhni.

Since when has the *Bibi* turned a *Bāmhni (i.e.* an upright woman)? "*Bibi*" is the usual title of a Musalmān lady, here used for a woman with indifferent reputation, in opposition to a *Bāmhni*, who, being the wife of a Hindu priest, is supposed to be strictly virtuous. Said when one of indifferent reputation suddenly affects a respectable rôle. The following story is told in illustration of the above saying. A sarāi (or inn) was kept by some Musalmān *Bhattiārins.* They found that they were not patronized by Hindus, so to attract Hindu customers they set up one woman among them as a Brāhmani; and in consequence of this subterfuge they soon had a Brāhman visitor, and the newly-made "*Bāmhni*" was told off to attend him. In course of talk the "*Bāmhni*" asked the newly-arrived guest how long ago it was that he had become a Brāhman. "Since when have you become a *Bāmhni?*" asked the suspecting Brāhman. "Only last week," was the reply. The Brāhman did not stay long in the sarāi after this information.

7. Shamming to shirk.

७ सींग झारे और खुर घिसे पीठ न बोझा ले
ऐसे बूढ़े बैल को बाँधि कवन भुस दे

Sīng jhāre aur khur ghise pīth na bojha le
Aise būrhe bail ko bāndhi kawan bhus de ?

Who is going to feed such an old (useless) bullock that shakes its horns, rubs its hoofs on the ground, and refuses any weight on its back? These are the signs of a lazy (*korhi*) bullock that refuses to work; there is no use in feeding such a useless animal. Said of a worthless man who will not work from laziness.

8. She knows nine but not six.

८ नव जानेली छव ना जानस
Nao jāneli chao na jānas.

Knows nine but not six!

Said of one who shams ignorance—pretends not to know simple things, but really knows a great deal. Applied usually to women.

9. Sinking low indeed!

९ कहावे ले सैयद चोरावे ले छुच्छी
Kahāwe le saiyad chorāwe le chhuchchhi.

She styles herself a *saiyad*, but she can be low enough

to steal even a nose stud. Said sarcastically when one who is commonly accepted as a respectable person descends to do a low act. सैयद् "*Saiyad*" is the most respectable sect (the priest-class) among the Mohamedans. Another proverb of similar application is कहावे के बीबी चोरावे के चमरख *Kahāwe ke bibi chorāwe ke chamrakh*, i.e. calls herself a lady, but can stoop to steal the leather of the spinning axle. चमरख "*Chamrakh*" is the leather on which the spinning axle rests in passing the upright.

10. Pretended delicacy.

१० कहावे के बुलबुल लीले के गूलर
Kahāwe ke bulbul, līle ke gūlar.

She calls herself a *bulbul*, but swallows a *gūlar!* बुलबुल "*Bulbul*" is a nightingale, and is used to represent a delicate creature. A *bulbul* is too small to be able to swallow a *gūlar* (*i.e.* a wild fig). Cast at those who pretend to be delicate and small, but are really the opposite.

11. Old in sin and yet a novice.

११ लड़िका खाइत खाइत बूढ़ी भेलीँ लोग कहे बकडाइन
Larika khāit khāit būrhi bhelīñ; log kahe, bakdāin.

I have grown old in experience (*lit.* in eating children), still people call me a novice (*lit.* a semi-witch; not a "full" witch). डाइन *Dāin* is "a witch." Her favourite occupation would seem to be to kill (metaphorically " to eat") children. A बकडाइन "*bakdāin*" is not a full *dāin*; something wanting to make one a full *dāin*.

One who prides herself on possessing a life-long experience in anything (chiefly in evil practices), but finds her experience questioned, is supposed to express her indignation in this ghastly metaphor. It is of course uttered by a third party, as if coming from the person to be ridiculed. The point of the sarcasm lies in the person being represented as boasting of her misdeeds (which she really does not).

Avarice, Parsimony, Covetousness, Greed, etc.

12. A life's hoarding lost at a stroke.

१२ साङ्क बटोरे कौड़ी कौड़ी राम बटोरे कुप्पा

Sāhu batore kauri kauri, Rām batore kuppa.

The *sāhu* (or shopkeeper) collects (*ghi* or oil) little by little (a *kauri's* weight) at a time, but Rām (the god) sweeps away a whole *kuppa*. कौड़ी कौड़ी "*Kauri kauri*" means a very small weight at a time: the weight of a *kauri*, or a shell, which is the lowest current coin. कुप्पा "*Kuppa*" is a leather vessel used for keeping oil or *ghi* in large quantities; and contains about a maund. Said in derision of the *sāhu* or *baniya* who laboriously gathers *kauri* by *kauri*, while misfortune with one stroke sweeps away the whole of his hoard.

13. "Almighty dollar."

१३ गुरु ना गुरभैया सब तेँ बरा रुपैया

Guru na gurbhaiya
Sab teñ bara rupaiya.

Neither the spiritual guide nor the fellow disciple are of any account; greater than they all is the rupee.

गुरभैया *Gurbhaiya*. The son of the religious teacher is regarded in native society with the same respect and affection as one's own brother.

14. The miser's loss is sudden.

१४ कौड़ी कौड़ी कैल बटोर   रुपया भैल त ले गैल चोर

Kauri kauri kail bator
Rupya bhail ta le gail chor.

He gathered a shell at a time, and when he had gathered enough to make a rupee a thief stole it.

Said to laugh at a miser when he loses what he has toiled and pinched himself to gather.

15. The miser and his wife.

१५ सूमिन पूछे सूम से काहे बदन मलीन
का गाँठी का गिर पड़ा का काहू को दीन
ना गाँठी का गिर पड़ा ना काहू कछु दीन
देत लेत पर देखिया ता तैं बदन मलीन

Sūmin pūchhe sūm se, kāhe badan malīn
Ka gānthi ka gir para, ka kāhu ko dīn
Na gānthi ka gir para, na kāhu kachhu dīn
Det let par dekhiya, ta teñ badan malīn.

The miser's wife asked her husband, "Why are you looking so sad? Has anything dropt out of your pocket, or have you given away anything to anybody?" "No," was the reply, "nothing has dropt out of my pocket, nor have I given away anything to anybody. I saw another parting with his money, and that has made me sad!" *i.e.* A miser feels unhappy at seeing others generous.

बदन "*Badan*" face; some people say "*deh*," body, instead of "*badan.*"

16. Take one and give two.

१६ लेना एक न देना दू
Lena ek, na dena du.

To take one and give two; *i.e.* not to hold any intercourse, not to have any transaction.

"I will not take one and give two."

The following story is told in illustration of the above
proverb:—Once upon a time a peacock and a tortoise
became great friends. The peacock lived on a tree on the
banks of the stream in which the tortoise had his home;
and daily the peacock after he had a drink of water danced
near the stream and displayed his gay plumage for the
amusement of his friend. One unfortunate day a bird-
catcher who was on the prowl caught the peacock and was
about taking him away to the market. The unhappy bird
begged of his captor to allow him to bid his friend the
tortoise good-bye, as it would be the last time he would
see him. The bird-catcher allowed him his prayer and
took him to the tortoise, who was greatly moved to see his
friend a captive. The tortoise asked the bird-catcher to
let the peacock go; but he laughed at the request, saying
that was his means of livelihood. The tortoise then said,
"If I make you a handsome present, will you let my friend
go?" "Certainly," answered the bird-catcher, "that is
all I want." Whereupon the tortoise dived into the water
and in a few seconds came up with a handsome pearl,
which, to the great astonishment of the bird-catcher, he
handed to him. This was beyond his expectations, and he
let the peacock go immediately. A short time after the
avaricious man came back and told the tortoise that he
thought he had not paid him enough for the release of his
friend, and threatened that unless a match to that pearl
was obtained for him, he would again catch the peacock.
The tortoise, who had already advised his friend to betake
himself to a distant jungle on being set free, was greatly

enraged at the greed of this man. "Well," said the tortoise, "if you insist on having another pearl like it, give it to me and I will fish you out an exact match for it." The cupidity of the bird-catcher prevented his reasoning that "one in hand was equal to two in the bed of the stream," and he speedily gave the pearl to the wily tortoise, who swam out with it, saying, "I am no fool to take one and give two!" and forthwith disappeared, leaving the bird-catcher to be sorry ever after for his covetousness.

17. When gaining he is discontented, when losing contented.

१७   आवत हाही जात सन्तोख

Āwat hāhi, jāt santokh.

When it is coming in (*i.e.* he is gaining), he is discontented; when it is going out (*i.e.* he is losing), he becomes contented—*i.e.* the more an avaricious man gets, the more he is anxious for, and is consequently discontented. But he learns to be contented when he begins losing. Then he would be content with what is left, if he should only lose no more.

Aping.

18. Aping a losing game.

१८   कौवा गेला हंस के चाल सीखे

अैला अपन चाल गँवाय

Kauwa gela hans ke chāl sīkhe,
Aila apan chāl gañwāy.

The crow went to learn the ways ("walk") of the goose, but lost its own!

चाल " *Chāl,*" *lit.* " walk," hence " ways," " habit." The waddling gait of the goose is much admired.

One who abandons his natural ways to ape those of others is very apt to lose his individuality and make himself ridiculous.

19. Aping your betters causes discomfort.

१९   बिना बान तिलक लिलार चरचराय

Bina bān tilak lilār charcharāy.

Whoever applies a *tilak*, being unaccustomed to it, will find his forehead skin-chapped. Said to ridicule one who apes the habits of his betters and finds that he is not made comfortable thereby. (तिलक " *Tilak* " is the sandal-wood mark that a Brāhman applies to his forehead. When it dries, the skin shrinks with it. The sandal paste is made by rubbing sandal-wood.) Another proverb of similar application is बे बान के खरिका बाँस बरोबर *Be bān ke kharika bāns barobar*, "To one not in the habit of using a toothpick, it is like a bamboo ! " *i.e.* he feels when using it as uncomfortable as if he were forcing a bamboo between his teeth. Said to ridicule those who take to a habit in imitation of others and find that it makes them very uncomfortable.

20. Paying dearly for aping.

२०   अनकर सेन्दुर देख के आपन कपार फोरीं

Ankar sendur dekh ke āpan kapār phorīñ.

If I see vermilion on another's forehead, am I to crack my own ? (*i.e.* cause it to bleed so as to appear as if I have also applied vermilion ?). An admonition to those who cannot afford it, but strain their utmost to appear like others, and really suffer thereby.

Aimed at those who ape others.

Bullying, Oppressing, Venting Rage, etc.

21. The weak bullying the weaker.

२१ कदुआ पर सितुआ चोख

Kadua par situa chokh.

The *situa* is sharp enough for the pumpkin.

सितुआ "*Situa*" is a "spoon" or "scraper," generally made out of a shell. A kind of primitive spoon with a blunt edge; here it is meant for a blunt instrument.

The "*situa*" with its blunt edge is an instrument sharp enough to cut the soft pumpkin, though not sharp enough to make any impression on a hard surface. One who takes advantage of the weakness of his inferior and bullies him may fitly be compared to the *situa* operating on the pumpkin. *E.g.*, when a petty police constable visits a village, among the villagers he is the very embodiment of authority.

22. The cunning bully the weak.

२२ चतुर के खीस अबरे पर उठेला

Chatur ke khis abare par uthela.

The rage of the cunning man is (usually) vented on the weak, *i.e.* on those unable to resent it.

23. The anvil bears the missing stroke.

२३ झकल चोट नेहाई पर

Hukal chot nehāi par.

The missing (or empty) stroke falls on the anvil. Usually said when a man is angry with one and vents his rage on another weaker than himself—on one who is usually the butt of his anger. ·

24. The fallen are trampled.

२४   परल पाईं मुँगरे मुँगरे ठठाईं

Paral paiñ muñgre muñgre thathaiñ.

The fallen are cudgelled repeatedly.

One who is found weak and fallen is constantly beaten with a mallet. Those who are down are always apt to be kicked. (The use of *muñgre* twice denotes repetition of the act.)

25. Entirely at your mercy.

२५   मार काट पिया तोरे आस

Mār kāt piya tore ās.

Whether you kill or save, I am at your mercy (*lit.* all my hope rests in you).

मार काट "*Mār kāt*" is *lit.* "to beat" and "to cut up."

26. Venting one's rage on the innocent.

२६   ठेस लगे पहारे घर के फोरौं सिलवत

Thes luge pahāre, ghar ke phoriñ silwat.

I hurt myself against a rock (*lit.* I receive a knock from a rock), but vent my rage on the grinding-stone at home by breaking it. Usually said by the wife who has to put up with the rage of the husband if he has met with any reverse or disappointment in the world.

Bad Hand-writing.

27. Bad hand-writing.

२७   लिखें मूसा पढ़ें खोदा

Likheñ Mūsa parheñ Khoda.

What is written by *Mūsa* (Moses) can only be read by God (*lit.* Moses writes and God reads). Said when the hand-writing is so bad that nobody can read it.

A slight variation in the pronunciation of the words *Músa* and *Khoda* (pronouncing the syllables separately, *Mú-sa* and *Khod-a*) gives a ludicrous turn to the meaning of the passage. "He writes as fine as hair, and, in order to read it, has to come himself" (*i.e.* he writes so badly that no one else can read his writing except himself), where *mu* (Persian) is "hair." The same idea is got by substituting *Īsa* (Jesus) for *Músa* (Moses)—**लिखें ऐसा पढ़ें खोदा** *Likheñ aisa parheñ khoda*, "He writes so (badly) that he has to come himself to read it."

Blabbing.

28. A blabber dying to blab.

२८ कहे विना रहा ना जाय   सारा भगवा जरा जाय

> *Kahe bina raha na jãy*
> *Sāra bhagwa jara jãy.*

When the loin-cloth is burning, it is impossible to refrain from speaking out.

Puts in a quaint way the failing of one who is affected with *cacoethes loquendi* and cannot keep himself from blabbing, just as one whose loin-cloth takes fire, must needs jump and cry out; also said when any one suffers a wrong from another's hand and finds it impossible to refrain from complaining. Also said when one feels compelled to speak.

29. The tell-tale causes the downfall of a kingdom.

२९ घर का भेदिया लंका डाह

> *Ghar ka bhediya lanka dāh.*

The man who divulges home secrets (the tell-tale) brings about the ruin of a house (as Bibhīkhan caused the downfall of Lanka).

The allusion is to the Hindu mythology. Bibhīkhan, the brother of Rāban, by joining Rāmchandra and giving out the secrets of his brother, caused the downfall of Lanka.

Counting the chickens before they are hatched, Anticipating, etc.

30. The son is born before the father.

३० बाप जमबे ना कैले पूत पिछुआरे ठाढ भैले

Bāp jambe na kaile, pūt pichhuāre thārh bhaile.

The father is not yet born, but the son has taken his stand behind.

This is said as a riddle, meaning "smoke." The father is the fire and the son the smoke, which usually precedes the fire.

Said when one anticipates an event by a long period.

A similar Urdu proverb is गाछ पर कटहल होँठ मेँ तेल *Gāchh par katahal, hoñth meñ tel,* "The jack fruit is yet on the tree, but the oil has been already applied to the lips." (The "jack" being a very glutinous fruit, oil is usually applied to the lips to prevent it sticking.)

E.E. "Counting the chickens before they are hatched."

31. The father is still unborn, but the son attends a wedding (safflower).

३१ बाप रहल पेटे पूत गैल बरियात

Bāp rahal pete, pūt gail bariyāt.

While the father was still in the womb (*i.e.* pod), the son went to a wedding party.

The father is the seed of the safflower in pods; the son is the safflower dye (Grierson).

32. Proclaiming before the son is born.

३२ वेटा भैवे ना कैल पहिले डन्डा डोर

Beta bhaibe na kail, pahile dandu dor.

The son is not yet born, but a beat of the drum proclaims the event beforehand.

Of similar application to Proverb No. 30.

33. Crying before he is hurt.

३३ लौर कपार का भेँट ना बाप बाप श्रगते

Laur kapār ka bheñt na, bāp bāp agate.

Before the cudgel and his forehead have met, he cries
out, "O father, O father," the usual cry of a native when
he is hurt.

i.e. Crying before one is hurt.

34. Anticipating evil.

३४ वाग लगवे ना कैल मंगरन डेरा देल

Bāg lagbe na kail mañgran dera del.

The trees in the orchard have not yet been planted,
but the woodworms have settled down there beforehand.

मंगर "*Mangar*" is a longish kind of insect destructive to trees in general. It has a hard beak with
which it burrows into the wood, and destroys the pith.
Applied when destructive agents are already present
before anything is begun. "Canker in the germ."

Conceit about one's wisdom.

35. Conceit about one's wisdom.

३५ विधि रचल बुद्धि साढ़े तीन
तेह मेँ श्राधा जगत श्रापन तीन

Bidhi rachal buddhi sārhe tīn
Teh meñ ādha jagat āpan tīn.

God made wisdom of three parts and a half, of which the half went to the world, the rest to him; *i.e.* according to the person aimed at, the whole world has got only the half, while he possesses the remaining three parts.

This is a sarcastic reference to a conceited man.

Extravagance.

36. Can't afford rice-gruel, but drinks toddy.

३६　माँड़ न जूरे ताड़ी

Māñr na jūre tāri.

He cannot afford rice-gruel, yet he (drinks) toddy! Extravagance in a drunkard.

37. Expenditure on a thing more than its worth.

३७　दमड़ी के वुलबुल टका चौथाइ

Damri ke bulbul taka chothāi.

The bird is not worth more than a *damri*, but the "plucking" costs a *taka*.

दमड़ी *Damari* = eight kauris, or $3\frac{1}{8}$ *dām.*

टका *Taka* = two (Gorakhpuri) pice.

Said when the expenditure in connection with a thing is more than it is really worth.

38. Cost of the wood is nine pice, but he spends 90 on it.

३८　नव के लकड़ी नब्बे खरच

Nao ke lakari nabbe kharach.

The wood is worth nine only, but the expenditure thereon is ninety.

(Variation of No. 160, meaning to imply that the expenses in connection with an object are more than it is really worth.)

39. Useless appendage.

३९ चाकर का चूकर मँड़ई का ओसारा

Chākar ka chūkar mañraï ka osāra.

Servant to a servant is like a portico to a hut.

Useless, unnecessary, out of place.

चूकर "*Chūkar*" is a word coined to agree in sound with चाकर "*Chākar*," *i.e.* a servant.

An unnecessary appendage.

40. Servant to a servant.

४० नोकरो के चाकर तेकरो लमैचर

Nokaro ke chākar tekaro lamaichar.

Servant to a servant and on him another dependent.

"*Lamaichar*" is probably connected with लमेरा "*lamera*," which Mr. Grierson defines as " the seed which falls on the ground in the field at harvest time, and which germinates next year;" a wild uncared-for plant; extra; not in the regular order. Hence a servant's servant would be one out of the regular order, an extra, unnecessary appendage.

Exaggeration.

41. Critics say more than the poet.

४१ थोर कैलन तुलसीदास बहुत कैलन कविता

(या) थोड़ा करैँ वाली मियाँ बहुत करैँ डफ़ाली

Thor kailan Tulsīdās bahut kailan kabita

(ya) Thora karaiñ Bāli Miyāñ bahut karaiñ dafāli.

Little was said by the poet Tulsīdās, but a great deal was added by the (other) poets (and commentators).

Tulsīdās was the well-known author of the Rāmāyan. Commonly said when the original story is greatly exaggerated.

42. Making a mountain of a mole hill.

४२ सिआर के गूह परवत

Siār ke gūh parbat.

The dirt of the jackal is made into a mountain (*i.e.* to magnify trifles).

E.E. To make a mountain of a mole hill.

43. A lakh is on the lips of a brag.

४३ लवार का मुँह में लाख रुपैया

Labār ka muñh meñ lākh rupaiya.

A *lākh* is on the lips (mouth) of a liar; *i.e.* a fibber, who is all talk, can give you as high a figure as you wish without the least hesitation; that is, a liar has no scruple in exaggerating. *Labār* is a braggart.

Gluttony.

44. A greedy daughter-in-law.

४४ सात बासी सात तेवासी बहुरिया कहवथ रात के उपासी

Sāt bāsi sāt tewāsi, bahuriya kahawath rāt ke upāsi.

The daughter-in-law has fed seven times on the remnants of yesterday's meal, and seven times on the remnants of the day before; still she makes out she is fasting from last night.

बासी *"Bāsi"* is what is left over-night from the previous day's meal, and तेवासी *"tewāsi"* is what remains the third day.

This ungracious speech is supposed to be uttered by the mother-in-law who is always at "daggers drawn" with her daughter-in-law.

45. Pretended fasting before her husband.

४५ सात बेरी सतौन पिया आगे दतौन

Sāt beri sataun, piya āge dataun.

Seven times has she breakfasted, and yet before her husband she is only brushing her teeth (*i.e.* preparing to eat for the first time).

Natives as a rule never eat before cleaning their teeth. Hence हम अभी तक दतौन ना करलीं "*Ham abhi tak dataun na karlīñ*" implies that "I have not yet broken my fast even." दतौन "*Dataun*" is a tooth brush made of a twig of *Nim.* सतौन "*Sataun*" is from सतनजा "*satanja,*" or 7 *ans*, or kinds of grain mixed, which is usually eaten as an early breakfast. This mixture of 7 kinds of grain is also eaten on other occasions, such as during the paddy transplanting time in some parts of Bihār.

Also a sneer cast at the wife by either her mother-in-law or sister-in-law.

46. Ambition dying for name; greed for belly.

४६ नामी मरलन नाम ला पेटू मरलन पेट ला

Nāmi maralan nām la petu maralan pet la.

The ambitious man dies for fame: the glutton for his belly!

47. The greedy advised to eat with eyes closed before children.

४७ आँख मूंद के खाईं लड़िका ना परिकाईं

Ānkh mūnd ke khāīñ ; larika na parikāīñ.

Shut your eyes and eat; and do not encourage children.

This is thrust at a glutton who does not offer what he is eating to the children standing by. He is advised (in bitter irony) to shut his eyes lest he may, seeing the

children, feel induced to share with them what he is
eating, and thus encourage them.   (Shame is supposed to
dwell in the eyes, by shutting them, therefore, one does
not feel any shame ; and thus he can play the rôle of a
tender-hearted and liberal man and also make the excuse
that he does not wish to encourage children.)

48. Hunger to be appeased before devotion.

४८ चार कवर भीतर तब देवता पीतर
Chār kawar bhītar, tab deota pītar.

First eat (*lit.* put inside you) four mouthfuls, then think
of deities and ancestral heroes.

This is hit at those who think of their belly more than
the household gods.

कवर *"Kawar"* or कौर *" kaur "* is a mouthful or mor-
sel. देवता पीतर *"Deota pītar"* are deities and deceased
ancestors who are worshipped after their death.   The
household gods.

49. " Enemy to food."

४९ काम के न काज के दुसमन अनाज के
Kām ke na kāj ke, dusman anāj ke.

Fit for no work, but an enemy to grain (*i.e.* destroys
food).

One who lives to eat ; cast at a lazy fellow who fills
his belly and does no work.

Ingratitude.

50. The young of a cuckoo will after all be a cuckoo.

५० कोइली के बचवा कोइली होइहैँ कौआ मूहैँ छाय
Koili ke bachwa koili hoihen kaua muhen chhāy.

The young of the cuckoo will (after all) be a cuckoo,

and cause the crow (its foster-mother) grief and disappointment.

मूहैं छाय "*Mūheñ chhāy*" *lit.* is to put ashes on the face. Besmearing one's face with ashes or dust is a token of sorrow and penitence. "Covering of the head with ashes has been long a common sign of mourning among Eastern nations, indicative of the greatest distress and humiliation." E.E. "Birds of a feather flock together." "Like will produce like."

51. A snake bites its charmer.

५१   उलटा साँप सपहेरिये काटे
Ulta sāmp sapaheriye kāte.

When a snake turns he bites the snake-charmer (its keeper), *i.e.* "stings the bosom that warmed it."

Said of "ingratitude" (or उलटा "*ulta*" may be rendered "on the contrary," *i.e.* contrary to what it ought to do, which would give the same idea of "ingratitude").

52. A viper is never grateful.

५२   साँप के दूध पियाईं तवहूँ बीखे उगली
Sāmp ke dudh piyāiñ tabahūñ bīkhe ugali.

The snake even if fed (all its life) on milk will always when it bites give out venom. *Ugali* is to vomit, "to spit out."

E.E. "The leopard cannot change his spots."

53. Like a horse which grumblingly neighs when given *ghi*.

५३   घीउ देत घोड़ नरियाय
Ghīu det ghor nariyāy.

When given *ghi* the horse grumblingly neighs!
Said of one, who, instead of being grateful for favours,

scorns them like a horse that is not thankful for being fed on a dainty like *ghi* (clarified butter).

Ignorance.

54. Poor attainments taunted.

४८   कोदो दे के पढ़ल है

Kodo de ke parhala hai ?

Have you paid *kodo* for your education ?

कोदो " *Kodo* " *(Paspalum frumentaceum)* is one of the small millets.   It is very cheap, and the usual food of the poorest classes ; hence despised by the well-to-do.   The idea is that if his education has been purchased at so cheap a price, it cannot be worth much.   Said to quiz one of his ignorance.

Improvidence.

55. An improvident man overtaken by the flood.

५५   सिरकी एक देलन्हि तानि

    ताहि बेर में ँ आएल पानि

    सिरकी उठावे क रहल ना बेरा

    आगू नाँथ न पाछू पगहा

Siraki ek delanhi tāni

Tāhi ber men āel pāni

Siraki uthāwe ka rahal na bera

Āgu nānth na pāchhu pagaha.

He pitched his hovel, and it began to rain, nor could he get an opportunity for striking it ; he was (like an ass) without nose-string or tether.

सिरकी " *Siraki* " is a hut or tent made of reeds of that name (Grierson).

The meaning of this proverb comes out better with the

following variation: instead of "*āgu nānth na pāchhu pagaha*" read "*na āgu nāo na pāchhu bera*," which is the form sometimes used.

"He pitched his hovel, when down came the flood; he had no time to strike it, nor had he a boat or a raft to save himself." Said of course to ridicule those who are so improvident as to make no provision for the future and suffer in consequence. बेरा "*Bera*" is a raft usually made by joining plantain trees.

Inability to appreciate worth, merit. (Pearls before swine.)

56. Can a low caste appreciate *bāra*?

५६   राड़ जाने बारा के सवाद
Rār jāne bāra ke sawād.

What do the vulgar (low caste) know of the taste of the *bāra*? बारा "*Bāra*" are cakes of *urid* pulse fried in *ghi* or oil, and considered a great delicacy among the respectable people. E.E. "Casting pearls before swine."

57. Can a monkey appreciate ginger?

५७   बानर जाने आदी के सवाद
Bānar jāne ādi ke sawād?

What does the monkey know of the taste of the ginger? (A variation of Proverb 56.)

58. The hubble-bubble in the hands of a monkey.

५८   बानर के हाथ में नरियर
Bānar ke hāth meñ nariyar?

The hubble-bubble in the hands of a monkey!

नरियर "*Nariyar*" is cocoanut—hence hubble-bubble made of the cocoanut shell.

A man who does not know the use of a thing, which he

has probably come by accidentally, is sure to spoil it, just as a monkey would a *nariyar*, which he could not appreciate.

59. Music hath no charms for a buffalo.

५९   भैंस के आगे बेन बजावे बैठो भैंस पागुराय (या भैंसो
पागुलावे)

Bhaiñs ke āge ben bajāwe, baithi bhaiñs pāgurāy
(ya bhaiñsi pāgulāwe).

(He) plays the flute before the buffalo, but the buffalo sits (unconcernedly) and ruminates !

Perfectly indifferent to the charms of music (expresses want of appreciation). *Pāgurāy* chews the cud.

बेन *"Ben"*—the correct word is बेणु *"Benu,"* which means bamboo; hence all musical instruments made out of it, such as वाँसुरी *bāñsuri*, etc., derive their names.

60. Useless to adorn before a blind husband.

६०   का पर करौँ सिंगार पुरुख मोर आँधर

Ka par karoñ siñgār, purukh mor āndhar.

What is the use of adorning myself, my husband is blind? का पर *"Ka par," lit.* " on what." This is a peculiar idiom among the common people, meaning " on what strength or hope," " relying on what strength."

61. To the blind day and night are the same.

६१   (१) आँधर का लेखे दीन रात बरोबर
      (२) जे दीये ना देखी से दीया ले का देखी

      (1) *Āndhar ka lekhe dīn rāt barobar.*
      (2) *Je diye na dekhi se diya le kā dekhi.*

(1) To a blind man day and night are alike.   (2) The other proverb is a play on the words दीये *diye*, " even the

light," and देखी *dekhi*, "to see." He who cannot see the
light itself, what can he see with the light?

The well-known Urdu proverb दीया ना दीया *diya na diya*
is a play on the word *diya*, and has two meanings: (1) You
have not given me a light. (2) Your giving is the same
as not giving, *i.e.* you have given under such conditions
(perhaps so late), that it amounts to not giving; the gift
has no value. Also said when anything is given nominally,
with the object of being taken away.

62. Worth unappreciated.

६२ जहाँ बूझ ना बड़ाई तहाँ से भाग चल रे भाई

    Jahāñ būjh na barāi tahāñ se bhāg chal re bhāi.

Brother! let us flee from a place where there is no
appreciation of worth. बूझ ना बड़ाई *Būjh na barāi, lit.*
neither understanding nor honour or respect (paid to the
worthy).

63. Merit not recognized (illustrated by an allegory).

६३ अँधेरपूर नगरी कुबुद्धी राजा
    टके सेर भाजी टके सेर खाजा

    Andherpūr nagari kubuddhi rāja
    Take ser bhāji take ser khāja.

The country is one of unreason; the ruler is Folly.
Both भाजी *bhāji* and खाजा *khāja* are sold at the same
price (*lit.* at a टका *taka* a seer).

अँधेरपूर "*Andherpūr*" is an allegorical name (from
अँधेर *andher*, unjust, unreasonable, senseless, and पूर *pūr*,
city) for a country where there is no sense of justice;
and कुबुद्धी "*kubuddhi*" (from कु *ku*, bad, and बुद्धी *buddhi*,
sense) for one wanting in sense.

भाजी *Bhāji* or *sāg* is a very common herb used for

pottage and found often growing wild, and of little or no value: whereas खाजा *khāja* is an expensive sweetmeat made of flour, *ghi*, milk and sugar.

The meaning is that in such a country as the above no distinction is made between the good and the bad, the deserving and the undeserving, the worthy and the unworthy. Another proverb of similar import is No. 64.

64. Making no distinction.

६४ सब धान बाइसे पसेरी
Sab dhān bāise paseri.

To him every kind of paddy is the same (*lit.* worth 22 paseries per rupee).

There are of course different classes of धान *dhān* or paddy, and like most things the price varies with the quality. When this is not recognized and all are treated alike, no distinction being made according to merit, this saying is used.

Inattention.

65. Enquiring who is the hero after the whole tale is finished.

६५ सारा रामायन कह गये सीता किस की जोय
Sāra Rāmāyan kah gaye, Sīta kis ki joy ?

After the whole Rāmāyan has been repeated, (he enquires) whose wife is Sīta ?

राम "Rām," the husband of सीता "Sīta," is the principal character in the रामायन "Rāmāyan." "The whole plot of this great Epic poem, the 'Rāmāyan,' rests on a rash promise given by Dasaratha, king of Ayodhya, to his second wife, Kaikeyi, that he would grant her two boons. In order to secure the succession to her own son, she asks that Rāma, the eldest son of the king's other wife, should be banished for fourteen years. Much as the king repents his promise, Rāma, his eldest son, would on no account let his father break his word, and he leaves his kingdom to wander in the forest with his wife Sīta and his brother Lakshmana. After the father's death, the son of the second wife declines the throne, and comes to Rāma to persuade him to accept the kingdom of his father. But all in vain. Rāma will keep his exile for fourteen years, and never disown his father's promise." (Professor Max Müller.)

A man who had sat through the play of Hamlet, and at the end of it asked, "Who was Hamlet?" would be a parallel instance. Used towards one who discovers a joke long after it is made.

Love of False Display, Empty Boast, Foppishness, etc.

66. Affecting high-sounding names.

६६   वाप के नाम साग पात पूत के नाम परोरा खाँ

Bāp ke nām sāg pāt pūt ke nām parora khāñ.

The father's name is "*Sāg pāt*"; the son (assumes) the name of "*Ghendhāri Dās*" or "*Parora Rām*" or "*Parora Khāñ.*"

साग पात "*Sāg pāt,*" *lit.* leaves and trash, *i.e.* something small and insignificant or trivial. गेन्धारी "*Ghendhāri*" and परोरा "*Parora*" are superior kinds of vegetables much liked by the people. Hence "*Ghendhāri Dās*" and "*Parora Rām*" mean simply high-sounding names.

If the father is a common low-caste man, and the son assumes a high-sounding name of a higher caste, this saying is cast at him.

Usually said of an upstart. It is a common thing to

find low-caste people when they rise in the world assume
the title of the higher classes, *e.g.* a *Pāsi* or a *Baniya*
styles himself " Lāl," and a " *Dom* " or " *Dosādh* " adds
" Rām " after his name.

67. Foppishness in dress.

६७   वाप पूत बिसनी तेरह गज के इजार

Bāp pūt bisani terah gaj ke ijār.

Father and son (pose) as stylish people; they wear
(luxurious) *paijāmas* made up of 13 yards of cloth.

बिसनी *Bisani* means here people who make an outward
show of cleanliness. Also a debauchee—a man of the town,
or man of fashion who overdresses himself from foppishness.
(The meaning of this proverb is not clear. If *bisani* be
taken for an ascetic, the sense is clear. They call themselves ascetics, but they wear clothes usually worn by
fashionable men of the world.)

68. One who asks for alms should not enquire after the
rent-roll of a village.

६८   माँगौं भीख पूछौं गाँव के जमाँ

Māngiñ bhīkh pūchhiñ gāoñ ke jamāñ.

He sues for alms, yet asks the rent-roll of the village.

He is really a "make believe," who, while he has not
a penny in his pocket, pretends to ascertain the rent
of a village, in order to give the impression that he
wishes to purchase it.

69. Dying to eat pan.

६९   वाप दादा न खाइल पान दाँत निपोरले गेल प्रान
(या) बाप जनम ना खिलैं पान दाँत निपोरले गैले प्रान

Bāp dāda na khāil pān dānt niporale gel prān
(*ya*) *Bāp janam na khaileñ pān dānt niporale gaile prān.*

His ancestors (*lit.* father and grandfather) have never tasted *pān* (betel-leaf), yet for want of it he is dying (*lit.* showing his teeth in his eagerness to get it).

Said in sarcasm of one who apes gentility or hankers after anything (*e.g.* comfort or luxury) which his ancestors have never had. पान "*Pān*," betel, is always eaten by the fashionable and well-to-do, rarely by the poor, to whom it is a luxury.

70. A vain woman's love for display.

॰७० सौखीन बहुरिया चटाई के लहँगा

Saukhīn bahuriya chatāi ke lahanga.

The woman is so fond of show, that although she can't afford a better dress, she still wears a *lāhanga* made out of mat (to gratify her vanity).

लहँगा "*Lāhanga*" is a loose petticoat worn by the women of the better class.

The vain woman, determined to make a show, will wear a *lāhanga* at any cost, though it be only one of straw mat ! An exaggerated way of ridiculing a woman who cannot afford it, but still decks herself, though it be in tatters.

71. False outward display.

॰७१ नेम टेम गोपाल ऐसन हाँड़ी चरुई चमार ऐसन

Nem tem Gopāl aisan, hāñri charui chamār aisan.

The rules he observes outwardly are those of "*Gopāl*," while his cooking pots and pans are (dirty and unclean) like those of a *chamār.*

Said of one who makes an outward show.

नेम टेम "*Nem tem.*" नेम "*Nem*" is a corruption of *niyam* = rule. टेम "*tem*" is simply a meaningless word put in for the sake of rhyme. The expression means " outward behaviour," " outward show."

गोपाल "Gopāl" is a name of the god Krishna. A Gopāl is a devout hermit who observes cleanliness—who keeps his house and everything about him clean and tidy, unlike a *chamār* or leather-worker, who is the opposite.

72. Fashionable father and son, with frogs for kettle-drums.

७२   वाप पूत बिसनोँ बेँग के नगाड़ा

Bāp pūt bisanīñ beng ke nagāra.

The father and son call themselves *Bisanīñ*, and they have for drums (the croaking of) frogs.

बिसनोँ *"Bisanīñ,"* a debauchee, a fashionable man. Said in ridicule of one who affects to make a display without the means. Every great man is supposed to sport a kettle-drum at his gate. A Bisanīñ, *i.e.* one who sets himself up for a man of fashion, ought if anything to have a better kettle-drum than the ordinary, instead of which he has " croaking of frogs."

73. One who cannot afford it keeping up a dance at his gate for display.

७३   घर मेँ खरची न डेउढ़ी पर नाँच

Ghar meñ kharchi na, deurhi par nānch.

He cannot afford to carry on his daily house expenses, yet keeps up a dance at his gate (for show).

Said derisively of one whose expenditure is beyond his means ; or one who makes a display when he cannot afford it.

74. Falsely calling himself a Benares man.

७४ आरसी न पारसी भैया जी बनारसी

Ārsi na pārsi, bhaiya ji banārasi.

Acquainted with neither Arabic nor Persian, yet my friend calls himself a " Benares man."

बनारसी " *Banārasī*," *i.e.* " one of Benares," is looked up to as a highly-polished man with a finish to his education. Said to ridicule one who tries to pass himself off as a polished citizen.

75. The cock after four days' absence returns home a peacock.

७५ चारे दिन के गैले मुरगा मोर हो के ऐले

Chāre din ke gaile murga, mor ho ke aile.

The cock goes (from home) for four days only, and returns a peacock !

A rustic who goes to town for a short while, and fancies on his return that he is a great swell. The following story also holds up to ridicule those who on returning to their homes after a short absence give themselves airs and pretend to have forgotten their own patois.

अरब गये मोगल होइ आय
बोले अरबी बानी
आब आब कहि पिया मोर मुअलेँ
खटिया तर रहल पानी

Arab gaye Mogal hoi āy
Bole Arbi bāni,
Āb āb kahi piya mor mualeñ
Khatiya tar rahal pāni.

My beloved, he went to Arabia and returned quite the Mughal; he talked Persian (which nobody understood). He died from thirst, calling out اب اب " *Āb, ab* " (water), while all the time the water was under his bed !

76. Display in borrowed plumes.

७६   छावल छोपल घर पौलीँ बाँधल पौलीँ टाटी
     अनकर जामल बेटा पौलीँ चूमा लेउँ की चाटी

Chhāwal chhopal ghar pauliñ bāndhal pauliñ tāti
Ankar jāmal beta pauliñ, chūma leuñ ki chāti.

Like one who has found a ready furnished house (*lit.*
a house thatched and *tatti* walls secured), he has (without
trouble) come by another's son; he is so elated that he
does not know how to express his affection.

Aimed at one who makes too much of anything which
really does not belong to him, or which he has got without
any trouble or exertion.   चाटी "*Chāti*" is (*lit.*) " to lick,"
as the lower animals (such as cows) do when showing
affection for their young ones.

77. A vain woman thinks of adorning herself only.

७७   सगरे गाँव परायल जाय घूरा बहु कहस जे माँग टीक द:

Sagare gāoñ parāyal jāy ghūra bahu kahas je māng tik dah.

The whole village is fleeing, but Ghura's wife says
" Please put the vermilion on my forehead."

टीक द: "*Tik dah*" or टीका द: "*tika dah*" is to put the
vermilion mark on a woman's forehead over the parting.
It is considered a necessary part of the toilet of a woman
whose husband is living (सोहागिन *sohāgin* or एहवाती
ehwāti).   A widow (बेवा *bewa* or राँड़ *rānr*) never decks
herself in that fashion; indeed, she is never supposed to
wear ornaments of any kind or adorn her person.   Her
life is one long penance.

Said of a vain woman who will deck herself at all
hazards.

78. A beggar and a beggar at his door.

७८ आप मीयाँ माँगनेँ दरवाजे दरवेस

Āp mīyāñ māngneñ, darwāje darwes.

Himself a beggar, (can he afford to have) one asking for alms at his door?

दरवेस "*Darwes,*" a Mahommedan *fakir.*

79. Love of worthless finery.

७९ हाथ मेँ ना गोड़ मेँ टकही लिलार मेँ

Hāth meñ na gor meñ takahi lilār meñ.

No (ornaments) on her arms or feet; and yet a two-pice trinket (*tikuli*) on her forehead!

i.e. She cannot afford ornaments for her arms and feet, yet such is her love for finery that she decks herself prominently with a worthless टिकुली *tikuli* worth two pice only. टिकुली "*tikuli*" is a spangled circular and wafer-like ornament gummed on to the forehead. The two-pice ones are bigger and more gaudy, about the size of a shilling piece.

टकही "*Takahi*" is one worth a *taka* or two Gorakhpuri pice.

80. When out he wears long *dhotis*, at home he eats *masur* bread.

८० वाहर लम्बी लम्बी धोती घरे मसुरी के रोटी

Bāhar lambi lambi dhoti ghare masuri ke roti.

When out he wears long *dhotis*, at home he has nothing better to eat than *masur* bread.

धोती "*Dhoti*" is a cloth worn round the waist and between the legs. Long *dhotis* are worn only by the well-to-do and fashionable.

मसुरी "*Masuri*" or मसूर "*Masur*" (*Ervum hirsutum,*

3

or *Cicer lens)* is one of the common pulses which furnishes the well-known *dall* of that name. Bread made out of the flour of this pulse is commonly eaten by the poorest, and hence despised by the well-to-do.

Said of one who affects to make a vain display when he really cannot afford it.

81. Tall talk outside and Kodo porridge at home.

　　८१　वाहर लम्बी लम्बी वात घरे कोदई के भात

　　　Bāhar lambi lambi bāt ghare kodai ke bhāt.

Abroad he is full of big talk : at home his food is porridge of *kodai !*

कोदई "*Kodai,*" or **कोदो** "*Kodo,*" **भात** *bhāt* is porridge made of *kodo,* a millet (*Paspalum frumentaceum*). It makes a coarse kind of porridge which is only used by the poor as food.

82. Boasting of three-seer anklets.

　　८२　बाहर पुआवै तीन सेर के नेउरा घरे सूप ना दौरा

　　　Bāhar puāwai tin ser ke neura, ghare sūp na daura.

Outside she boasts of possessing three-seer anklets : at home she has not even the very necessary articles for cleaning and keeping rice.

पुआवै "*Puāwai*" is to boast, to talk big (Feminine colloquialism in Sāran and Shahabad).

नेउरा "*Neura*" are heavy anklets worn as ornaments by the lower classes. They are sold by the weight and serve as ornaments as well as provision for a rainy day. As in the proverb :

　　　सूखी के सिँगार भुखे के अधार

　　　Sukhi ke singār bhukhe ke adhār.

i.e. Ornaments to those in easy circumstances and means of food to those who are hungry.

दौरा "*Daura*" is a basket for holding grain.

सूप "*Sūp*" is a basket for sifting grain.

Every house has a *sūp* and a *daura*; she must be poor indeed who does not possess these necessary domestic articles. An exaggerated way of expressing poverty.

83. Demanding a torch at another's house.

८३ अपना घरे सँझवत ना अनका घरे मूसर ऐसन वाती

Apna ghare sanjhwat na
Anka ghare mūsar aisan bāti.

In his own house he cannot afford the "evening light"; at another's he pretends to want a torch as thick as a pestle.

सँझवत "*Sanjhwat*" is "evening light." There is a widely prevailing superstition among natives that it is unlucky to commence the evening without a light. Even the poorest light a *chirāg* for a few minutes only.

84. A blind woman owning three collyrium boxes.

८४ आँख हैये नाँ तीन तीन गो कजरौटा

Ānkh haiye nāñ tīn tīn go kajrauta.

She is blind, yet she sports three collyrium boxes !

कजरौटा "*Kajrauta*" is an iron box or receptacle for keeping lamp-black to be applied to the eyes. It is warmed in it too.

It is a grim and exaggerated way of deriding one who loves to make a display, but lacks the means.

85. The needy keeping company with the great.

८५ खाये के साग पात बैठे के अमीर का साथ

Khaye ke sāg pāt, baithe ke amīr ka sāth.

He has barely enough to keep himself alive, yet he moves in the company of the great. Applied to a "toadeater," a mean sycophant.

साग पात " *Ság pát* " are pot herbs, common vegetables which the poor eat with their rice.

86. Rags to wear and carpets to spread.

८६   ओढ़े के लुगरी बिछावे के गलैचा

Orhe ke lugari bichhãwe ke galaicha.

For covering he has rags, but spreads on the ground an expensive carpet.

False love of display.

87. Proud of her chundari sári.

८७   चूँदरी फाट गैल चमकल मेट गैल

Chũndari phát gail

Chamakal met gail.

When the *chũndari* is torn the shine is gone!

चूँदरी " *Chũndari* " is a variegated sheet with white spots, which are caused by tying small knots in the cloth to be dyed, so that the spots tied remain white. It is very much prized by the village women.

The meaning is when the sheet gets torn, the pride is gone. She has nothing left then to make a display with. Said to ridicule those who boast about empty nothings, or things which are evanescent.

88. A poor fop.

८८   गाँठी में दाम नाँ बाँकीपूर का सैर

Gánthi meñ dám nañ, Bánkípúr ka sair.

He hasn't a *damri* in his pocket, yet he would go to saunter about in Bánkípúr !

बाँकीपूर " *Bánkípúr*," the chief town of Bihár, and the Divisional headquarters where the Commissioner resides. One of the derivations given of Bánkípúr is बाँके "*Bánke*" and पूर "*Púr*," *i.e.* "the town of the fop or coxcomb,"

on account of its once being the part of the town (Patna)
where women of ill-fame resided, and gaily-dressed men
were in the habit of frequenting it. A similar bazaar in
Gaya is called *Terhi bazār*, or the " crooked " bazaar.

89. The poor man at the prow of the boat.

८९ जिनिका खेवा नहीं से अगिला माँगि सवार

Jinika khewa nahiñ, se agila mañgi sawār.

He who hasn't money to pay his fare is seated on the
prow of the boat. खेवा *" khewa "* is ferry charge.

Said to ridicule one who takes up a prominent position
unbefitting his circumstances, while others who can really
afford it better, remain in the background. The prow of
a boat is the most conspicuous seat one can take in a
country boat, and boatmen worship the bow.

90. Vain boast.

९० लिखे न पढ़े नाम मोहमद् फाजिल

Likhe na parhe, nām Mohamad Fāzil.

He neither knows how to read nor write, but styles
himself Mohamad Fāzil.

फाजिल *" Fāzil "* (Persian), learned.
Aimed at those who affect to be clever.

91. An upstart affecting gentility.

९१ बाप ना दादा तीसर पुस्त साहुजादा

Bāp na dāda, tīsar pust sāhujāda.

Neither his father nor his grandfather (was rich), but
he behaves as if he were the son of a rich man !

i.e. Can one whose ancestors were poor suddenly acquire
the ways, tastes, and habits of one born amidst wealth ?

Cast at an upstart who affects to be habituated to wealth
from his very infancy.

92. Affecting familiarity with the great.

९२   वाप भुसङ्डला पूत चौपार नाँती वैसले माँह दरवार

Bāp bhusahula pūt chaupār
Nānti baisale mānh darbār.

The father's sitting place was in the chaff house; the
son used to sit in the open air (yard in front of the house)
in front of the verandah ; but the grandson has taken to
sitting in the great darbār, *i.e.* he will sit nowhere else.

Said to ridicule an upstart who affects the intimacy of
the great, and shuns his former friends and resorts.

Pot calling the kettle black.   Alike faulty or defective.

93. The sieve blaming the *sūp*.

९३   चलनीँ दुसलन सूप के जिनका सहसर छेद्

Chalanīn dusalan sūp ke, jinka sahasar chhed.

The sieve with a thousand holes finds fault with the *sūp*.
चलनीँ "*Chalanīn*," a sieve.
सूप "*Sūp*," a basket, usually in the shape of a horse-
shoe, used for sifting and cleaning grains of various sizes.
E.E. "Pot calling the kettle black."

94. Equally miserable and poor.

९४   जैसने दिगम्बर पाँड़े वैसने रसुल्ला
       उनका न छान छपर उनका न चूल्हा

Jaisane Digambar Pānre, waisane Rasulla
Unka na chhan chhapar, unka na chūlha.

Both Digambar Pānre and Rasulla are similarly circumstanced ; the former has no roof to his hut, the latter
no cooking place ; *i.e.* both are equally destitute, so that
one has nothing to boast over the other.

दिगम्बर पाँड़े "*Digambar Pānre*" and रसुल्ला "*Rasulla*" are empty high-sounding names, *i.e.* names of people who are really poor.

"*Digambar*" *lit.* means "naked," from दिग "*dig*," sides, the four points of the compass, and अम्बर "*ambar*," dress, *i.e.* one who has nothing else but the four sides—North, South, East, and West—for his covering or dress; *i.e.* the destitute.

Another saying of opposite signification is सावन ला भादो दूबर "*Sāwan la Bhādo dūbar*." Is the month of Sāwan weaker than Bhādo? (both being heavy rainy months).

95. Both alike defective.

९५ जिसने उद्दी वैसने भान इनका पोंछ न उनका कान

> *Jaisane Uddi waisane Bhān*
> *Inka ponchh na unka kān.*

As *Uddi* so *Bhān*; one is tailless and the other earless.

उद्दी "*Uddi*" and भान "*Bhān*" are the names (after the sun and the moon) of a pair of oxen that are yoke-fellows.

96. Blind to one's own faults.

९६ आपन टेटर नाँही देखे अनके फूलो निहारत फिरे

> *Āpan tetar nāñhi dekhe*
> *Anke phūli nihārat phire.*

He does not see the speck in his own eye, but stares at the mote in another.

i.e. Blind to his own defects and faults while ready to point out those in others.

Presumption, Audacity, Cheek, Arrogance, Over-confidence,
Impudence, etc.

97. Where the big have failed, the pigmy has come to try his strength.

एº७ बड़ बड़ गेला गजौर अिला

Bar bar gela gajaur aila.

The great have failed, the pigmy (*lit.* one yard long) has (now) come (to try his strength).

Said of a small man, or one of inferior position and abilities, who attempts a work in which his superiors have failed.

98. Where camels are drowned, the donkey ventures to ford.

एº८ बड़ बड़ उँट दह़ायल गेला गद्हा पूछे कतेक पानीँ

Bar bar ūnt dahāyal gela,
Gadaha pūchhe katek pānīñ.

Huge camels have been washed away by the current; the donkey (has the "cheek") to inquire what is the depth!

Where his betters have utterly failed, it is presumptuous for the donkey to ask even the depth of the stream with an intent to ford it.

99. Falsely claiming kinship.

एº९ चीन्हौँ न जानौँ मेँ दुल्हह की चची
      मँड़वा मेँ कोइ बात न पूछे कोहबर दुलहा की चची

(1) *Chinhoñ na jānoñ maiñ dullah ki chachi.*
(2) *Manrwa meñ koi bāt na pūchhe kohabar dulaha ki chachi.*

(1) Though unknown, she calls herself the (paternal) aunt of the bridegroom, *i.e.* claims kindredship.

The paternal uncle's wife of a bridegroom is an especially privileged individual in the marriage feast among the people ; she lords it over all. Thus it comes to be applied when one who, being a mere casual acquaintance, claims the familiarity of kinship and its rights.

(2) Nobody even speaks to her in the *Manrwa* (where all have ingress), but she claims the treatment of the bridegroom's aunt in the *Kohabar* (where only the near relatives of the bride and bridegroom are allowed).

100. While the superior spirits are weeping from hunger, Mūa has the "cheek" to ask for cakes.

१०० वड़ बड़ भूत कद्म तर रोवे ँ मूत्रा माँगे पूत्रा

Bar bar bhūt kadam tar roweñ,

Mūa mānge pūa.

The superior ghosts are crying (weeping) under the *kadam* (tree), *Mūa* (has the "cheek") to ask for *pūa*. The कद्म "*kadam*" tree, and the नीम "*nīm*" tree, etc., are the favourite resorts of evil spirits, as the पीपल "*pīpal*" ; the वेल "*bel*" and the वर "*bar*" are of the good.

मूत्रा "*Mūa.*" Among the host of evil spirits and deities worshipped by the people some are of very inferior rank, and almost incapable of doing any harm. Mūa is one of them ; low down in the scale, and invoked only to frighten children (chiefly in South Bihar).

पूत्रा *Pūa* is wheat and rice flour and molasses mixed and cooked in ghi or oil. It is considered a delicacy, and is used in *pūjas* or other festive occasions.

(Used as a satire on presumption in asking for anything which his betters would not dare to.)

101. Breeze of the fan pitted against the hurricane.

१०१ आँधी के आगे बेना के बतास

Āndhi ke āge bena ke batās.

Before a gale the breeze from a fan has no effect!

i.e. when a weak man presumes to oppose an immensely powerful one, the light breeze from the fan may metaphorically be contrasted with the hurricane to mark the disproportionateness of the opposing force put forth.

102. The goat of a *jolaha*, and addicted to butting!

१०२ जोलहा के छेर मरखाही

Jolaha ke chher markhāhi.

The goat of a *jolaha*, and addicted to viciousness!

In the first place a goat is harmless and is not usually addicted to butting; and then the goat of a जोलहा *jolaha* (the proverbial fool) ought to be particularly quiet and inoffensive.

103. Impudence in a young girl.

१०३ देखले छौंड़ी समधिन

Dekhale chhaunri samdhin.

Yesterday a (mere) girl, and to-day a "*samdhin*."

समधिन "*Samdhin*" is the mother of the son-in-law or daughter-in-law.

The father of the bride and the father of the bridegroom call each other समधी "*samdhi*." Their wives call each other समधिन "*samdhin*" (Grierson).

Said to snub "cheek" or "impudence" in a young person (also to express surprise at the sudden growth of a girl).

Similarly the saying कास्हे बनियाँ आजे सेठ *Kālhe baniyāṅ*

āje seth. "Yesterday a petty shopkeeper and to-day a banker."

104. Can the dance get on without Gāngo?

१०४ वे गाँगो के झूमर
(या) बिना जोलहेँ ईद्

(1) *Be Gāngo ke jhūmar (ya) Bina jolaheñ īd.*

(1) Can the dance (*jhūmar*, see proverb 126) take place without Gāngo? (2) Can the *īd* take place without weavers?

गाँगो "*Gāngo*" is a fictitious female name.

Both these sayings are used in a good-humoured way when one is playfully said to be indispensable to an occasion.

105. Cricket on a bundle.

१०५ उचरुङ चढ़लन बकुचा कहलन के सब हमरे धन

Uchrung charhlan bakucha
Kahlan ke sab hamre dhan.

The cricket mounted on a bundle says, "I am the owner of this wealth."

A small-minded man suddenly raised to power gives himself unjustifiable airs, and considers he has more authority than he really possesses.

106. Making free with another's property.

१०६ अनकर मद् अनकर मङ आ
नाँचे चोर बजावे सङआ

Ankar mad ankar mahua
Nānche chor bajāwe sahua.

Another's wine and another's *mahua*; the wine-seller plays to the dancing of the thief.

मङआ "*Mahua*" is the flower of the *mahua* tree (*Bassia latifolia*) used for distilling country spirits.

The idea is that the thief steals the *mahua* and makes it over to the wine-seller, and both enjoy themselves at another's expense (To dance to the playing of the wine-seller, who pulls the string, is comically suggestive).

107. The barber's wife's lament.

१०७ राज हो राज तोरा विनाँ नगरिया के मूँड़ी हो राज

Rāj ho rāj, tora bināñ nagaria ke mūnri, ho rāj !

Without you, my lord, how will the town get shaved ?

The barber's widow, in bewailing her husband, praises him inordinately.

Said to ridicule one who considers some one else indispensable, as the barber's wife thought when her husband was dead that there was no one left to shave the towns-people !

108. Can the sea-gull support the falling skies with its tiny feet ?

१०८ टिटही का टेकले वादर थम्ही

Titahi ka tekale bādar thamhi ?

Would the sea-gull support the sky (with her feet) in case it fell ?

There is a common story about the sea-gull, that it goes to sleep at night on its back with its feet held upwards, in order to hold the sky in case it comes down.

Applied when ridiculously feeble efforts are made to effect great results.

109. He does not know the charm for a scorpion, yet ventures to put his hand in a snake's hole.

१०९ बीछी के मन्तर नाँ जानाँ साँप के विल में हाथ डालीँ

Bichhi ke mantar nāñ jānāñ,
Sāmp ke bil meñ hāth dālīñ ?

He is unacquainted with the charm for scorpions (*i.e.* for curing scorpion sting), yet is foolhardy enough to put his hand into a snake's hole.

i.e. He has not the ability to do an easy thing, and yet has the "cheek" to try his hand at something far more difficult.

It is easier to cure scorpion sting than snake bite. The belief is universally prevalent in Bihār that snake bites and scorpion stings can be cured by spells and charms, if only the patient be subjected to them in proper time. Marvellous instances of cure (even after life was extinct) are related in every village, and one or two *ojhās* (charmers or wizards) are always to be found in a village, who are supposed to possess the secret charm. The *ojhās* are also employed in exorcising evil spirits, and are believed in by the women of even well-to-do and educated men. Faith in the efficacy of charms of every kind is universal among the peasantry. Scarcely any malady is too severe to be cured by the charmer, and the means adopted are as various as the diseases to be cured.

110. Self-praise is no praise.

११० अपनेँ मुँह मियाँ मिट्ठू

Apaneñ munh miyāñ mitthu.

Perfect in his own estimation.

मियाँ मिट्ठू "*Miyāñ mitthu*" is one who is self-satisfied, thinks himself a hero. A parrot is also familiarly called *mitthu.*

E.E. "Self-praise is no praise."

111. Arrogating superiority over one's teacher.

१११ गुरु गुरे रहले चेला चीनी हो गैले

Guru gure rahale, chela chīni ho gaile.

The teacher has remained the same coarse sugar (as before), but his pupil pretends to have become clean sugar. This is a play on the words गुरु "*guru*" (teacher) and गुर "*gur*" (the coarse brown country sugar).

Cast at those who affect superiority over their betters.

112. Presumption of the inexperienced.

११२ सावन जमले सियार भादो आइल बाढ़
बाप रे बाप ऐसन बाढ़ कबहुँ नाँ देखलो

Sāwan jamle siyār bhādo āil bārh ;
Bāp re bāp aisan bārh kabahu nāñ dekhli.

The jackal pup was born in the month of *Sāwan* (August), there was a flood in *Bhādo* (September), he has the impertinence to say, " Good gracious! I never saw such a high flood."

113. The young crow wiser than its mother.

११३ कौआ ला कबेलवे गाढ़

Kaua la kabelwe gārh.

The young crow is more cunning than its mother!

A crow was advising its young to fly away for safety's sake, as soon as it saw any one stoop to pick up a stone, so as not to give him a chance of pelting it. "But," said the precocious young bird, "supposing the man comes provided with a stone in his hand."

The old bird stopped giving further advice to one possessed of so much foresight.

114. Born but yesterday and to-day a giant.

११४ कब जमले कब राकस भैले

Kab jamale kab rākas bhaile ?

Born but yesterday and to-day a giant!

(*Lit.* When was he born? When did he turn a demon?)

115. An old goat quizzing the wolf.

११५ वूढ़ बकरी ङुँड़ार से ठठा

Būrh bakari hunrār se thatha.

The old goat has the impudence to quiz the wolf!

Said when weakness audaciously pits itself against strength, and runs the risk of being made to pay the penalty. (An old goat is presumably more feeble than a young goat, and therefore he ought not to defy a wolf.)

Recklessness.

116. Recklessness of those who have nothing to lose.

११६ लँगटा नाचे फाटे का

Langta nāche, phāte ka ?

If the naked dance, what can they tear?

Applied to those who, having nothing to lose, are very ready to venture all. The following sayings are used to laugh at the readiness of people who have nothing to carry, to start on a journey at a moment's notice. हेल बाँड़ा, पोंछ अलगाँले बानी "*Hel bānra, ponchh algaule bāni,*" the tailless bullock on being told to get ready says, "I have already lifted my tail!" (*i.e.* preparatory to entering the water). नागा भाइ कूँच लँगौटियो निखे "*Nāga bhāi kūnch langautiyo naikhe.*" Similarly, the naked (who has nothing) is asked to get ready to start on a journey, says he has not even the small rag round his loins, *i.e.* he has nothing to get ready.

117. One who has nothing to lose can be reckless to any extent.

११७ लँगटा नाँचे तीन तीन बेरिआ अनगुत साँझ दुपहरिआ

Langta nānche, tin tin beria
Angut, sānjh, dupaharia.

The shameless can afford to caper three times a day:
morning, noon, and night.

i.e. those who have nothing to lose can always afford to
be reckless. It is only those who have their reputation
at stake that have to be careful of what they do.

"To dance" is here synonymous with "playing pranks,"
"being up to mischief." Dancing among themselves is
not considered a respectable amusement by the natives.
Those who take to it as a profession are looked down upon
by society. "To dance" is therefore synonymous (in its
opprobrious use) with "To behave vulgarly."

118. Reckless waste of another's property.

११८   करवा कोहार के घीव जजमान के ढरकौले जा:

Karwa kohār ke, ghīw jajamān ke ; dharkaule jāh.

It is the pot of the potter and the *ghi* of the follower ;
go on pouring it.

This speech is supposed to be made by the Brāhman who
has come to officiate at the *pūja* and is performing the
oblation ceremony (होम "*Hom*") of pouring ghi into the
fire. A very small quantity of it is necessary to be poured.
A Brāhman who is reckless will pour and waste a lot.

Said when one is reckless with another's property.
जजमान "*Jajmān*" is a customer, a follower of a Brāhman.
It is the Sanskrit यजमान: *yajamānaḥ.*

Selfishness, Heartlessness, Obstinacy, Self-willed, having one's
own way, etc.

119. What is play to one is death to another.

११९   चीरई के जीव जाय लड़िकन के खेलौनाँ

Chiraiñ ke jīw jāy, larikan ke khelaunāñ.

It is play to the children, but death to the bird.

120. Dying man asked to sing.

९२० मरल जाईँ रास गाईँ

Maral jāīñ, rās gāīñ.

Can a dying man sing love songs ?

Lit. I am dying, and I am to sing love songs !

राम *"Rās."* The love stories of the Hindu god Krishna are related and acted in *" Rās Līla."*

Supposed to be said by one who is unhappy or sick, but is expected to be jolly notwithstanding.

121. A self-willed man.

१२१ मन माना घर जाना

Man māna, ghar jāna.

He goes home when he likes (*lit.* to go home when the mind likes or wishes).

Said in reference to a self-willed man, or one who pays no heed to the wishes or advice of others.

122. Requiring full weight when the shopkeeper does not come to terms.

१२२ बनियाँ दे ना पूरा तौल

Baniyāñ de na : pūra taul.

The shopkeeper does not agree to sell ; yet he says, give full weight.

i.e. The seller does not agree to give at the terms offered, yet he tells him to weigh out correctly.

Said sarcastically when any one takes for granted, or neglects the most essential thing in any transaction which requires to be settled first, before any steps can be taken. Cast at one who takes an entirely selfish view of anything.

123. The goat has paid with its life, yet its meat is not appreciated.

१२३ खसी के जीव गइल खवैया का सवादे ना मिलल

Khasi ke jiw gail khawaiya ka sawāde na milal.

The (poor) goat has lost its life; and still the *gourmand* declares that the meat is not to his taste! *i.e.* the poor goat has done its very best, it can do no more.

Said when one has done his very utmost and still gets blamed, or fails to give satisfaction. Cast at one who is difficult to please.

(The final " e " in सवाद " *sawāde* " is to emphasize it.)

124. The poor dog is dying, but the Raja thinks of his sport only.

१२४ पिल्ली के जीव जाय राजा के सिकारे भागल जाय

Pilli ke jiw jāy, rāja ke sikāre bhāgal jāy.

The bitch is dying, but the Raja (declares that his) game is running away.

i.e. The sufferings of the poor bitch do not cause any concern to the Raja; all he thinks of is his enjoyments, lest the game may escape.

Aimed at those who are so inconsiderate and selfish as to think of their own pleasure and purpose only.

125. The Rani has thoughts of the Raja only.

१२५ आनो के आन चिता रानी के रजवे के चिता

Āno ke ān chita, rāni ke rajawe ke chita.

Others have other thoughts, but the Rani has thoughts of the Raja only.

Applied to one who is intent on his own thoughts only, regardless of others.

१२० मरल जाईँ रास गाईँ

Vain or impotent desire, vain expectations, useless labour.

126. Vain desire of the handless woman to dance.

१२६ सब मिल के झूमर पारे तूठी कहे हमहूँ

Sab mil ke jhūmar pāre, thūthi kahe hamahūñ.

(When) all are dancing the *jhūmar* the handless woman says, "I also (shall join)."

झूमर *"Jhūmar"* is an aboriginal dance in which the women go round in a circle with joined hands. A woman with a stump is evidently unfit to take part in it. Her wish, therefore, to join is on the face of it absurd.

Said of one who has a wish to do anything, but lacks the essential power.

127. Wife vainly waiting for the collyrium to put in her eyes.

१२७ काजर गेल बिहार बहुरिया आँख निडेरले हथ

Kājar gel bihār, bahuriya ānkh niderale hath.

The *Kājar* has gone to Bihār, while the wife (woman) has wide spread her eyelids to (receive it).

काजर *"Kājar"* is collyrium or lamp-black applied to the edges of the lower eyelids.

It places in a comical and ridiculous light the situation of one who has let an opportunity slip, and is still fondly waiting for it, by depicting humorously the not very comely attitude of the vain wife, who, in the act of applying the lamp-black to her eyes, has wide-spread them, while the collyrium is nowhere at hand.

Applied to ridicule one who is waiting for the past or any lucky turn of events, instead of exerting.

128. Fruitless labour in spinning.

१२८   मर मर कातीँ माल्हे जाय

Mar mar kātīñ mālhe jāy.

With the greatest hardship I spin cotton, but all (my earnings) are wasted in mending the spinning machine (*lit.* the driving band of the spinning machine).

माल "*Māl*" or माल्ह "*Mālh*" is the driving band "which goes twice round the driving wheel and the spinning axle. It is rubbed with resin, and is then blackened with charcoal" (Grierson).

It is a constant source of annoyance to the woman who spins, because it frequently breaks.

A quaint way of expressing that all earnings are lost in the cost of production, in repairing the machinery.

129. The earless woman wishing for earrings.

१२९   नाक ना कान वाली के अरमान

Nāk na kān
Bāli ke armān.

She has neither nose nor ears, yet hankers for ear and nose rings.

130. An old cow's desire to take part in the Sohrāi festival.

१३०   वूढ़ गाय सोहराई के साध

Būrh gāy, sohrāi ke sādh.

An old cow with a longing to take part in the *sohrāi*!

सोहराई "*Sohrāi*" is a Hindu festival held on the 15th of Kārtik (October–November) of each year, chiefly by the *goālas* (milkmen). Its object is to make the cow dance, hence also called गोंञ्चर्थू "*Goñarthu*," गोक्रीड़ा "*Gokrira*," or गैडार "*Gaidār*." Various means are adopted to induce the cow to dance, really to run. A young pig is made to squeal near a calf, at which the mother, followed by all the herd, attack the pig and gore it to death. Sometimes this cruel sport is humanely varied by dragging a large gourd, or a black blanket, at which the cows run to butt. Applied to one who is too old or incapable to take part in a pleasure, yet has a longing for it.

Compare also the following saying :

बूढ़ी गाय सहिजनी चरली

माँके लगली ढहि के परली

Būrhi gāy sahijani charali

Mānke lagali dhahi ke parali.

i e. The old cow having grazed on the horse-radish tree, began to gambol, but dropped down forthwith.

Another proverb of similar application is

वुढ़िया सराहे घीव खिचड़ी

(1) *Burhiya sarāhe ghīw khichri !*

A variation of it is

वुढ़वें सवादल घीउ खिचड़ी

(2) *Burwen sawādal ghīn khichri.*

The former (1) means "The old woman is too fond of *ghi* and *khichri*" (*lit.* praises it, takes to it kindly).

The variation of (2) is "The old man has found the *ghi* and *khichri* to his taste."

खिचड़ी "*Khichri*" is a very favourite dish with the natives of all classes. It is made of a mixture of rice and dall (cooked together). The poor people can seldom afford to use *ghi* in it, which adds greatly to its flavour. The well-to-do always mix *ghi* with their *khichri*. The idea is that it becomes the old not to show excessive fondness for such delicacies.

Said sarcastically when any one shows an overfondness for a thing which does not become him. To ridicule unbeseeming taste.

CLASS II.

PROVERBS RELATING TO WORLDLY WISDOM AND MAXIMS,
EXPEDIENCY AND CUNNING, AND WARNINGS AND
ADVICE.

131. A circuitous route.

१३१ गया के राह कोरमथू

Gaya ke rāh Kormathu ?

The (straight) road to Gaya (is not through) Kormathu.

कोरमथू *"Kormathu"* is a village near Gaya, but not
on any of the high roads leading to it. Any man who
adopts a circuitous route or style instead of the straight
one might be asked sarcastically, "Are you going to Gaya
through Kormathu ?"

132. Absurd sight or situation.

१३२ एक हाथ के ककरी नव हाथ के बीया

Ek hāth ke kakri nao hāth ke biya.

The *kakri* is one cubit long; its seed nine cubits !

The seed contained inside the ककरी *"kakri"* (a longish
cucumber) ought in all reasonableness to be much smaller
than the *kakri* itself. Said to mark disproportionateness,
ludicrous effect, or absurdity of a sight; also to ridicule
the presumption of a small or insignificant man who
attempts to do anything much beyond his power.

133. A new washerwoman applies soap to rags even.

१३३ नयी धोबिनियाँ आवेली
चिर्कुटवे सावुन लावेली

Nai dhobiniyañ āweli
Chirkutwe sābun lāweli.

A new washerwoman applies soap to rags even (*lit.* when a new washerwoman comes she applies soap in washing rags even, which are seldom washed with soap).

E.E. "A new broom sweeps clean."

134. The barber's wife with a wooden nail cutter.

१३४ नई नाउन बाँस के नरहनी

Nai nāun, bāns ke narahani.

A new (female) barber; she has a bamboo nail cutter!

नरहनी "*Narahani,*" a chisel-like instrument made of iron for cutting finger-nails. It is never made of bamboo. Said of a "new broom," who wants to effect impossibilities.

135. A chip of the old block.

१३५ बाप के पूत सिपाही के घोड़ा नाँ तो थोड़म थोड़ा

Bāp ke pūt, sipāhi ke ghora ; nāñ to, thoram thora.

A chip of the old block; like the steed of the trooper, if he is not up to very much still he is above the average.

136. All that glitters is not gold.

१३६ उपर के छाम छूमँ मत भूल: तरे लुगरिये बा

Upar ke chhām chhūmeñ mat bhūlah, tare lugariye ba.

Do not be carried away by the outward specious appearance; below (the outward finery) are rags (as underclothing).

छाम छम "*Chhām chhūm,*" specious appearance.

137. A good man needs speaking once.

१३७ भला घोड़ा के एक चाबुक भला मानुख के एक बात

Bhala ghora ke ek chābuk
Bhala mānukh ke ek bāt.

The good (*i.e.* spirited) horse needs but once to be whipped, just as the good man needs but once to be spoken to.

138. All in the same plight.

१३८ केकर केकर लीहौँ नाँव कमरा ओढ़ले सगरे गाँव

Kekar kekar līhiñ nāoñ
Kamra orhle sagare gāoñ.

Whom am I to name? All the villages are similarly circumstanced! (*lit.* all are alike covered with blankets, *i.e.* poor, in the same boat).

Said *e.g.* when all in a place are more or less implicated or blameworthy (or almost all are poor), and are trying to sham. The poorer class only use the country made blankets as a covering, and consequently it is taken as a sign of poverty by the people. The better classes always, when they can afford it, use shawls, and people not so well off use दोहर "*Dohars*" (thick sheets), लेहाफ "*lehāfs*" (light quilts), धूसा "*Dhūsas*" (woollen sheets), etc.

A story is told of a former Tikāri Raja, illustrating that blankets are considered as fit covering for the poor only.

One day the Maharaj was belated in his evening walk, and had to take "a short cut" through a village of Ahirs, who are proverbially thick-headed. He wore a highly valuable black shawl, which, to those who had never seen a shawl, seemed like a black blanket. He had scarcely passed the village when an old Ahir ran up to him and,

with tears in his eyes, supplicated the chief to accept all
he had, namely, the few rupees he had gathered together.
Still weeping, he added that he could not bear to see the
old Maharaj in a common blanket; that he had heard a
great deal about his being in debt and his income having
been much reduced of late, but until now he had no idea
that the Maharaj had come down to such straits as to
cover a blanket. Saying this, he earnestly besought the
Maharaj to accept his offering, and suggested that he
should make immediate use of it, in making for himself
a few red *lehāfs* and *dohars*, and not cause pain to his
loyal subjects by going about in that style. The Maharaj
very gracefully accepted the gift, and asked the Ahir to
accompany him to his palace. It is pleasing to know (so
the story says) that the Maharaj rewarded the Ahir's
loyalty by granting him the village in which he had his
home, and his descendants are now said to be well-to-do
zemindars in those parts.

139. An old parrot never gets tame.

१३९   बुढ़ सूगा पोस मानेला?

Būrh sūga pos mānela ?

Can an old bird (parrot) ever get tame?

Said when one advanced in years is ungrateful.

140. After meals wait awhile.

१४०   खा के पसरीँ मार के ससरीँ

Kha ke pasarīñ mār ke sasarīñ.

Stretch yourself after your meal, but disappear ("slope")
after beating (any one).

i.e. Rest after your food, but do not tarry after you have
thrashed anybody lest he may return it. It is a piece of
cunning advice.

पसरव "*Pasarab*" is to spread, to stretch out.

ससरव "*Sasarab*" is to slope, to disappear, to clear out, to remove.

141. A dog is brave at his own door.

१४१ अपनाँ दुआरी कुकुरो बरियार

Apanāñ duāri kukuro bariyār.

A dog is brave at his own door.

An equivalent saying in Urdu is घर का कुत्ता शेर "*Ghar ka kutta sher*," "A dog is brave as a lion at his own door!"

E.E. "A cock on his own dunghill."

Adding insult to injury.

142. Grinding corn on the dead.

१४२ मुअला पर कोदो दरे अैले

Muala par kodo dare aile.

He has come to grind corn (*kodo*) over the dead.

i.e. over the corpse.

i.e. to add insult to injury.

143. The *Karaila* climbing on the *nīm*.

१४३ एक तो करैला अपने कड़ुई दुसरे चढ़लो नीम

Ek to karaila apane karui, dusare charhali nīm.

The *karaila* is itself bitter enough, but it becomes worse when it climbs the *nīm*.

करैला "*Karaila*" (*Momordica charantia*), a very bitter kind of vegetable of the gourd family. It is a creeping plant.

नीम "*Nīm*" (*Azaderachta indica*), a common tree with very acrid fruit and juice.

The idea is that the *karaila*, which is itself bitter, adds to its bitterness by climbing the *nīm*.

Said of anything that aggravates an injury.

E.E. " Adding insult to injury."

A similar idea is expressed in the sayings:

(1) **एक तो मीयाँ खुद बौड़ाहै (या अपने रहे) दोसरे खाइन भाँग**

Ek to miyāñ khud baurāhe (or, apne rahe) dosare khāin bhāng.

The **मीयाँ** *miyāñ* is really mad, and adds to it by drinking **भाँग** *bhāng.*

(2) **एक तो नयना मद भरे दूजे अञ्जन सार**
ऐ बौरी कोई देत है मतवारे हथियार

> *Ek to nayana mad bhare, dūje anjan sār*
> *Ai bauri koi det hai matwāre hathiyār.*

Your eyes are full of intoxicating wine. You increase their power by applying antimony. Stupid! does any one ever place a weapon in the hands of a drunkard?

To say that a fair one's eyes are full of wine is a figurative way of expressing that they possess the power of intoxicating or captivating others.

144. A bear, and he with a spade on his shoulders.

१४४   एक भाल दुसरे काँध कुदार

> *Ek bhāl dusare kāndh kudār.*

The bear and he to shoulder a spade!

i.e. Makes him ten times more dangerous.

Said when one who is already inclined to be a bully gets power.

145. Insulting the dead.

१४५   मरे पर साैं दुरा

> *Mare par sau durra.*

On the dead (or after he is dead) he lays a hundred stripes with the whip.

i.e. Heaping injury on the helpless; on one who cannot return.

"*Durra,*" it is said, was a lash made of a long narrow bag stuffed with pice, rupees, or gold mohars, according to the social position of the man who was to be chastised.

146. A demon and a torch in his hand.

१४६ एके राकस दुसरे हाथ में लुकवारी

Eke rākas dusare hāth men lukwāri.

A demon and with a burning torch in his hand !

राकस "*Rākas*" is a demon who is supposed to emit fire from his mouth.

Said when any one viciously inclined is placed in a position which enhances his power of doing mischief.

147. A bad workman quarrels with his tools.

१४७ नाचे (या चले) न जानीँ अँगनवेँ टेढ़

Nāche (or chale) na jānīñ anganwen terh.

One who cannot dance blames the floor.

A variation of it is,

One who cannot walk straight says the compound is crooked.

E.E. A bad workman quarrels with his tools.

148. A barking dog seldom bites.

१४८ करिञवा बादर गरजे के ढेर बरसे के हइये नाँ

Kariawa bādar garaje ke dher barase ke haiye nāñ.

Black clouds thunder a great deal, but rain little.

E.E. A barking dog seldom bites.

A thundering cloud gives little rain.

149. A black goat has no heart.

१४९ करिया खसो का कारेजे नाँ

Kariya khasi ka kāreje nāñ.

A black goat has no heart.

Said of one who has no courage : who cannot be trusted or is not equal to an occasion.

A black goat is supposed to possess mysterious virtue. It is a favourite offering to the gods (especially भैरो *Bhairo*, and to the goddess काली *Kāli*, etc.), and its bile is believed to possess healing properties, *e.g.* those who suffer from night blindness are strongly recommended to apply its bile to the eyes and to eat its liver.

This proverb is ascribed to the following tale :

Once a tiger, who had grown sick and feeble from age, and was unable to hunt owing to failing strength, was strongly recommended by his physician to try the liver of a black goat. Thereupon the monarch of the forest ordered his vazīr, the jackal, to get him a black goat. The wily "Jack" by many false promises managed to inveigle a black goat within reach of his infirm master, who took no time in killing it. The cunning jackal, who was himself eager to eat the liver, having heard of its marvellous powers, suggested to his master a preparatory bath before taking the remedy. The tiger approving of the suggestion went to have a bath. In the meantime "Jack" devoured the liver of the black goat. When the tiger came back, he was surprised to find that the goat had no liver. Turning to the jackal the tiger asked what was the meaning of this. "Sire," exclaimed the "Jack," "I thought your majesty was aware that black goats had no liver : otherwise how could your servant have deceived a black goat into your presence ?"

150. A ludicrous attempt to frighten.

१५० पोआ देखाइ गरुड़ के देरवाईं

Poa dekhāi, garūr ke derwāiñ.

By showing a young snake to the adjutant will you (ever) frighten him?

गरूड़ "*Garūr*" is a large species of crane (*Leptoptilos argala*); its exceedingly voracious habits render it valuable as a scavenger. It swallows up large snakes. पोंआ *Poa* is a young snake. It is absurd therefore to think of frightening it with a young snake.

Said when an absurd attempt is made to intimidate any one. Another saying of the same import is

जेकरा पीठ पर अगरधत के नगारा बाजे

से का सूप का भड़भड़ौते भागे

Jekara pīth par agardhat ke nagāra bāje;

Se, ka, sūp ka bharbharaute bhāge?

"Will one on whose back is played a kettledrum, made of several metals, be frightened at the noise made with a winnowing basket?" As the camel is said to have remarked to the old woman who was trying to frighten him away from grazing her field by using her winnowing basket.

अगरधत "*Agardhat*" is said by natives to be a corruption of अष्टधातु "*ashtdhātu*," *i.e.* or eight metals. A drum made of an alloy of many metals makes a great noise.

151. A rat skin is not sufficient to cover a kettledrum.

१५१ मूँस का चाम से दमामा छवाला

Mūns ka chām se damāma chhawāla.

Is it possible to cover a kettledrum with the skin of a mouse?

The following couplet in Theth Hindi makes use of the same proverb to illustrate the impossibility of getting men of inferior ability (men of low caste) to fill honourable places.

कसे छोटे नरन से सरै बड़न को काम
मढ़ो दमामा जात कहुँ सौ चूहाँ को चाम

Kaise chhote naran se sarai baran ko kām
Marho damāma jāt kahuñ sau chūhoñ ko chām !

How can the low do the work of the high, can the
kettledrum ever be covered with the skin of 100 mice even?

i.e. even 100 low-caste men can't fulfil the duties of one
high-caste man : just as impossible it is to cover the
kettledrum if the skins of 100 mice were pieced together.

152. A prophet is with honour save in his own country.

१५२   गाँवँ के कोरेया लोग कहें इन्दर जव

Gāoñ ke koreya, log kahe indar jao.

This is the (common) *koreya* of the village, and people
style it the "*Indar jao !*"

i.e. It is the common produce that grows in every
village, commonly called "*koreya*" by the people, but
medically it is known by the high-sounding name of
"*Indar jao.*"

इन्दर जव "*Indar jao,*" literally, "barley fit for *Indar,*"
King of the Fairies.

Applied when something common is dignified with a
sonorous or euphemistic name.

A short time ago a medicine was advertised as a recent
discovery and very much lauded (as all new patent
medicines are) as a specific for asthma.   It was called
"Kalikarpa."   A respectable Hindu gentleman who was
suffering from this chest malady was advised to send for
a box of it.   He did so.   It was not bigger than half the
size of an ordinary tin of sardines.   On his opening the
box and examining this high-priced specific, great was
his surprise to find that it was the rind of the common

dhatūra plant (*Stramonium*), which he knew very well before. On this occasion he made use of this proverb.

153. Among butchers a devout man can never be happy.

१५३ जहाँ सगरे गाँव कसाई तहाँ एक राम दास के का बसाई

Jahāñ sagare gāoñ kasāi
Tahāñ ek Rām Dās ke ka basāi.

Where the whole village consists of butchers, how can one devout man find it pleasant to live?

राम दास *Rām Dās* is the declared servant of *Rāma*, the god; he who leads a devout life and never touches animal food.

154. Annoying an old man.

१५४ चल लरिके दादा के बिरा आईं

Chala larike, dāda ke bira āiñ.

Come along, children! let us go and mock at grandpapa! Said when people join together to annoy another.

155. Whatever is in the vessel will come out of the spout.

१५५ जे करवा में रहे से टोंटी से बहे

Je karwa meñ rahe, se tonti se bahe.

Whatever is in the pot flows out of the spout!

करवा "*Karwa*" is a pot with a spout.

E.E. "Out of the fulness of the heart the mouth speaketh."

156. Beneath notice is *Bhak Bhaun Puri*.

१५६ कौन गने भक भौन पुरी के

Kaun gane Bhak Bhaun puri ke.

Who counts (poor) *Bhak Bhaun Puri*?

भक भौन पुरी "*Bhak Bhaun Puri*" is the supposed name of one of the sects of सन्यासी *Sanyāsi*. The *Sanyāsi*

faqīrs are divided into several sects. The following are
the titles of some of these sects or clans :

गीर " *Gir*," पुरी " *Puri*," भारथी " *Bhārthi*," अरण्य
"*Arnya*," बान " *Bān*," परबत " *Parbat*," etc., etc.

Applied when any one owing to his insignificance is of
no consequence.

Installation of a *Mohant* :

The following is a short account of the ceremony of in-
stalling a *Mohant* or abbot as head of the मठ *math* or abbey.
The ceremony is called चदर उराएव " *Chaddar Urāeb*,"
lit. "to cover with the sheet." The *Mohant* of a *math*, who
is vowed to celibacy, has usually some चेला *chelas* or
disciples attached to him. They are adopted in the
following ways : they are either made over to him when
young by their parents to become his *chelas*, or come of
their own accord and enlist as his disciples, or are sometimes purchased by him (as in the case of the Boklahar
Mohant in Champāran). On being received as disciples,
their heads are shaved. This forms the initiatory step,
and is commonly called मूँड़ मुड़ाना " *Mūñr Murāna*," which
therefore is equivalent to becoming a disciple. When
the *Mohant* wants to appoint a successor, he chooses from
among his disciples the one whom he thinks capable of
conducting the duties appertaining to the mat. The most
senior disciple (usually the son of a Brāhman or any other
respectable caste), if capable and otherwise qualified, is
chosen ; but the *Mohant* is not bound to appoint him
unless he thinks him fit for the post. He has power to
choose *any one* among his disciples. This is done by inviting
on a fixed day the neighbouring well-to-do men, and the
principal tenants in the estates attached to the monastery.
After worshipping the gods in the *math* or monastery the

chosen disciple is made to sit on a **मसनद** *masnad* (carpet)
with a **कलसी** *kalsi* (earthen chatty) of water in front of
him. At the appointed hour and before the assembled
guests the *Mohant* wraps a **पगड़ी** *pagri* or head dress round
the disciple's head. After this ceremony is over he pro-
ceeds to apply a **तिलक** *tilak* or forehead mark, and then
salutes him as the new *Mohant*. This being done, as a
final ceremony he covers him with a shawl and takes his
seat alongside of him. Then the guests offer presents
and also cover him with shawls or sheets. This com-
pletes the ceremony, and the disciple is henceforth the
Mohant elect and the recognized heir to the old *Mohant*,
and succeeds him in due course in the *gaddi* or manage-
ment seat of the monastery and the property attached to
the *math*.

157. Bamboos make the clump.

१५७ वाँस गुने बँसउर चमार गुने अधउर

Bāns gune bansaur
Chamār gune adhaur.

The (value of the) bamboo clump depends on the quality
of the bamboos, just as the quality of the hide depends on
the (skill of the) tanner.

158. Beating is pleasant, all but the consequences.

१५८ हँसी हँसी मारीं कूकुर रोइ रोइ फेंकीं गूह

Hañsi hañsi marīñ kūkur
Roi roi pheñkīñ gūh.

All smiles when killing the dog, but all tears when
having to throw out the dirt!

The idea is taken from killing a dog or a cat, which
usually makes a mess on being chevied, and so the dirt

has to be cleaned or removed afterwards. It means, so long as you are winning or enjoying it is all very pleasant, but the time comes when the consequences are far from pleasant and make you weep.

Said as a warning to those who oppress; that a time may come when the tables may be turned upon them.

159. Bound to do it.

१५९ ए गूड़ खायेँ कान छेदायेँ

E, gūr khāyeñ, kān chhedāyeñ.

You *must* eat this sugar, and must have your ears bored! Refers to the practice of giving a little sugar to a child whose ears are to be bored: while she is eating it the operation is performed. Said when one has under any circumstance to perform a thing, *nolens volens*, when there is no possibility of escape and he must do it.

160. Constant repetition not conducive to conviction.

१६० गाइ गाइ का होखह बाउर
भूसा कुटले निकसी चाउर

Gāi gāi ka hokhah bāur
Bhūsa kutale niksi chāur ?

Why are you making yourself mad by singing (over and over the same thing)? Can rice be got by pounding husk?

वाउर " *Bāur*," mad, that is, why repeat the same thing over and over again and behave like a mad man? You can't convince him, no good can be served: no more than rice can be got by pounding husk.

Said to one who cannot bring conviction to another by constant repetition, and is therefore advised not to waste his breath.

161. Can meat be kept on trust with a jackal?

१६१ गीदर रखे माँस के थाती

Gīdar rakhe māns ke thāti.

Would you keep meat on trust with a jackal? *i.e.* Can the jackal ever be trusted to keep meat safely in his charge?

थाती " *Thāti*," or थाथी " *Thāthi*," a trust charge.

Said when any one altogether untrustworthy is expected to keep faith.

162. Drowning the miller.

१६२ दे दाल मेँ पानी पैगा बह चले चुल्हानी

De dāl meñ pāni
Paiga bah chale chulhāni.

Pour water into the dall (so much so) that the whole village of Paiga may be washed into the cooking place.

Said when the dall (brose) is very watery.

The following story is said to account for this saying:

Once a very large number of people came with a marriage procession to the village of Paiga. As the dall cooked was not sufficient, water was freely added to make up the quantity, upon which it was sarcastically said: जेकर सहारा पानी सेह घटला *Jekar sahāra pāni, sehu ghatala,* i.e. can a thing fall short which can be increased by adding water! (lit. the chief support of which is water).

163. Diamond cut diamond.

१६३ जतने गाँगू लाम ततने सोहाइक चाकर

Jatne Gāñgu lām, tatne sohāik chākar.

Gāñgu is as long as *Sohāik* is broad! *i.e.* One equals the other in craftiness.

गाँगू " *Gāñgu*" and सोहाइक " *Sohāik*" were two notorious

knaves in the fable who vied with each other in artful
dodges and in deceiving people. When any one attempts
to out-do another in cunning (and both are equal), this
saying is used: in a case of "diamond cut diamond."

164. Dear at its native place and cheap at the market.

१६४ ताल महँगा हाट ससता

Tāl máhanga, hāt sasta.

Costly at the place where it is produced, and cheap at
the market! Another version of the proverb is got by
substituting the word टाल for ताल.

टाल *tāl* means "a stack, a rick": "dear at the stack,
but cheap in the market."

ताल " *Tāl* " is lit. a field in the outskirts of a village;
hence the place of production. Another meaning of *Tāl*
is a pond, or lake, a deep collection of water also called
मन " *Man.*"

Said when a thing commands a higher price at the
place where it ought naturally to be cheap.

Hājīpur, for instance, is famous for its excellent mangoes,
but if any one goes to buy its best mangoes there, he
invariably finds that these command a higher price in
Hājīpur itself than in Patna city, where they are im-
ported by wholesale dealers. The reason is, of course,
that the crop is always sold beforehand, and what remains
is usually kept for private use. Knowing this fact, the
owners ask exorbitant rates.

In such a case this proverb may be used when the order
is reversed.

165. Do in Rome as Rome does.

१६५ जैसन देस तैसन भेस

Jaisan des, taisan bhes.

Suit your behaviour (lit. appearance) to the country.

भेस "*Bhes*" assumed likeness, disguise, mask, hence behaviour.

166. Do what he may, he is still a beggar.

१६६ माथो मुड़ौले गरीब गोर नाँव

Mātho muñraule garīb gir nāoñ.

Although he has had his head shaved, yet they name him *Garībgīr*.

Refers to the story of the poor man who thought he would be well off by joining a convent of faqīrs; but on being shaved (the usual preparatory step), and renamed, he found to his disappointment that he was still called गरीब गोर "*Garībgīr*," *i.e.* the poor Faqīr.

Said when poverty does not forsake one whatever he may do.

167. Prescription for keeping health.

१६७ खा के मूती सूती बाँव काहे के वैद् बसावह गाँव

Kha ke mūti, sūti bāoñ,
Kāhe ke baid basāwah gāoñ?

If after eating you (make it a practice to) pass water and always sleep on your left side, there is no use of having a physician in your village (*lit.* getting a physician to settle in your village), *i.e.* you will not fall ill (if you take to this habit) and need the service of a physician.

Extent of one's power.

168. The *Parās* (tree) has but three leaves.

१६८ परास मेँ तीने पात

Parās meñ tīne pāt.

The *Parās* tree has but three leaves to each branch.

परास "*Parās*" (*Butea frondosa*) is trifoliate.

Said derisively of one the extent of whose powers is limited. "He can go to this extent and no further!"

169. However strong the grain, it cannot break the cooking-pot.

१६९ कॆतनॊ बूँट बरियार हॊइ भनसार नाँ फॊरी

Ketnon būut bariyār hoi, bhansār nañ phōri.'

However hard the grain may be, it cannot burst the parching house.

i.e. The utmost strength one can exert may fall far short of another's ordinary power.

भनसार "*Bhansār*" is the fireplace in the parching house where grain is parched.

There is usually one general fireplace where all the village women bring their grain to be parched. The parching is usually done by the "*Kāndu*" women, who receive their wages in grain. It is strange that while the Hindu is so scrupulous about the cooking of his food, and will not eat what has not been cooked by his own or higher castes, he does not object to his grain being parched by a Kāndu or a Kahār, and in the earthen pot in which the grain of all the castes of the village is parched. The excuse of course is that water, which is the contaminating medium, is absent from parching.

170. Follows the rich and feeds on the poor.

१७० धनी कॆ बात सुनॊँ गरीब कॆ भात खाइँ

Dhani ke bāt sunañ, garīb ke bhāt khāiñ.

He hears the rich (*i.e.* he acts according to their wish), but feeds on the poor.

Cast at him who fawns and flatters the wealthy, but has to rely on the poor and insignificant (whom he despises) for his support. A sycophant, a parasite.

171. Fate and self-help equally shape our destiny.

७१ करम बौसाव आधे आध

Karam bausāo ādhe ādh.

Fate and self-exertion are half-and-half in power. *i.e.* We must not solely depend on fortune for our success, because all our actions owe half their success to self-help. In other words self-help and confidence in our good fortune must go hand in hand. The meaning is, that they are both equally powerful in shaping our destiny.

Highly Improbable.

172. Can a dead horse eat grass?

७२ मुअलो घोड़ा घाँस खाला

Mualo ghōra ghāns khāla?

Does a dead horse ever eat grass?

Said when one tries to do an impossibility.

173. Can a frog catch cold?

७३ मेँढक को भो जोकाम

(या) बेँगो के सरदी

Meṅrhak ko bhi zokām?

(Ya) Bengo ke sardi?

A frog with a cold or cough (*i.e.* Is it possible for a frog to catch cold or get a cough?)

A derisive way of expressing "unlikelihood" or "improbability": when any one who is used to anything pretends that he cannot stand it.

174. Can a goat eat nine maunds of flour?

७४ का कहूँ कुछ कहा न जाय नव मन आँटा वकरी खाय

Ka kahūṅ kuchh kaha na jāy,

Nao man ānta bakari khāy?

What am I to say?   I am dumb, is it possible for a goat to eat nine maunds of flour?

175. He who holds the ladle commands everybody.

१७५ जेकरा हाथ में ँ डोई तेकरा हाथ में ँ सब कोई

Jekra hāth meñ doi
Tekra hāth meñ sab koi.

He who holds the ladle commands everybody.

डोई *"Doi,"* a wooden ladle, to stir the cooking, also to help out food with.

176. He who has suffered can sympathize with those in pain.

१७६ जानेली चोलम जिनका पर चढ़ेला अँगारा

Janeli chīlam jinka par charhela angāra.

The fire bowl (of the hubble-bubble), which holds the burning embers, knows (the pain of burning)!

चीलम *"Chīlam"* is the bowl of a हुक्का *"huqqa,"* which contains the tobacco and fire.   *i.e.* He who has never experienced the pain of burning can afford to laugh at it, but let him ask the *chīlam* what it feels with a live coal inside it.

177. He thatches his roof whose house leaks.

१७७ जेकरा पर चूएला सेही नूँ छावेला

Jekra par chūela sehi nūñ chhāwela.

He whose house leaks thatches his roof.   *i.e.* He who suffers tries to find a remedy.

178. How money may be got rid of.

१७८ विप्र टहलुआ चोक धन औ बेटिन के बाढ़
ए हु से धन ना घटे करों बड़न से रार

Bipra tahalua, chīk dhan, au bētin ke bārh
E hu se dhan na ghate, kari baran se rār.

If you cannot get rid of your wealth by having a Brāhman servant, keeping possession of money received from a butcher, or from excess of daughters, you will do it by fighting with bigger men (Grierson).

i.e. A Brāhman servant being of superior caste cannot be checked in his reckless expenditure as one of an inferior caste can ; it is considered very unlucky to receive money from butchers, it will even take away what one has ; and the extravagant expenditure a Hindu incurs at his daughter's wedding is proverbial. It is ruin for a Hindu to possess several daughters.

This proverb is meant as an admonition to those who engage in a quarrel with the great. If one is determined to get rid of his money the best way he can do it is to pick up a quarrel with a great man : he will then be more certain to do it than from any of the causes enumerated above.

179. Happy medium.

१७९ ना अति बकता ना अति चूप
ना अति बरखा ना अति धूप

Na ati bakta, na ati chūp
Na ati barkha, na ati dhūp.

Neither too much talk nor too great a silence, neither continuous rain nor continuous sun, is desirable.

180. Indifference to loss.

१८० गेंडुँआर के कतेक गोड़ टूटी

Genruār ke katek gor tūti.

How many feet can you break of the earth-worm?

गेंडुँआर "*Genruār*" or गेंड़गोआर "*Ganrgoār*" is a worm which has like the centipede many feet. It probably takes its name from मेंड़ुरी *genruri* (a round twisted pad, usually made of grass, for supporting water-pots, etc., on a woman's head) from the fact that this worm when touched coils up like a *genruri*.

The meaning is that the *genruār* has many feet and can therefore suffer the loss of a few without much harm coming to it.

Said of a rich man who can afford to lose some of his riches without feeling the loss.

181. "Ifs" and "Ans."

१८१ मरते नहीँ तो घर भर होते

Marte nahīñ to ghar bhar hote.

If they did not die, they would fill the house.

Certainly they would, but the "if" comes between. Said when one makes everything conditional on impossibilities.

E.E. If "ifs" and "ans" were pots and pans,
There would be no work for tinker's hands.

182. "Ifs" and "Ans."

१८२ हमरा के केहू ना मारे तो हम सन्सार के मार आईँ

Hamra ke kehu na māre to ham sansār ke mār āīñ.

If there was no one to oppose me, I could beat the world.

Said to deride an excessively ambitious man, who, but for the restrictions imposed, would domineer everybody.

183. In the friendship of asses look out for kicks.

१८३ गदहन के यारी लातन के सनसनाहट

Gadahan ke yāri, lātan ke sansanāhat.

In the friendship of the ass expect (nothing else but) a shower of kicks (or constant kicks).

सनसनाहट "*Sansanāhat*" is tingling, whizzing : it means the whizzing sound caused by swiftly flying kicks without pause; also refers to the tingling pain. A variation of this (in Shāhābād) is लौण्डन के यारी ढेलन के सनसनाहट *Laundan ke yāri dhelan ke sansanāhat.* "In the friendship of boys expect nothing else but a shower of clods."

184. In a treeless country the castor-oil plant is a big tree.

१८४ रूख ना बिरिच्छ तहाँ रेंड़ँ परधान

Rukh na birichchh tahāñ reñr pardhān.

Where there are no trees the castor-oil plant is looked upon as a big tree.

i.e. In a place where there is no one of particular distinction a man who is a little elevated above his fellows is considered a great man, just as a small hillock is raised to the dignity of a mountain in a level country.

185. If a woman of ill fame gets angry with you, so much the better.

१८५ बेस्या रूसल धरमें वाँचल

Besya rusal, dharmeñ bānchal.

If the woman of ill fame gets angry with you, so much the better : your virtue is saved. *i.e.* By her getting angry and stopping intercourse with you, you are prevented from committing further sin which might have ruined you morally.

बेस्या "*Besya*" or वेस्वा "*beswa*" is a prostitute.

Said derisively when the anger of any one is rather a blessing than a loss to us, affects us rather for good than injuriously.

186. It is a *sarkāri* dog: do not oppose: let it do as it likes.

१८६   ई पिल्ली सरकारी हः लौर जन लह
       टुकुर टुकुर ताकत रहह चूल्ह कोड़तिया त कोड़े दह

I pilli sarkāri ha, laur jan lah
Tukur tukur tākat raha,
Chūlh koratiya ta kore dah.

This bitch belongs to the landlord: do not lift a stick (to beat it). If it is digging up the cooking place, put on a good face over it (*lit.* stare only).

सरकारी "*Sarkāri*" is belonging to the Government. Here a public servant or a servant of the great or of some one in authority is meant. Even if he should encroach a little on your rights, it is the best policy to remain quiet.

187. If benighted, go where the dog barks and not where the light is seen.

१८७   कुकुर भूके जाईँ दीया लौके नाँ

Kukur bhūke jāiñ, diya lauke nāñ.

If benighted, go where the dog is barking and not where the light is shining.

This is a warning to benighted travellers not to be led astray by the *ignis fatuus,* or as popularly called Jack-with-the-Lantern, the spontaneous phosphoric exhalation so often seen in marshy lands; a dog's bark is more certain to lead to a village.

188. Kill the snake as well as save the stick.

१८८   साँपो मारह लौरो जोगावह

Sāmpo mārah lauro jogāwah.

Kill the snake as well as save your stick.

In attempting to kill a snake one is apt to break his stick. The aim therefore should be to preserve your stick as well as kill the snake. Said metaphorically when one has to effect his purpose and see that no harm may come by it.

E.E. "Kill two birds with one stone."

189. Like to like.

१८९ जैसन के तैसन सुकठी के वैगन

Jaisan ke taisan sukthi ke baigan.

One to his deserts; just as brinjal suits a curry of dried fish.

i.e. One deserves to be treated according to his deserts or merits, just as brinjal is the proper vegetable to be served with dried fish.

This is a piece of worldly wisdom greatly appreciated by natives of all classes, to treat each one according to his social position.

190. Like to like.

१९० जैसन पस वैसन घास

Jaisan pas waisan ghās.

As the animal, so the grass. *i.e.* Suited to it : according to his deserts.

तस पूजा चाही जस देवता *Tas pūja chāhi, jas deota.*

As the deity, so the worship, *i.e.* according to his merit.

191. Little things are great to little men.

१९१ चिउँटी का मूँते पैराव

Chiunti ka mūnte pairāo ?

A little water (urine) is sufficient for the ant to swim in. Said when a little is sufficient for any purpose.

192. *Laddus* (sweetmeat) in both hands.

१९२ दूनो हाथ में लड्डू

Dūno hāth men laddu.

Sweets in both his hands.

Said when one is so circumstanced that he profits either way he turns: any course he takes he gains, like a saw that cuts both ways.

193. Leading an unhappy life.

१९३ नकटा जीये बुरी हवाल

Nakta jiye buri hawāl.

The noseless man lives, but such a life! *i.e.* His life is a misery, being always laughed at.

Said of one who exists, but under very unhappy circumstances.

194. Let's see on what side the camel sits.

१९४ कौना करे तो ऊँट बैठेला

Kauna kare to ūnt baithela.

Let's see on what side the camel sits.

The story is that once a *kunjra* (a greengrocer) and a *kumhār* (a potter) jointly hired a camel; and each filled one side of the pannier with his goods. The camel as he went along the road every now and again, when he had a chance, took a mouthful from the greengrocer's bag of vegetables. This provoked a laugh from the potter, who thought he had the best of the bargain. But the time came for the camel to sit, and he naturally sat on the heavier side, bearing down on the pots, and also to have his mouth free to operate on the bag of greens. This caused the pots to break in the bag, and then the greengrocer had all the laugh to himself.

Hence the saying, "Let's see on what side the camel sits," means

E.E. "He laughs best who laughs last."

Might is Right.

195. The strong can strike in the most vulnerable part.

१९५ बरियार के लाठी माँह कपार

Bariyār ke lāthi māñh kapār.

The cudgel of the strong (always falls) on the middle of the forehead.

i.e. The powerful man can always deal a blow at the most vulnerable part and with effect. He has you in his power.

196. The strong not only strike, but prevent you from complaining.

१९६ बरियर का मारे रोइँ नाँ दे

Bariyar ka māre rohuñ nāñ de.

The powerful man strikes and does not even let you cry out.

i.e. The powerful man not only strikes but prevents your complaining.

197. The strong, even if he should be in the wrong, strikes you.

१९७ हाकिम हारे मुँह में मारे

Hākim hāre muñh meñ māre.

If the powerful man loses even, he still strikes you in the face.

Similar proverb to above.

198. Right or wrong the mighty bully.

१९८ हारों तो हारों जीतों तो थूरों

Hāroñ to hāroñ jitoñ to thūroñ.

6

If I lose I shall strike ; if I win I shall crush !

हरब "*Hūrab*" is to thrust.   थूरब "*Thūrab*" is to pound.

i.e. Under any circumstances the powerful man punishes you, whether he wins or loses.

199. Necessity has no law.

१९९ नेह न जाने ओछी जात भूख न जाने जूठा भात
प्यास न जाने मूर्दा घाट निन्द न जाने झिलंगा खाट

Neh na jāne ochhi jāt ; bhūkh na jāne jūtha bhāt ;
Pyās na jāne mūrda ghāt ; nind na jāne jhilanga khāt.

Love knows no lowly caste ; Hunger minds not stale repast ; Thirst knows not the "ghāt" where the dead are burned ; Sleep objects not to a broken cot.

झिलंगा "*Jhilanga*" means "loose," broken, with the ropes hanging loose and broken "baggy."

200. No good to be got out of him.

२०० एह तीसीँ तेल नाँ
Eh tīsīñ tel nāñ.

This linseed has no oil !

i.e. Will not yield what is wanted, will not answer the purpose. Usually applied to a miser out of whom nothing can be got.

201. Not the sugar that flies will take to.

२०१ ऊ गुड़ न: की मक्खी खाय
Ū gur nah ki makkhi khāy.

It is not that sugar that flies will take to !

He is not such a one as you can get anything out of.

Said when no encouragement is met with ; where one expects encouragement, but is disappointed : where one has tried and failed.

Out of Place, Incongruous, mal apropos, etc.

202. The wedding of the sickle and song of the hoe!

२०२ हँसुआ के वियाह खुरपा के गीत

Hansua ke biyāh khurpa ke gīt.

It is the wedding of the sickle and all the song is for the hoe!

हँसुआ "*Hansua*," sickle.

खुरपा "*Khurpa*," a kind of hoe for weeding.

In the wedding of the *hansua*, the song (praise) should be for the *hansua* and not for the *khurpa*. Said to mark the inappropriateness of an act or speech (mal-apropos). This proverb appears somewhat quaint to us, but in the mouths of people, whose chief pursuits are agricultural, the allusion to implements of agriculture is but natural.

203. Same thing right or wrong according to situation.

२०३ ठावँ गुने काजर कुठावँ गुने कारिख

Thāoñ gune kājar kuthāoñ gune kārikh.

In the right place they count it collyrium, in the wrong place soot.

i.e. The same thing may be right or wrong according to situation or differing conditions.

E.E. "A place for everything and everything in its proper place."

204. *Mūnj* stitches on velvet.

२०४ मखमल पर मूँज के बखिया

Makhmal par mūnj ke bakhiya.

Stitch of *mūnj* on velvet (ground).

मूँज *Mūnj* is a kind of long grass used for making string and mats. Its stitches on velvet would be coarse work to say the least of it and out of place.

Evidently said to mark incongruity or want of harmony.

205. Pestle has nothing to do with curd.

२०५ दही में मूसर
(या) दाल भात में ऊँट के ठेहुन

Dahi meñ mūsar

(Ya) dāl bhāt meñ ūñt ke thehun.

The pestle in the tyre!

or The knee of a camel in pease-porridge and rice.

These proverbs put in a striking though quaint way the incongruity of things.

The मूसर *mūsar* or pestle for pounding rice has nothing on earth to do with tyre, nor the knee of a camel with pease-porridge and rice.

206. A cummin seed in the mouth of a camel.

२०६ ऊँट का मुँह में जीरा

Ūñt ka muñh meñ jīra.

A cummin seed in the mouth of a camel!

E.E. "A drop in the ocean."

207. Can the bark of one tree fit another?

२०७ आन काठ के बोकला आन काठ में कहुँ सटेला

Ān kāth ke bokla, ān kāth meñ kahuñ satela.

Can the bark of one wood ever be made to fit another?

i.e. Can anything that does not naturally come to one ever be fitly adopted by him? It will always appear out of place and far from natural.

Once Bit Twice Shy.

208. Will the bald head again go under the *bel* tree?

२०८ फिर मुँड़लो बेल तर

Phir muñrlo bel tar.

Will the bald head (*lit.* the woman with a shaved head) again go under the *bel* tree (never!)?

The वेल "bel" fruit, or wood apple, is said to have an especial attraction for the shaven head. She who has once had a bel drop on her shaven head will, you may be certain, never again venture under a bel tree. "O" in muñrlo marks the feminine gender.

E.E. "Once bit twice shy."

Burnt Child Dreads the Fire.

209. " A scalded cat dreads cold water."

२०९ दूध के डहल मठा फूक पीहीँ

Dūdh ke dahal matha phūk pīhīñ.

One scalded by (hot) milk drinks (cold) buttermilk even after blowing into it.

फक is blowing in order to cool anything.

Those who have suffered severely in any way are apt to have unreasonable apprehensions of suffering the like again.

"He that has been stung by a serpent is afraid of a rope."

E.E. "A burnt child dreads the fire."

210. A dog once struck with a firebrand dreads even the sight of lightning.

२१० लुआठ के मारल कूकुर लौका देख पराय

Luāth ke māral kūkur lauka dekh parāy.

A dog which has been once beaten with a firebrand will flee even at the sight of lightning.

Luāth or *luāthi*, a stake burnt at one end.

211. On the horns of a dilemma (the snake and the musk rat).

२११ भइ गति साँप छुछुन्दर केरी

Bhai gati sāñp chhuchhundar keri.

Circumstanced as the snake and the musk rat.

i.e. His situation is similar to that of the snake and the musk rat in the fable. The popular idea is that a snake places himself in a fix when he lays hold of a musk rat. If he should swallow it he is sure to suffer from blood poisoning (become a leper), if he should let it go he is certain to become blind.

Said of one who is in a quandary or on the horns of a dilemma.

Note. "This is a line from the Tulsi Krit Rāmāyan. It is in the Ayodhya Kānd. Chaupāi 54, in Rām Jasan's Edition."—Grierson.

212. One man's meat is another man's poison.

२१२ केकरो भंटा बैरी केकरो भंटा पन्थ

Kekro bhanta bairi kekro bhanta panth.

To some the brinjal is a poison (enemy): to others it is a regimen.

i.e. What is one man's meat is another man's poison.

Brinjal, or egg-plant, is considered especially hurtful in certain ailments, while in others it is prescribed as a special diet. *Panth* is regimen prescribed for the sick. Also the first light meal a patient is allowed to make when he is convalescent. It is usual for patients to fast for days. The idea is that by starving the patient the disease is starved out.

213. One never reveals his defeats and the beating he has received from his wife.

२१३ आपन हारल मेहरी के मारल केह कहला

Āpan hāral mehri ke māral kehu kahala.

Who ever speaks of his own defeat, or the beating he has received from his wife? *i.e.* one's defeat, like the beating one receives from his wife, is kept a dead secret.

214. A full belly makes a heavy head.

२१४ पेट भारी से माँथ भारी

Pet bhāri se mānth bhāri.

When the belly is full, the head is heavy!

Also said figuratively, when one has no wants, he usually becomes proud. It is also literally true. Too full a stomach gives a heavy head.

माँथ भारी "*Mānth bhāri*," a heavy head, is used towards one who carries his head high: opposed to "light-headed."

215. Out of all reckoning.

२१५ तीन में न तेरह में सुतरी के गिरह में

Tīn men na terah men sutri ke girah men.

Neither in the three, nor in the thirteen, but in the knot of the string.

i.e. Out of all reckoning. The "three" are the three highest गोत्र *gotras*, or clans, of Brāhmans. They are— 1 *Gārg*, 2 *Gautam*, and 3 *Shāndilya*.

And the "thirteen" are the next in order of merit, namely, 1 *Payāsi*, 2 *Samadari*, 3 *Chauri*, 4 *Brihadgrām*, 5 *Dharma*, 6 *Kanchani*, 7 *Mālu*, 8 *Supāla*, 9 *Triphala*, 10 *Pindi*, 11 *Itiya*, 12 *Itāri*, and 13 *Rārhi*.

He is neither among the three nor among the thirteen Brāhmans that are recognized; the account of the rest (being so numerous) is kept by tying knots to a string.

Said contemptuously of one who arrogates to himself a high position, but is so insignificant as not to be reckoned in the regular order. Out of reckoning.

"Out of the running."

216. One with a wax nose is easily led.

२१६ मोम के नाँक जेने नवाइँ तेने नवे

Mom ke nāṅk jene nawāiñ tene nawe.

A wax nose : whichever side you bend it, it bends.

i.e. One easily led, one who has no will of his own, but is a tool in the hands of others.

नवाएव *nawaeb,* " to bend."

217. One good turn deserves another.

२१७ नाँच परोसिन मोरा त मैं नचबूँ तोरा

Nānch parosin mora ta maiñ nachbūñ tora.

Neighbour, if you dance at my house, I shall dance at yours.

E.E. One good turn deserves another.

" If you scratch my back I shall scratch yours."

नाँच *Nānch* refers to the custom of dancing the *jhūmar* dance at wedding feasts.   It is gone through by the lower classes only.

218. Plain speakers not favourites.

२१८ साँच बात सदुल्लह कहे सब के चित से उतरल रहे

Sānch bāt sadullah kahe, sab ke chit se utral rahe.

Because Sadullah speaks the truth he is disliked by all (*lit.* is " out of favour " with all).

219. Truth at times parts the best of friends.

२१९ साँच कहले संग विधुआय

Sānch kahle sañg bidhuāy.

If you speak the truth, even your friend gets angry with you.

i.e. Plain speaking causes a breach between the best of friends.

220. Pain preferable to remedy in some cases.

२२० फूटल सहाला आँजन नाँ सहाय

Phūtal sahāla, āñjan na sahāye.

Rather bear the pain than the remedy! (He can bear the pain but not the remedy.)

फूटल "*Phūtal,*" *lit.* cracked, refers to the eye being blind.

आँजन "*Āñjan*" is collyrium or an application to the eyelids when inflamed or to improve them. Antimony is also used. Another proverb of similar import is

आँखिये फूटी त आँजन का लगाइ्ब

Āṅkhiye phūti ta āñjan ka lagāib.

If the eye is blind, what is the use of applying collyrium?

221. Purchasing troubles.

२२१ ढेबुआ दे के दुख बेसाहीँ

Dhebua de ke dukh besāhiñ.

To give money and purchase pain!

i.e. To be out of pocket and at the same time not to get any return; to pay as well as suffer. *Lit.* to "buy troubles."

ढेबुआ "*Dhebua*" is one pice in the language of the common people.

222. Right question, wrong answer.

२२२ चाउर के भाव पूछे गेहूँ छव पसेरी

Chāur ke bhāo pūchhe gehūñ chhao paseri.

He is asked the price of rice, but he answers " wheat is sold at 10 paseri!"

Said to laugh at a funny mistake, as for example when

a wrong answer is given that has nothing whatever to do
with the question.

223. Riches count for virtue.

२२३ जेकर चून तेकर पून

Jekar chūn tekar pūn.

He who possesses grain (to give away in alms) is
reckoned the virtuous man.

i.e. He who can afford to give alms is considered a
virtuous man.

चून "*Chūn*" is the corrupted form for चूर्ण *chūrṇa*,
"broken grain." Alms are usually given in grain or kind,
hence *chūn* stands for the means of giving alms. It is
a sarcastic reference to the fact that riches covereth a
multitude of sins.

224. Requiring constant service with adequate return.

२२४ दाना न घास दूनौँ साँझ दुमकजा

Dāna na ghās dūnoñ sāñjh dumkaja.

No grain or grass and the bearing-reins on morning
and evening !

दुमकजा *Dumkaja* (from *dum*, tail, and *qāiza*, corruption
of the Persian دُم قايزه کرنا or simply قايزه کرنا as in the
expression گھوڑیکو قايزه کرنا, means to tighten the bearing-
reins). Bearing-reins tightened, *i.e.* the state in which
we often see the horses of native gentlemen led out. A
string is tied to the reins and passed round under the tail
and tightened in order to cause the horse to arch his neck
and appear showy. Said when one is required to keep up
to the mark, or do his utmost, and suffer a constant strain
without being adequately remunerated.

225. Splendour but short-lived.

२२५ चार दिन की चान्दनी फिर अँधारी रात

Chār din ki chāndni phir andhāri rāt.

Four days of moonshine, and then comes again dark night!

One who makes too great a boast of or is too much elated by his short-lived success, may appropriately be reminded of the darkness that will follow apace.

226. Straightforwardness not always expedient.

२२६ सोझे अँगुरीं घीव निकल है

Sojhe angurīñ ghīu niklā hai.

Can you take *ghi* out with a straight finger?

In order to get anything good in this world, the proverb implies one must be a little crooked.

The meaning is, if you are quite straight and good, you cannot get on very well in this world, just as you cannot get much clarified butter out of a bottle by dipping your straight finger: you must bend it slightly.

Some amenable to kicks only.

227. Some amenable to kicks only.

२२७ लात के अदमी बात से ना माने

Lāt ke ādmi bāt se na māne.

One who is used to kicks will never listen to reason (words).

i.e. The man who is used to receiving kicks in order to make him do his work will never be influenced by mere words.

228. Give him betel and he won't offer you meal even, but give him kicks and he will give you sweets.

२२८ पान देले सातू नाँ पनही देले पूत्रा

Pān dele sātu nāñ, panhi dele pūa.

If you give him betel leaves, you will not even get
meal out of him; but if you give him a shoe beating, he
will be ready to supply you with cakes!

पान "*Pān*" is betel leaves, and पूत्रा "*pūa*" a kind of
cake made of flour, *ghi*, and sugar. To give *pān* is to
treat one with civility and kindness.

सातू "*Sātu*" is parched grain reduced to meal. It is a
common food of the poor.

Said of the low caste people who will not give you anything good unless they are beaten. It points to the
prevalent idea among the people of the treatment the
lower class ought to be subjected to in order to get anything good out of them.

229. Call him "father," and he will not give you oil
even; but abuse him and he will offer you clarified butter.

२२९ वावा कहले तेल नाँ समुर कहले घीव

Bāba kahle tel nāñ, sasur kahle ghiu.

Call him "father," he will not give you oil (even); but
call him "father-in-law" (*i.e.* abuse him), and he will offer
you *ghi* (clarified butter). To call one "father-in-law"
is a serious abuse.

Same remark applies to this Proverb as to No. 228.

230. Straight as a sickle!

२३० बड़ सोझ त हँसुत्रा नीयर

Bar sojh ta hañsua nīar.

If he is very straight, he is still like the sickle!

i.e. Even when he is in his best behaviour he is still
"crooked." Said in sarcasm of a man who is by nature

"crooked" in his dealings; one who cannot possibly be straightforward; evilly disposed.

The shape of a हँसुश्रा *hansua* is a curve. The metaphors, it will be noted, are invariably drawn from agricultural implements by a people whose chief avocation is tending the soil.

231. Sing his praise who gives you food.

२३१ जेकर खाईँ तेकर गाईँ

Jekar khāīñ tekar gāīñ.

Sing his praise who gives you to eat!

i.e. It ought to be your policy to side him or speak in his favour who gives you to eat.

232. Slay your enemy without scruple.

२३२ हने को हनिये दोख पाप न गनिये

Hane ko haniye, dokh pāp na ganiye.

Spare him not (*lit.* kill or slay him) who tries to harm you, and do not feel any scruple that you are committing a sinful act. *Lex talionis* is regarded as perfectly justifiable.

233. Too many cooks spoil the broth.

२३३ बारह डोम तेरह नाई से बजाये सिंग सहनाईं

Bārah dom terah nāi ; se bajāye sing sahnāi.

Even twelve *doms* and thirteen barbers : can these play on the *sing* or *sahnāi* ?

i.e. Twelve *doms* and thirteen barbers may attempt it, but can they possibly play on the *sing* or *sahnāi* ?

सिंग "*Sing*" and सहनाईं "*sahnāi*" are musical pipes; a kind of flute.

The *doms* and barbers are never employed to play on instruments in marriage processions, but *chamārs* and sweepers; therefore the meaning seems to be that although so many as twelve *doms* and thirteen barbers may be assembled to play on these musical instruments, yet they, whose occupation it is not, will only produce discord. When men attempt to do anything that is not their business, the result is always a failure, be they ever so many who engage in it.

234. The blusterer lords it over all.

२३४ नाँचे कूदे तूरे तान तेकर दुनियाँ राखे मान

Nānche, kūde, tūre tān, tekar duniyān rākhe mān.

The blustering man is always thought a great deal of in this world.

Lit. The man who dances, jumps, and makes a noise is respected much.

तूरे तान " *Tūre tān,*" lit. is to bring the note to a close or fall in right time.   (It is a musical term.)

235. The weevil gets crushed with the wheat.

२३५ जव का साथे घुनो पीसाले

Jau ke sāthe ghuno pisāle.

Along with the wheat the weevil is also ground down.

i.e. Along with the great (people from whom they derive their support, the patrons) their hangers on are crushed although they may be innocent.

236. The grass suffers in the fight of the tiger and buffalo.

२३६ वाघ भैसा के लड़ाइ मेँ नल खगड़ा के माैत

Bāgh bhaisa ke larāi meñ ; nal khagra ke maut.

In the fight between the tiger and the buffalo the long grass and weeds perish (by being crushed).

i.e. When two great men quarrel and fight, the " small fry " about them suffer.

237. The sweet ones he swallows, the bitter he rejects.

२३७ मीठा मीठा गब कड़ुवा कड़ुवा थू

Mitha mutha gab, karua karua thu.

All the sweet ones he swallows; the bitter ones he spits out.

Said when one selfishly picks out the good things and rejects all the bad ones, *i.e.* does not take his share of bad things.

238. Tongue—source of honour and shame.

२३८ जेहि मुहेँ पान तेहि मुहेँ पनही

Jehi muhen pan, tehi muhen panhi.

The very same tongue brings us honour (*pan*) or shame (*lit.* gets us a " shoe beating ").

A variation is *bhat* " rice," and *lat* " kicks," instead of "*pan*" and "shoe beating."

पान "*Pan*" is betel leaf; to give *pan* is to honour one. It is offered only to equals and superiors. It is therefore a special mark of regard shown to guests and friends.

पनही "*Panhi*," shoes; "to give one a shoe beating " is to disgrace him.

The meaning is that if one is guarded and careful in his speech and says the right thing in the right place, he will meet with success and favour; if, on the other hand, he does not control his tongue, " that restless thing of shame and mischief fatal spring," he is sure to meet with disgrace.

Another saying, illustrating that one may either get an elephant as a reward, or meet with his death, owing to his tongue, is the following play on the word पैयाँ *paiyan*, " you will get," or पाँव *paon*, " feet."

वातें हाथी पाइयाँ वातें हाथी पाँव

Bāteñ hāthi pāiyāñ, bāteñ hāthi pāoñ.

i.e. Words will secure you an elephant, and words will
also bring you to the feet of an elephant.

The meaning is that you will be trampled to death by
an elephant.   One of the many cruel ways of torturing a
guilty man to death under the Mahomedan Government
was to tie him to the leg of an elephant and thus get him
trampled.

There are many proverbs in English recommending due
control of the tongue.

1. " Confine your tongue, lest it confine you."

2. " Keep your purse string and tongue close."

3. " Better to slip with the foot than the tongue."

239. A needy troupe of dancers.

२३९ गरजू किरतनियाँ अपने तेले नाँचे

Garju kirtaniyāñ apne tele nāñche.

The needy dancing people use their own oil.

किरतनियाँ " *Kirtaniyāñ*," are a troupe of dancers who
usually perform by torchlight, the oil for which is sup-
plied by those who engage them to dance ; therefore the
meaning is, that one who is in need will go out of his way
to get his object.

240. The meanest can harm.

२४० ठिकरिश्रो से घड़ा फूटेला

Thikrio se ghara phūtela.

The ghara can be cracked by a small piece of potsherd
even ; *i.e.* the meanest thing can sometimes do you harm.

घड़ा " *Ghara*," is an earthen vessel used for holding
water.

241. The less the grain to be parched the more noise it makes.

२४१ थोर भूँजिया बहुत भड़भड़हट

Thor bhūñjiya, bahut bharbharhat.

The less the quantity of grain to be parched the more noise it makes in parching.

भूँजिया "*Bhūñjiya*" is parched grain. It is usually parched with an admixture of sand to equalise the heat and roasting. The sand is then separated by winnowing or in a sifting basket. When grain is parched without sand it is called उलाएब "*Uláeb.*" भड़भड़हट "*Bharbharhat*" is the crackling noise the grain makes in being parched.

E.E. Empty vessels make the most sound.

242. Things to be always guarded against.

२४२ गोएँड़ा के खेती सिरवाँ के साँप
मिभा कारन बाड़ी वाप

Goeñra ke kheti, sirwāñ ke sāñp
Maibha kāran bādi bāp.

The field nearest the village, the snake at the head of the bed, and the father who is against you on account of a step-mother (are all to be feared or guarded against as leading to danger).

गोएँड़ा के खेती "*Goeñra ke kheti*" is the belt of land near the homestead, which is better manured, more carefully cultivated and adapted for a superior kind of crop. —(Grierson).

It is the most frequent source of contention among villagers. Being nearest the village any stray cattle or goat easily finds its way into it, and sows the seed of a quarrel, which often ends in litigation and riot.

7

सिरवाँ के साँप "*Sirwān ke sāñp.*" By "the snake where your head rests," is meant, figuratively, your close relative or one on whom you repose confidence, but who is really your enemy ; a secret foe, a pretended friend, a wolf in sheep's clothing.

मैभा "*Maibha*" is a step-mother. A father, who marries a second time, usually takes the part of his new wife, and ill uses the children by his former marriage.

243. Things we ought to pray to be saved from.

२४३   चैत के जाड़ राड़ के बोली
       बिखम कहार छोटके डोली
       रामेश्वर आसिन के घाम
       ई मति कबहूँ सहावः राम

Chait ke jār ; rār ke boli.
Bikham kahār ; chhotke doli.
Rāmeshwar āsin ke ghām
I mati kabhūñ, sahāwah rām.

O Rām ! Never make me suffer (says Rāmeshwar) from the heat of the month of *Āsin* (September-October), from the cold of the month of *Chait* (March-April), from the hard words (reviling) of the low caste, from an uneven set of palki bearers (*i.e.* of unequal height), and from a small *doli* (litter) (*i.e.* in which I can't fit).

244. Taking a pleasant view of everything.

२४४   सावन के आँधर का हरियरे सूझेला
Sāon ke āñdhar ka, hariyare sūjhela.

The man who becomes blind in the month of Sāwan (July-August), fancies that he sees everything fresh and green.

Said of one who always takes a pleasant and one-sided

view of things; who is so biassed that it is a foregone
conclusion he will take a particular view of a question.
Also said of one who has a tendency to take a rosy view
of everything. The allusion is to the popular idea that
one who becomes blind when nature is green always
fancies that he sees everything fresh and green.

245. The staves of ten men make the load of one.

२४५ दस का लाठी एक का बोझ

Das ka lāthi ek ka bojh.

The staves of ten are equal to the weight of one man !
i.e. Equal distribution of work or labour is not felt as
a burden.

246. The word of a man, like the tusk of an elephant,
can never be withdrawn.

२४६ मरद के वात हाथी के दाँत जे निकलल से निकलल

Mard ke bāt hāthi ke dānt ; je niklal, se niklal.

The word of a man, like the tusk of an elephant, when
once out, it is always so, *i.e.* he does not "eat it."

The tusk of an elephant in Proverb No. 3 has been made
use of to illustrate the opposite character, namely, of dissembling or hypocrisy.

Unconcern or Indifference.

247. If the *bel* fruit is ripe, it matters little to the crow.

२४७ बेल पकल कौआ के बाप ला का

Bel pakal kaua ke bāp la ka.

What is it to the crow (*lit.* to the crow's father) if the
bel (fruit) is ripe?

The crow, which usually pecks at all (ripe) fruits, finds

the *bel* (wood-apple), with its hard shell, too tough for its beak ; therefore it is of very little concern, interest, or profit to the crow whether the *bel* is ripe or not.

वाप "*Bāp*" is the "intensive" form with the common people, as you are naturally supposed to look after the interest of your father, who is taken for granted to be greater than the son—the inference being that if anything does not concern the father, it ought not the more to concern the son. Said when one can afford to regard anything with perfect indifference.

248. If she disappoints, the bed only will remain empty.

२४८ आई तो आई नहीँ तो खाली चारपाइ

Āi to āi, nahīñ to khāli chārpāi.

If she comes (well and good), otherwise the bed will remain unoccupied.

Expressing indifference or unconcern at one's coming or not coming. (Said usually in reference to a female.)

249. Without restraint.

२४९ आगा नाथ न पाछा पगहा
जैसे धूर मेँ लोटे गदहा

*Aga nāth na pāchha pagha
Jaise dhūr meñ lote gadha.*

Neither has he the nose string nor the heel rope (tethering rope) : like an ass that rolls about in the dust (*i.e.* without any check or restraint, uncared for like an ass).

पगहा "*Pagha*" is the rope generally used for tethering cattle. The नाथ *nāth* and *pagha* are used for the better class of cattle: never for the ass, who is usually hobbled.

250. What is in a name?

२५० गाँव सिकटिया महतों जीयन
ज्यों ज्यों उकटीं त्यों त्यों तोञ्रन

Gāoñ sikatiya, mahtoñ jīyan

Jyoñ jyoñ uktīñ, tyoñ tyoñ tīan.

The village is called *sikatiya* and its *mahtoñ jīyan*, but the more you rake up the more you come by pleasant things (*lit.* savoury curry), *i.e.* which repays search.

सिकटिया "*Sikatiya*," *lit.* means a bit of potsherd, stands for a mean name (there is a village of this name in Champāran).

जीयन "*Jiyan*" is a very common name among natives of the lower class: it is used here to denote an insignificant name.

Said when any one discovers good things where he least expected them. (Both the village and its *Mahtoñ*, or headman, have unpretending names, still the village has some good things in it.) Compare also the following saying:

वाइस टोला के गाँव नाँव फुचटी *Bais tola ke gāoñ, nāoñ phuchti*, *i.e.* the village has twenty hamlets, but its name is "*Phuchti!*" (a common meaningless name of a village in the Hājīpur subdivision). Ridiculing an unpretending name, especially when it belongs to one who is of substance.

Warnings against Naturally Defective and Certain other Classes of Men.

251. The cunning of the dwarf, the squint-eyed, and the one-eyed compared.

२५१ साठ कोस नाटा के दौड़ अस्सी कोस बड्डकान
वा के अन्त न पाइये जो एक आँख के कान

Sāth kos nāta ke daur, assi kos bahukān
Wa ke ant na pāiye, jo ek āṅkh ke kān.

Sixty *kos* is the depth (*lit.* run = tether) of the dwarf
and eighty of the squint-eyed; but one who is blind of
one eye can never be fathomed. "*Ant*," end, bottom.
The *kos* or distance is simply used by way of comparison.
It is the common measure of distance in India—usually
taken to be two miles, but it varies immensely in different
parts of India. For example in Chutia Nāgpur it is the
distance a branch could be carried green. A traveller,
when starting on a foot journey, broke a branch from the
nearest tree and reckoned the number of *koses* he went
by renewing the branch when it withered. A "*Gāu kos*"
(so called in the north of Bihār) is the distance at which the
lowing of a cow can be heard. It means "a small *kos*."

In the above proverb the palm for deep cunning is
given to one blind of one eye, who would seem to be
especially obnoxious. Another proverb says of him :

बिरले कान भए भल मानुख *Birle kān bhae bhal mānukh*, i.e.
Rarely do you meet with a one-eyed man who is a gentleman (a good man).

Compare also the following Urdu saying on the same
subject, where a forced pun is made on the Arabic word
كان = " is."

كانے كي بدذاتيان　هين ميري دل مين يقين
آيا هي قران مين　كان مـن الـكـافـريـن

कानै की बद्ज़ातियाँ　हैं मेरे दिल में यकीन
आया है कोरान में　कान मिनलकाफरीन

Kāne ki badzātiyāñ haiñ mere dil meñ yaqīn,
Āya hai Qurān meñ, kān min alkāfrīn.

"Of the wickedness of the one-eyed I am thoroughly convinced, because even in the Korān it is said that 'the one-eyed is among the unbelievers!'"

Also compare the following warning against a bastard:

सात हाथ घोड़ा से डरिये चौदह हाथ मतवाल
हाथ अनगनित वा से डरिये जेकर जात फेटवाल

Sāt hāth ghora se dariye, chaudah hāth matwāl
Hāth anganit wa se dariye, jekar jāt phetwāl.

i.e. Keep seven cubits away from a horse and fourteen from a drunkard, but ever so far (literally, "innumerable hands") from a bastard (literally, "a mixture")!

The following story is related of the acuteness of a one-eyed man: He laid a wager with a man who had both his eyes, that he, with his one eye, could see more than his friend with two eyes, and proved it thus: he, with his one eye, saw his friend's *two* eyes, whereas his friend with his *two* eyes could only see his one! This specious reasoning is a good illustration of what the logicians call the fallacy of division. The fallacy turns on the word "*more.*"

252. Beware of grey eyes.

२५२ सौ में फूली सहसर में कानाँ
सवा लाख में ऐंचा तानाँ
ऐंचा तानाँ कहे पुकार
कांसा से राहियो होशिआर

Sau men phūli, sahasr men kānāñ
Sawa lākh men aiñcha tānāñ,
Aiñcha tānāñ kahe pukār,
Kaunsa se rahiyo hoshiār.

The man with a cataract in his eye is one in a hundred

(for rascality), the one-eyed is one in a thousand, the squint-eyed is one in a lakh and twenty-five thousand; but the squint-eyed man proclaims to all the world, " beware of the grey-eyed man."

(Meaning that there is one even more wicked than himself.)

253. Warnings against men with certain peculiarities.

२५३   कोतह गरदन कल्ला दराज   नखुनाँ नैन कबूतर-बाज
       करिया ब्राह्मन गोर चमार   बानर कान ऊँट भुँइहार
       इनका संग न उतरौं पार   भोरे बिसरे गोता मार

Kotah gardan, kalla daráj, nakhunán nain kabútar-báj,
Kariya Bráhman gor chamár, bánar kán únt bhuiñhár,
Inka sang na utrín pár, bhore bisre gota már.

Never go on a journey with any of the following (*lit.* never cross a river, meant figuratively for never associate or travel in company of the following) :—One with a short neck, one with a wide mouth (or one who has a long tongue), one who has a cataract in his eye, a pigeon fancier, a black *Bráhman*, a fair *Chamár*, a monkey, a one-eyed man, a camel, and a *Bhuiñhár Bábhan* : otherwise you will be duped before you are aware and come to grief (*lit.* any slip, mistake, or forgetfulness on your part will be taken advantage of by them and you will find yourself floundering (diving) in water).

A black *Bráhman* and a fair *Chamár* are proverbially untrustworthy.

There is a story about a camel and a monkey crossing in a boat. The monkey frightened the camel by attempting to get on to his neck and in moving about in his fright he sank the boat.

254. When there is a will there is a way (mind compared to a blacksmith).

२५४ मनवाँ लोहार जो मन के धरे
ढेढर पीट के चोखा करे
मनवाँ लोहार जो मन मन करे
चोखो में कुछ धोखा करे

Manwāñ lohār jo man ke dhare,
Dhedhar pīt ke chokha kare,
Manwāñ lohār jo man man kare,
Chokho meñ kuchh dhokha kare.

If the blacksmith called "Mind" makes up his mind, he can hammer very inferior iron and improve it; but the same blacksmith, if unwilling, will spoil the best of iron.

E.E. Where there is a will there is a way.

This is a play on the word मन "*Man*," mind or will. ढेढर and चोखा "*Dhedhar* and *Chokha*" are inferior and superior iron respectively. The former is unmalleable: the latter malleable.

मन मन करे "*Man man kare*" is to hesitate, to be unwilling, to falter, to be lukewarm and half-hearted over a matter. The metaphor is taken from the oil lamp, which, when the oil is nearly burnt, flickers with a murmuring sound before going out, "uncertain whether it should burn on or go out."

255. What houses are on the certain road to ruin (according to *Ghāgh* the poet).

२५५ बनियक दाता ठकुरक हीन
वैदक पूत ब्याध नहिँ चीन्ह
भाटक चुप चुप बेस्वक मेल
कहिँ घाघ पाँचो घर गेल

Baniyak dāta thakurak hīn,
Baidaka pūt byādh nahīñ chīnh,
Bhātak chup chup beswak mail
Kaheñ Ghāgh pāncho ghar gail.

A generous *baniya*, a mean landlord, a son of a physician ignorant of the diagnosis of disease, a silent *bhāt*, and an unclean courtezan, are all five, according to Ghāgh, on the road to ruin (*i.e.* not up to their calling)! क "*K*" marks the possessive case, *e.g.* (lit.) the generosity of a *baniya*, the meanness of a landlord, etc. चुप चुप "*Chup chup*" means speaking in a hesitating manner, not outspoken. हीन "*Hīn*" is here little, the opposite of generous as all landlords ought to be.

i.e. It does not do for the niggardly *baniya*, whose sole object in life is to hoard money by disgraceful self-denials, to be generous. If a landlord, who, on the contrary, ought to be generous and noble-minded, takes to petty ways, he undoubtedly disgraces his position, or in other words a *baniya* cannot save money and at the same time be generous, nor can a landlord be niggardly and keep up his reputation of being generous. A son of a physician, if anything, ought to be able to recognize diseases. A *bhāt* or extempore bard lives by his wit and ready tongue; if he is therefore hesitating and not ready of speech, he is sure to fail in obtaining a livelihood. The courtezan, if unclean, will not be sought after.

CLASS III.

Proverbs Relating to Peculiarities and Traits, Characteristic of Certain Castes and Classes.

Ahīrs or Goālās (milkmen).

256. An *Ahīr* knows only how to sing his *Lorik* ballad.

२५६ केतनौँ अहिरा होहिँ सेयाना
लोरिक छाड़ि न गावहिँ आना

Ketnoñ ahira hohiñ seyāna,
Lorik chhāri na gāwahiñāna.

An *Ahīr* (milkman), however clever, will sing nothing else but his *Lorik*.

लोरी *Lori* is a deified *Ahīr* hero, in whose praise the *Ahīrs* always sing. It is their one tribal song. When an *Ahīr* is asked to sing, he invariably sings nothing else but the *Lorik* ballad.

Lorik, according to a legend told by Mr. J. C. Nesfield in a recent number of the Calcutta Review (quoted in the Pioneer of the 13th March, 1888), was an *Ahīr* hero or prince, who held the fort of Gaura, his native city. It was the stronghold of the *Ahīrs*. His adventures and his fight with the Cheru warrior King Makara, who had his fort in Pipri, are related at length by Mr. Nesfield. *Lorik* was subsequently killed by *Deosi*, one of the surviving sons of Makara, and the founder of the Musahar tribe, also called after him, Deosiya or children of Deosi. There is, therefore, a traditional enmity between the Ahīrs and the Deosiyas or Musahars, as shown by the following proverb still current among both tribes :

" *Jab tak jūre Deosiya*
Ahīr na chhāje gāī."

i.e. "As long as a Deosiya is alive the *Ahīr* will get no good out of his cows."

The story of *Lorik* is also given at length in vol. viii. of the Reports of the Archæological Survey of India.

257. Receipt given by the cunning *Kāeth* to the burly *Ahīr*.

२५७   कचहरी के बाकि बन के असूल
लाठी का हाथे राउत बेबाक

Kachahri ke bāki ban ke asūl,
Lāthi ka hāthe rāut bebāk.

What was due to the office (of the Zemindar) was recovered in the wood. The *Rāut*, who is armed with a club, is granted this receipt in full.

This was the ambiguous receipt given by the clever *Kāeth* (or man of the caste of scribes), who was waylaid by a burly राउत *Rāut* or *Goāla* in the jungle, and threatened with a thrashing if he did not grant him a receipt in full at once on the spot for any rent due from him, under the impression that he was thus over-reaching the wily *Patwāri* (accountant). But the *Kāeth* proved more cunning than the *Rāut*, and gave him the above receipt, which could be read between the lines. The *Rāut*, satisfied that he had got what he wanted, let the *Kāeth* go. The next day, to his great surprise, he found he had to pay in court more than all his due.

Rāut is the social title of a milkman.

Kachari=court. It is the office of the landlord of a
village where rent is paid in by the tenants and receipt
granted by the *Patwāri*.

Said when one has to give up under compulsion.

258. The young barber practises on the *Ahīr's* head.

२५८ कटे अहीर का सीखे बेटा नउआ का

Kate ahīr ka sīkhe beta naüa ka.

The barber's son learns to shave on the *Ahīr's* head,
which he cuts freely (*lit.* the *Ahīr's* head is, but the
barber's son learns !).

When the barber wants to teach his son his art he
usually chooses the foolish milkman to practise on.

Said to exemplify the stupidity of the *Ahīr*, who is
usually credited with little sense, also when one profits at
the expense of another.

Brāhmans.

259. Hair splitting about difference of castes.

२५९ तीन कनौजिया तेरह चूल्हा

Tin Kanaujiya terah chūlha.

Three *Kanaujiyas* (a tribe of Brāhmans) and thirteen
cooking places (*i.e.* for separate cooking) !

The **कनौजिया** *Kanaujiya* Brāhmans are the proverbial
sticklers about caste differences : with them a hundred
obstacles have to be overcome and shades of restricting
gotra rules have to be examined before two *Kanaujiyas*
can eat from the same pot. It is therefore an exaggerated
way of putting the differences which very often split up
a small community. Another way of saying the same
proverb in an accentuated form is *Tin Kanaujiya teñrāh
chūlha,* i.e. when three *Kanaujiyas* come together, adieu

to all eating (*lit.* "thou cooking place shalt be set aside, because there will be so much altercation about caste differences that there will be no cooking ").

260. The *Pāñre* does not practise what he preaches.

२६० ग्रान के पाँड़ सिखवन देस ग्राप ढिमिलिया खास

Ān ke pāñre sikhwan des, āp dhimiliya khās.

The *Pāñre* (teacher) would teach others; but he himself stumbles (*lit.* staggers and falls, trips).

पाँड़े *"Pāñre"* is a sect of Brāhmans : here for one who sets himself up as a teacher.

ढिमिलिया *Dhimiliya* or *dhammunyan khās* is staggers and falls, reels, stumbles.

The meaning is that he pretends to instruct and show the road, while he himself is stumbling.   Cast at one who does not practise what he preaches.

261. A *Kāeth* wants payment, a Brāhman feeding, and paddy and betel watering, but low castes only kicks to make them do their work.

२६१   काएथ किछु लेलें देलें बराहमन खिग्रौलें
        धान पान पनिग्रौलें ग्रौर राड़ जाति लतिग्रौलें

Kāeth kichhu leleñ deleñ, Barāhman khiauleñ,
Dhān pān paniauleñ, aur rār jāti latiauleñ.

A *Kāeth* does what you want on payment, a Brāhman on being fed, paddy and betel on being watered, but a low caste man on being kicked.

राड़ जाति *"Rār jāti"* are the low caste.—(Grierson.)
A variation of this is (in Shāhābād) :

काायथ के कुछ लेले देले बाम्हन के खिलवले
रजपूत के बोध बाध नान्ह लतिग्रवले

Kāyath ke kuchh lele dele, bāmhan ke khilaole,
Rajpūt ke bodh bādh, nānh latiaole.

Barber.

262. A barber's wedding.

२६२   नौआ के बरियात सब ठकुरे ठाकुर

Naua ke bariyāt, sab thkure thākur.

In the marriage procession of a barber every one is a
thākur; *i.e.* the marriage procession of a barber consists
of people who style themselves " lords and masters " only.

ठाकुर " *Thākur*,"—in common parlance a barber is styled
thākur, which literally means " a lord," " a master."

Said in joke when each one in a company thinks himself the leading spirit or master.   Barbers and boatmen are credited with being more helpful to their fellow
caste men than the high caste people, who are only good
for empty talk; they never help one another.

नौआ कँवट चीन्हे जात वड़का लोग के चिक्कन बात

Nauwa keñwat chīnhe jāt, barka log ke chikkan bāt.

The barber and boatmen are the only people who
recognize their caste fellows (*i.e.* who help them).   The
high caste are only good at fine talk !

In the polite language of the people each profession
has its civil style of address, *e.g.* a barber and also a
blacksmith are styled *thākur*, a washerman is *baretha*;
a carpenter is *mistri* (perhaps a corruption of ' *magister*,'
through the Portuguese); a tailor is *khalīfa*; a sweeper is
mihtar and also *jamadār*, etc.

(The word *thākur* in the proverb is used with a certain
amount of sneer.)

Baniya (shopman).

263. The owed *baniya* gives further tick.

२६३   अँटका बनियाँ सौदा करे

Antka baniyān sauda kare.

The owed *baniya* deals willingly (*i.e.* gives further tick) !

The meaning is, that the **वनिया** *baniya*, whom you owe money, will be very willing that you should not break with him, but continue dealing ; and hence he will be ready to give you further loans or things on credit.

Bābhan ("bastard" Brāhmans).

264. A *Bābhan*, a dog, and a *bhāt* are always at variance with their own castes.

२६४ बाम्हन कूकुर भाँट जाती जाती खाँट

Bāmhan kūkur bhāñt, jāti jāti khāñt.

Bābhans, dogs, and bards are always at variance with their own caste (kind).

A variation is

बाम्हन कूकुर हाथी जातो जाती खाथी

Bāmhan kūkur hāthi, jāti jāti khāthi.

Bābhans, dogs, and elephants can never agree with their own kind.

"*Khāñt*" in the first proverb means crooked, not coinciding or agreeing ; hence quarrelsome.

265. A *Bābhan* never to be believed.

२६५ सील सूत हरिबंस लि बीच गङ्ग के धार
एतेक लै बभना तौना करह इतिवार

Sīl sūt haribans lai, bīch gang ke dhār,
Etek lai babhna tauna karah itibār.

If a *Bābhan* swears by the ammonite, his son, the *Haribans*, and in the midst of the Ganges, don't believe him.—(Grierson.)

The reader is referred to an excellent note on the various forms of oaths prevailing in the Province of Bihar

in Mr. Grierson's "Bihār Peasant Life" (*vide* para. 1451,
page 401 of the "Bihār Peasant Life").

266. One *Bhuiñhār Bābhan* is equal to seven *Chamārs*.

२६६ सात चमार एक भुईँहार

Sāt chamār, ek bhuiñhār.

One *Bhuiñhār Bābhan* is equal (in meanness) to seven
Chamārs (leather-workers).

A variation is

सात चमार न एक भुईँनहार सात भुईँहार न एक नोनिआर

Sāt chamār na ek bhuiñhār, sāt bhuiñhār na ek noniār.

i.e. Seven *Chamārs* are not equal to one *Bhuiñhār Bābhan*,
and seven *Bhuiñhār Bābhans* are not equal to one *Noniār
Baniya* (a tribe of shopkeepers), who is said to beat them
all in meanness, parsimony, and the disgraceful self-
denials by which they save money.

Barhai (Carpenter).

267. A pretentious *barhai* or carpenter.

२६७ ईहे बढ़ैयू गाँव कमैंहेँ जिनका बसुला ना रुखान

Ihe barhaiyu gāoñ kamaiñheñ jinka basula na rukhān.

This carpenter would serve the village when he has
neither chisel nor adze.

Said of one who undertakes to do a thing without possessing the means.—(Grierson.)

Chamārs (Shoemakers and Cobblers).

268. When shoemakers quarrel, the king's saddle suffers.

२६८ मोँची मोँची लड़ाई होय फाटे राजा के जीन

Moñchi moñchi larāi hoe, phāte rāja ke jin.

In the fight of the saddlers (shoemakers) the saddle of

the Rāja gets torn, *i.e.* in contending who should have the work.

E.E. "Too many cooks spoil the broth."

The sad result to the object of dispute when two of the same trade fight over it, was once actually illustrated, though somewhat tragically, in Benares, the sacred place of pilgrimage, where previous to the ceremony each pilgrim has to be shaved. Two barbers fought hard for the possession of a poor pilgrim's head. At last one got hold of it, and, not to lose time, at once commenced operations, when his foiled brother also began shaving from the opposite side. In the scuffle which ensued, the unfortunate pilgrim received a deep gash, and had to be carried away to the hospital.

269. A shoemaker's daughter with an aristocratic name!

२६९   चमार के बेटी नाँव रजरनियाँ

Chamār ke beti nāoñ Rajraniyāñ.

The daughter of a shoemaker, and her name is *Rāja-rāni* (*i.e.* the Queen of a King) !

Said in ridicule of low-caste people, who have affected names, after the manner of their superiors. A low-caste man (*e.g.* a *Chamār*) will behave, it is said, after his low-bred fashion, no matter with whom he has to deal, because it is not in his nature to appreciate respectability. See, for instance, the treatment which the *Chamār* accords to the revered sandal wood and the use to which he puts it.

चन्दन पड़ा चमार घर नित उठि कूटे चाम
चन्दन बेचारा का करे पड़ा राड़ से काम

Chandan para chamār ghar, nit uthi kūte chām,
Chandan bechāra ka kare ? para rār se kām.

It fell to the lot of the sandal wood to be in a *Chamār's*

house. He used it daily for pounding leather. What could the helpless sandal wood do, having to deal with a low-caste man (this treatment was inevitable)?

Darji (Tailor).

270. Sticking to his last.

२७० दर्जी के पूत जब तक जीता तब तक सीता

Darji ke pūt jab tak jīta tab tak sīta.

The son of a tailor; he will sew as long as he lives. Said to express attachment to one's profession or to express in a sneering way that one will never rise above his low (class) habits.

Dhobi (Washerman).

271. The *Dhobi* and his ass.

२७१ ना धोबिआ के दूसर जनावर

ना गदहा के दूसर मौआर

Na dhobia ke dūsar janāwar,

Na gadha ke dūsar manār.

There is no other animal suited to a *Dhobi's* use (besides the donkey), nor is there another master who needs the use of the donkey (besides the *Dhobi*).

i.e. Each suits the other. No caste will keep an ass. In the social scale the *Dhobi* or washerman ranks the lowest, in one respect, because he washes the soiled clothes of women in childbed, who are ceremonially unclean. A *Dom* even (who is really of the lowest caste) will not eat food from a *Dhobi's* hand. One of his (*Dom's*) common oaths is to swear that if he does so and so, may he eat out of a *Dhobi's* hand. डोम का जनते धोबी नीच *Dom ka jante dhobi nich,* "To a

Dom a *Dhobi* is low," *i.e.* in the estimation of a *Dom* a *Dhobi* is lower than himself. But the *Aghori fakīr* (who eats out of everybody's hand, and is the filthiest living man) even beats the *Dom*. Compare, *e.g.* the saying डोम हारे अघोरी से *Dom hāre aghorī se*. A *Dom* is defeated by an *Aghori* only. A story is told of an over-credulous *Dhobi* (or washerman), who was childless, and was constantly upbraided for this misfortune by his scolding wife. This preyed upon his mind very much, and was a permanent cause of unhappiness to the couple. One day, in the course of his work, he went to the house of the town *Kāzi* (or magistrate). He heard the *Kāzi* reproaching one of his pupils in this wise: "Not long ago you were a jackass; I made a man of you," etc. The *Dhobi* did not wait to hear the rest. He hastened home with all speed and told his wife that he had made a discovery which they were to lose no time in utilizing. "The *Kāzi*, my dear," said the *Dhobi*, "can make a man of a donkey. Why should we fret any longer for a child? let us take our donkey to him and beg of him to transform him." The *Dhobi* and his wife, with their donkey, were shortly after this conversation on their way to the *Kāzi*. Their mission being explained, with many supplications, the *Kāzi*, quick-sighted, and with an eye to business, accepted the charge, and promised to effect the metamorphosis in a year. The *Dhobi* on his part promised to give his services free for that period. A year passed in waiting and in happy hopes. On the appointed day the *Dhobi* and his companion presented themselves before the *Kāzi*. The *Kāzi* took them aside and pointed out a strong young man among his pupils. "There," he whispered to the *Dhobi*, "is your donkey. You see the change: now persuade

him and take him home." The *Dhobi* and his wife flew
to their newly-created son, and with many endearing
terms prepared to embrace him and made other affectionate advances. Amazed at this unaccountable conduct of
these low people, the lad resisted at first, but as they
persisted he grew furious. After receiving many a cuff
from the lad, a happy idea struck the *Dhobi's* wife : turning to her husband she said, "Go you and fetch his peg,
rope, and grain bag; perhaps they may remind him
of what he was once." The *Dhobi* in hot haste went
home and fetched them. But it seemed to make
matters worse. The *Dhobi* held up each of these
articles to the young man's view, and said, in the
most persuasive tone he could command, " Come
home, my son, do you forget the day you were my
donkey ; this was the peg to which I would tether
you, this your tether rope, and this your food bag, come
to your home !" By this time a jeering crowd had
gathered round the young man, and this so infuriated
him, that he turned to and gave the *Dhobi* the soundest
thrashing he had ever received in his life. The poor
dupe of a *Dhobi* (the story says) went home thoroughly
convinced that it was far better to have a childless home,
than one with such a child ; and also convinced that
what fate had ordained it was useless to fight against,
looking upon his punishment as a just return for his
presumption.

272. Washermen wash best under competition.

२९२ धोबी पर धोबी बसे तब कपड़ा पर साबुन पड़े

Dhobi par dhobi base, tab kapra par sābun pare.

No soap ever touches clothes unless many washermen

live together (when, owing to competition, they wash well).—Grierson.

273. The washerman never tears his father's clothes.

२७३   धोबीक बाप केर किछु नहीँ फाट

Dhobik bāp ker kichhu nahīñ phāt.

Nothing belonging to a washerman's father is ever torn by him.

i.e. Those are the only clothes about which he is careful. A washerman's donkey is a bye-word, as in the proverb:

गद्हा के न दोसर गोसैयाँ धोबिया के न दोसर परोहन

Gadha ke na dosar gosaiyāñ, dhobiya ke na dosar parohan.

An ass has only one master (a washerman), and the washerman has only one steed (a donkey). This is a variation of Proverb No. 271. No other caste, except the *Dhobi*, will own the ass, as it is considered derogatory.

274. The *dhobi*, the tailor, and the barber are always careless.

२७४   धोबी नाउ दरजी इ तीनू अलगरजी

Dhobi nāu darji, i tinu algarji.

There are three careless people, the washerman, the tailor, and the barber.—(Grierson.)

अलगरजी "*Algarji*" means without care or concern; here it means that they are inclined to be independent. (It is a fact that these three workmen take everything as it comes in the most cool manner. They do not seem to trouble themselves much about pleasing their customers; it would seem to be all the same to them whether they get work or not. They never try to raise themselves above immediate want or provide for the future. Of improvident workers these three are no doubt the most improvident. It cannot be said that they do not work hard, but this they do fitfully, as necessity pinches them.)

275. A *dhobi* is likely to starve in the village of the nude.

२७५ जा के जहाँ न गुन लहे ता के तहाँ न ठाँव
धोबी बस के का करे दिगम्बर के गाँव

Ja ke jahāñ na gun lahe tā ke tahāñ na thāoñ,
Dhobi bas ke ka kare digambar ke gāoñ.

Where one cannot find a market for his talents, it is useless for him to stay (*lit.* his place is not there): for example, what occupation will a *dhobi* find in a village of people who possess no clothes?

दिगम्बर "*Digambar*," see note to Proverb No. 94.

Said sarcastically when an artisan or labourer does not find work, or his skill is not appreciated.

Kāyath.

276. A *Kāyath*, essentially a man of figures.

२७६ लेखे जोखे थाहे लड़िका बुड़लन काहे

Lekhe jokhe thāhe, larika burlan kāhe.

The depth was calculated and an average struck: why then was the child drowned? *i.e.* if the stream was found to be fordable, after sounding and calculating, how came the child to be drowned?

लेखा जोखा "*Lekha jokha*," arithmetic (lit. *lekha* is account and *jokha* is weighing).

There is a story connected with this saying illustrating that the *Kāyath* is essentially a man of figures.

Once a *Kāyath*, with his son, was going on a journey.

He came to a stream. As he was uncertain of its depth, he proceeded to sound it; and having discovered the depth to be variable, he struck an average. The average depth being what his son could ford, he ordered him, unhesitatingly, to walk through the stream, with the sad consequence that the boy was drowned.

Said sarcastically when great and elaborate efforts are put forth or great show is made with a barren or sad result.

277. Sinning in good company.

२७७ सात पाँच कायथ एक सन्तोख

गदहा खैने नाहिन दोख

Sāt pāñch kāyath ek santokh,

Gadha khaine nāhin dokh.

Among several (sinning) *Kāyaths*, if there happens to be one devout (contented) man, even if they should eat donkey's meat, it is no sacrilege.

There is a story told that once on a time the landlord of a village, chiefly inhabited by *Kāyaths*, had a tame deer, which his neighbours regarded with greedy eyes. The village took fire and every house in it was burnt to ashes. Among the ashes was found a roasted carcass, which all concluded to be that of the deer, as it was always, for safety's sake, kept tethered. Those who had so long had their eyes on the poor deer set to and had a good feast on it. But not long after, to their great surprise, the deer (which had broken loose) turned up. On subsequent inquiry it was found that what they had feasted on was not the deer, but an unfortunate jackass. Among the people who had so indulged there happened to be a *Bhagat* (a very religious man), so one of the

Kāyaths, quite equal to the occasion, explained that even eating donkey's meat was no sin, provided it was done in good company : hence the above saying.

It is a chaff against the *Kāyaths*; also said sarcastically when any one argues that sinning in good company is no sin.

278. A. *Kāyath* is helpless without pen and paper.

२७८ कायथ का कागजे में सूझेला

Kāyath ka kāgaje men sūjhela.

The *Kāyath* can only see in his paper.

The कायथ *Kāyath*, who is a born quill-driver, utterly fails in action. Said in chaff of a *Kāyath* or of any one who is nothing without his papers; useless in action.

279. *Kāyaths*, crows, and sweepings gather their own kinds.

२७९ कायथ कुरकुट कौवा तीनों जात पोसौवा

Kāyath kurkut kauwa tīnoñ jāt posauwa.

Kāyaths, sweepings, and crows are the three who stick (keep) to one another (पोसौवा " *Posauwa*," *i.e.* who help and support one another). A variation is

कायथ कौवा रोर जाती जात बटोर

Kāyath kauwa ror jāti jāt bator.

Kāyaths, crows, and jackals collect their own kind; *i.e.* wherever they are, they collect and support their own kind, are always to be found in numbers.

280. A *Kāyath*, when paying cash, is the very devil.

२८० नगद कायथ भूत उधार कायथ देओता

Nagad kāyath bhūt udhār kāyath deota.

A *Kāyath*, when paying cash, is the very devil (in ex-

acting a bargain); but when indebted he is as meek
as an angel.   This is an especial characteristic of the
Kāyath.

281. A *Kāyath* gains when fools quarrel.

२८१   लड्डु लड़े झिल्ली झरे कायथ बेचारे का पेट भरे

Laddu lare jhilli jhare kāyath bechāre ka pet bhare.

When *Laddus* come in contact (fight), bits drop out;
the poor *Kāyath* thus gets his living.

लड्डु "*Laddu*" is a sweetmeat made of sugar and cream
in the shape of a ball, which is a conglomeration of the
झिल्ली *jhilli*, or drops of cream and sugar, which united
together form the *laddu*.   Figuratively said of a "fool"
or "simpleton."

The *Kāyath*, like a lawyer, finds his living when two
rich men fight.   Their loss is his gain.   A *Kāyath's*
pickings are proverbial.

E.E. "When rogues fall out, honest men come by
their own."

282. Wherever three *Kāyaths* gather together, a
thunderbolt will fall.

२८२   बजर परे कहवाँ तीन कायथ जहवाँ

Bajar pare kahwāṅ tīn kāyath jahwāṅ.

Wherever three *Kāyaths* gather together, a thunderbolt
is sure to fall, *i.e.* some mischief is sure to result.   The
Kāyaths are notoriously people who instigate quarrels,
especially lawsuits.

283. Comparison of castes.

२८३   कायथ से धोबी भला ठग से भला सोनार
दे॒औता से कुत्ता भला पण्डित से भला सियार

Kāyath se dhobi bhala, thag se bhala sonār,
Deota se kutta bhala, pandit se bhala siyār.

A *Dhobi* is better than a *Kāyath*, a goldsmith better than a cheat, a dog better than a deity, and a jackal better than a *Pandit*.

Because a *Dhobi* can keep a reckoning of the clothes he has brought to wash in his head, and from memory can recognize the clothes of each when returning them; whereas a *Kāyath* cannot do anything without writing, *i.e.* without his pen, ink, and paper (see Proverb No. 278). A goldsmith is better than a cheat, because he cheats you more cleverly under the cover of his art, and is not known as a cheat at all. A dog is contented with whatever you give him and is always faithful; whereas a god always expects you to offer him of the best you have, and any remissness in your devotion brings down on you his wrath. A *Pandit* cannot foretell, unless he has his books and holy writs by him to consult, but a jackal (if you know how to interpret the omens) always foretells with certainty whether an undertaking will be successful or not.

Another proverb speaks of his (*Kāyath's*) sharp practices, and ranks him, for shrewdness, just below an "adulterer," who must be sharp to elude detection.

खत्री से गोरा पाण्डु रोगी कायथ से चतुर परभोगी

Khatri se gora pāndu rogi, Kāyath se chatur parbhogi.

An Albino only is fairer than a *Khatri*; and an adulterer only is sharper than a *Kāyath*.

खत्री "*Khatris*" are usually very fair. (It is commonly said that this caste originated in a *liaison* between a *Brāhman* woman and a *Kāyath*.) *Parbhogi* is *lit.* one who eats or enjoys another's property.

284. The three people who dance in other's houses.

२८४ पर घर नाचैँ तीन जने कायथ बैद दलाल

Par ghar nāchen tīn jane Kāyath, baid, dalāl.

The three people who dance in other's houses are the *Káyath*, the Physician, and the Broker.

i.e. The three classes of men who profit by the mis-fortune of others (in other words who "loot" them) are the *Káyath*, the Physician, and the Broker.

"To dance in another's house" is, figuratively, "to live on their earnings," "to enjoy at their expense."

Kurmi.

285. A *Kurmi* always untrustworthy.

२८५   पथल पर जो जामे घुरमी
         तबहूँ नाँ आपन होखे कुरमी

Pathal par jo jáme ghurmi,
Tabahūñ nāñ ápan hokhe kurmi.

It is sooner possible for the tender creeper *ghurmi* to take root on a rock than for the *Kurmi* to be your own, *i.e.* to be one whom you can trust.

The कुरमी "*Kurmis*" (a caste supposed to be allied to the *Kahárs*, but ethnologically, perhaps, quite different. Some say the *Kurmis* are an aboriginal race) are pro-verbially untrustworthy and selfish. It is commonly sup-posed that no amount of favour shown to a *Kurmi* will ever make him a reliable friend or grateful to you. Re-garding their deep-rooted litigiousness and obstinacy, an experienced Indigo Planter in Tirhut told the writer that he would rather have any other caste than the *Kurmi* to fight against in a lawsuit; for a *Kurmi* was so obstinate that he would fight to the last pice he possessed. He had, in his varied experience of the different Bihár districts, known instances where *Kurmis* had maintained an unequal lawsuit until reduced to beggary; and even then they would not rest quiet, but instigated others to fight. They are very spiteful. They are spread all over Bihār, but are found in great numbers in Patna, where they follow all manner of professions. They are great sticklers about caste, and pretend to be very strict Hindus. But they are looked down on by the higher castes and treated by them as a menial class.

Kumhār (Potter).

286. A *Kumhār* sleeps secure.

२८६ निचिन्त सूते कुम्हरा मटिया न ले जाये चोर

Nichint sūte kumhra matiya na le jāye chor.

The potter sleeps secure, for no one will steal clay.

He who has nothing to lose does not fear thieves.— (Grierson.)

A variation of this proverb is,

Gog (name of a man who had no one in this world) sleeps secure, as he has no children or family to cause him anxiety.

Musalmān.

287. A *Musalmān*, a parrot, and a hare are never grateful.

२८७ तुरुक तोता औ खरगोस
ई तीनौं नाँ माने पोस

Turuk tota au khargos,
Ī tinoñ nāñ māne pos.

A *Musalmān*, a parrot, and a hare, these three are never grateful.

A Mohamedan is still called a Turuk by the Hindus, no doubt from the fact of the early Mohamedans being Turks, just as the Europeans are still called Ferangis by the Indians from the early French (Franks).

288. To a *Musalmān* give toddy, to a bullock *kheñsāri*.

२८८ तुरुक तारी बैल खेँसारी

Turuk tāri, bail kheñsāri.

To a *Musalmān* (give) toddy, and to an ox *Kheñsāri*, *i.e.* each to his taste.

The following is quoted from Mr. Grierson's book on "Bihar Peasant Life."

खेँसारी "*Kheñsāri*" (*Lathyrus sativa*), a kind of pea. It is unwholesome for human beings, but bullocks eat it greedily, *e.g.* in the saying:

Turuk tāri bail kheñsāri Bāman ām Kāyath kām.

Toddy is necessary for a Musalmān's happiness, *kheñsari* for a bullock's, mangoes for a Brāhman's, and employment for a *Kāyath's*.

The Miyāñji (or Family Tutor).

289. When the *Miyāñji* is at the door, it is a bad look out for the dog.

२८९ जेकरा दुत्रार पर मीयाँ जी
तेकरा घरे कूकुर के जूठ फेँकल जाय

Jekra duār par miyāñ ji,
Tekra ghare kūkur ke jūth pheñkal jāy.

Is there ever any food thrown to the dogs in the house of one at whose door sits the family tutor? *i.e.* the family tutor eats up all the leavings, and there is nothing left for the poor dog.

मीयाँ जी "*Miyāñ ji*" is a typical character in the Bihar family circle. He is usually a poor Musalmān struggling for existence. Having acquired a smattering of Persian, he considers himself above manual labour; while on the other hand he is not sufficiently educated for any respectable intellectual employment. He therefore finds work as a teacher of children with some well-to-do family on a mere pittance and board. His place is at the door, where he instructs the children of the family in the rudiments. He is but tolerated and treated with scant courtesy. His share of food (for which he has often to wait very long) is doled out daily from the Zanāna; and he is not above accepting any remnants of food that may be added to his scanty meals. He is usually blessed with a good appetite, and no edibles need be thrown away when a *Mīyāñji* is at the door. It is therefore a bad look out for the dogs of the house if they happen to have such a voracious rival as a *Mīyāñji*.

This proverb is used sarcastically when anything need not be wasted owing to there being some one, who would, probably from poverty, be glad to accept it.

290. The *Mīyāñji* loses his beard in praise.

२९० मीयाँ के दाढ़ो वाह वाहे में गइल

Mīyāñ ke dārhi wāh wāhe men gail.

The beard of the *Mīyāñji* disappears in praising it! *i.e.* each student who wanted to pay him off laid hold of his beard and said, "What a fine beard, sir!" and gave it a tug, and thus every hair in the beard of the poor *Mīyāñji* was plucked! Said when anything disappears in simply tasting samples of it and praising it, or when anything is wasted.

The following story is told of a *Mīyāñji*, who was similarly served by one of his pupils whom he had left in charge of his dinner. A fowl had been cooked, but the pupil, instead of guarding the dish, went out to play, when a cat

walked off with a leg of the fowl. The *Miyāñji*, on missing
the piece, was greatly enraged, but the pupil maintained
that the fowl had only one leg. Notwithstanding this, he
got a severe whipping for stealing. Next day, while the
Miyāñji was comfortably taking his midday siesta, he was
rudely awakened by his aggrieved pupil, who came rush-
ing to inform him that he could prove that some fowls
had one leg only as he had said. The already enraged
tutor soon proved to his pupil, by throwing a stone at
the cock, which was resting on one of its legs (as fowls
are wont to do), that it had both. Upon which the poor
pupil got another sound beating. He remembered the
circumstance. Another day the same kind of accident happened, and the pupil discovered, before his master sat to his
meal, that a leg of the fowl cooked had again disappeared.
But this time he had got the secret of producing the lost
leg of a fowl. When his master turned angrily that
evening to him to demand what had become of the leg
again, the pupil, who had provided himself with a brick-
bat, threw it violently at the dish, saying, "There is the
other leg," expecting that the lost leg would be at once
forthcoming in the same way as the cock had produced
his under the stone of the *Miyāñji*. But the stone broke
the dishes and stunned the *Miyāñji*, and taught him to
respect the opinions of his pupils.

291. A *Miyāñji's* run is up to the mosque only.

२९१   मीयाँ के दौड़ महजीद ले

Miyāñ ke daur mahjid le.

The *Miyāñji's* run is as far as the mosque only, that
is the length he can go and no further; the extent of
one's reach; a *Miyāñji* is a tutor, who, when not engaged

in his work, is usually to be found in the **मसजिद्** *Masjid*.
He has no other place to go to. A *Miyañji* is always at
the door: if he goes out at all, it is to the mosque.

Said to mock one's effort: as much as saying, "That is
all he can do!"

Noniya.

292. A *Noniya's* daughter is born to labour.

२९२ नोनियाँ के बेटी का न नयिहरे सुख न ससुरे सुख

Noniyañ ke beti ka na nayihare sukh na sasure sukh.

The daughter of a *Noniya* has neither ease in her
father's house nor in her father-in-law's house.

नोनिया "*Noniya.*" The *Noniyas* are a labouring class
who find employment chiefly by extracting saltpetre,
hence their name.

"They are a poor and hardy race, and are the best
labourers, and especially sought after for digging"
(Hunter). The daughter of a *Noniya* would thus be
"born to labour." Their name is connected with *non*
salt. One usually enjoys more comfort in a father-in-
law's house than at home, so the expression "to be at
one's father-in-law's" means to be idle, to take things
easy and do no work. Hence if one is lazily inclined,
he is asked, "Do you fancy you are at your father-
in-law's?"

Rajpūt.

293. Thick-headed.

२९३ सूते रजपूत उठे अजगूत

Sūte Rajpūt uthe ajgūt.

When asleep, he is a Rajpūt; when awake, he is a fool
(literally, as if in wonderland), *i.e.* his senses are wool-

gathering, even when awake. Said of Rajpūts, who are proverbially thick-headed.

Suthrā fakirs.

294. Selfishness in *Suthrā fakirs.*

२९४   केहु मूए केहु जीए सुथरा घोर बतासा पीए

Kehu mūe kehu jīe Suthra ghor batāsa pīe.

Any one may live or die, the *Suthra sāhi* fakir must have his drink of *batāsa* and water.

The सुथरा साही *Suthra sāhis* are a sect of fakirs, the followers of सुथरा *Suthra*, who, it is said, was a disciple of नानक शाह *Nānak Shāh*. They sing and play on wooden batons and are very persistent in begging. Whatever may happen, they insist on their drink of शर्वंत *sharbat* before allowing the dead to be taken out of the house.

Said when any one selfishly insists on his object being served, regardless of circumstances.

The following story is told of Suthra. He was a favourite disciple of Nānak Shāh, and very popular with his fellow-disciples. He was always witty and spirited, and often indulged in practical jokes. On one occasion he paid dearly for his pranks by being ordered out of the monastery by his spiritual guide. After roaming about for some time, he appeared one evening before the monastery gate in the guise of a pedlar, with a pack-bullock, feigning he had come from a great distance with articles for sale, as well as offerings to the great Nānak. The gate-keeper was somewhat reluctant to announce him at that late hour, but was prevailed on by being promised half of what he would receive. On entering the presence of his patron, instead of saluting him, he thrice went

round his bullock and made a low obeisance to it, and
opened the panniers, when out fell a lot of bricks and
débris with which he had filled them. Then, turning
round to Nānak Shāh, he saluted him, and said it was to
these bricks that he owed the honour of coming again
into the presence of his revered patron; therefore his
first salutation was due to them. Enraged at this fresh
insult, Nānak ordered him a hundred stripes. Upon
which the cunning disciple said, "Half of it goes to the
gate-keeper according to my promise." His clever trick
so amused Nānak, that he pardoned Suthra and reinstated
him in his former favour.

Sonār (Goldsmith).

295. Hundred (strokes) of the goldsmith will not equal
one of the blacksmith.

२९५ सौ सोनार के न एक लोहार के

Sau sonār ke na ek lohār ke.

A hundred (strokes) of the goldsmith are not equal to
one of the blacksmith's.

The goldsmith uses a tiny hammer: a hundred strokes
from which would hardly equal one stroke from the
ponderous sledge hammer that the blacksmith wields.

i.e. One bold strong effort is better than a hundred
feeble ones!

Said to laugh at a feeble effort; or when one gains
success at the first trial where another's repeated efforts
have failed.

Teli (Oilman).

296. A *Teli*, though possessed of lākhs, cannot equal
Rāja Bhoj (in magnanimity or nobleness).

२९६ कहाँ राजा भोज कहाँ लखुआ तेली

Kahañ Rāja Bhoj kahañ Lakhua teli.

An oilman, however rich, can never be compared to
Rāja Bhoj.

राजा भोज "*Rāja Bhoj*" was a king of Bhojpur, from
whom it has taken its name.

लखुआ तेली "*Lakhua Teli*" was a rich oilman, who
amassed a large fortune, said to be several lākhs.

i.e. There can be no comparison between Rāja Bhoj
and a *Teli* (who is a low-caste man and proverbially mean),
though he may be possessed of lākhs. One is after all a
nobleman, and the other a shopkeeper.

Jolha (Weaver).

297. The weaver bearing the sins of others.

२९७ खेत खाय गदहा मारल जाय जोलहा

Khet khāy gadha māral jāy jolha.

The ass eats the crop, but the weaver is beaten for it.

The जोलहा *jolha* "weaver" is the proverbial scapegoat
of Indian society. A veritable "lodging-house cat"!

298. The weaver as a cultivator.

२९८ पावा हर का इमना खेती करबा अब

Pāwa har ka humna kheti karba ab.

I have found the rear peg of a plough, now I will at
once take to farming.

इमना "*Humna*" "is the peg which passes through the
shaft at the end of the plough" (Grierson). Meant for
the smallest part of a plough. This saying is ascribed
to a Mohamedan weaver (जोलहा *jolha*) who by accident
found a "*humna.*" He is the proverbial fool of Indian
stories.

299. The weaver penny wise and pound foolish.

२९९ सरबस हारौं गज भर ना फारौं

Sarbas hārŏñ gaj bhar na phārŏñ.

I will lose all, but still I shall not tear out a yard of cloth (or rather lose all than tear a yard of cloth). He is supposed here to be haggling for a yard of cloth which the customer wants, but which he under no circumstances will give.

This is another of the many proverbs aimed at the obstinacy of the Mohamedan weaver.

E.E. "Penny wise and pound foolish."

300. A whip does not make an equestrian.

३०० पड़ा पाया कोड़ा वाकी रहा थोड़ा जीन लगाम घोड़ा

Para pāya kora, bāki raha thora, jīn lagām ghora.

I have come by a whip accidentally: the rest is easy (to find), namely, a saddle, bridle, and a horse!

Similar proverb to No. 298.

Applied to those who having just made a beginning, or having got the least bit of anything, are so confident as to make light of the trouble required in attaining the rest.

301. A weaver's daughter aping her betters.

३०१ जोलाहिन के बेटी का बूबू के साध

Jolāhin ke beti ka būbu ke sādh.

The daughter of a weaver has a longing to call her sister "*būbu*" (in imitation of her betters).

बूबू "*Būbu*" is the familiar term by which elder sisters are called in respectable Mohamedan families.

Said when one tries to ape the ways of higher people.

302. A weaver proud as a king with a *gagra* full of rice only.

३०२   गगरीं अनाज भैल जोलहन राज भैल

Gagriñ anáj bhail jolhan ráj bhail.

As soon as a weaver gathers a vessel full of grain, he becomes as proud as a king, *i.e.* a weaver has only to get a vessel full of grain, when he feels as proud as a king.

Also cast at those who show pride on possessing very little.

303. The avaricious weaver.

३०३   जोलहा बटोरे नरी नरी खोदा मीयाँ लेस एके बेरी

Jolha batore nari nari khoda miyáñ les eke beri.

The *Jolha* (weaver) gathers laboriously very small quantities at a time, but God sweeps away all (his gatherings) at once.   (Compare Proverb No. 12.)

नरी "*Nari*" is the small tube inside the shuttle with the thread wound round it.   Aimed at those who take great pains to collect money, but lose it all at once. Mohamedan weavers are proverbially misers as well as everything nasty.

By "God" is meant Fate rather than God.   Said sarcastically, but with an air of earnestness.

A variation of this proverb is :

जोलहा चोरावस नरी नरी   "*Jolha choráwas nari nari.*"

खोदा चोरावस पोला   "*Khoda choráwas pola.*"

i.e. the *Jolha* steals little cotton at a time, but God takes away bales.

304. The weaver asks to be let off fasting, but gets saddled with prayers.

३०४ जोलहा गैले रोजा बकसावे निमाज परल गरे

Jolha gaile roja baksāwe nimāj paral gare.

The weaver went to have his fasting pardoned, but became burdened with prayers (*lit.* prayers fell on his neck).

The *jolha* went to his spiritual guide to beg that he may be let off keeping fast, but, on the contrary, he was saddled with prayers, *i.e.* he was directed, in addition to fasting, to pray five times a day according to the Mohamedan religion.

Said when one prays to be let off, but in answer gets burdened with additional penalty or trouble.

305. The weaver suffers on leaving his loom.

३०५ करिगह छोड़ तमाशा जाय नाँहक चोट जोलाहा खाय

Karigah chhor tamāsha jāy, nāñhak chot jolāha khāy.

The weaver leaves his loom to see the fun, and for no reason gets hurt. Alludes to the story of a *jolha* who got a thrashing on his going to see a ram fight, *i.e.* he is such a stupid that he never can step out of his house without getting into trouble. The "*jolha*" feels nowhere at home except at his loom.

306. *Īd* without weavers!

३०६ बिनाँ जोलाहे ईद

Bināñ jolāhe īd.

Īd without weavers! *i.e.* can there be ईद *Īd* without जोलहा *jolhas* (weavers)?

The *jolhas* and other low Mohamedans take the occasion of the *Īd* to indulge in uproarious merriment by drinking toddy. The *Īd* is a solemn festival in which good

Mohamedans never drink. Said when any one is indispensable on a festive occasion. Same application as Proverb 104.

वे गाँगो के झूमर *Be Gāngo ke jhūmar.*

307. A weaver makes a sad hash when required to reap a field.

३०७ जोलहा जानथि जव काटे

Jolha jānathi jao kāte.

Does a weaver know how to cut barley?

"Refers to a story that a weaver unable to pay his debt was set to cut barley by his creditor, who thought to repay himself in this way. But instead of reaping, the stupid fellow kept trying to untwist the tangled barley stems" (Grierson).

Another story told of the weaver as an agriculturist is that he, jointly with another man, sowed sugar-cane. When the crop was ripe, on being asked whether he would have the top or the stem, said, "Of course the top." When reproached by his wife for his stupidity, he said he would never again make such a mistake. The next crop they sowed was Indian corn. When the time for gathering came round, he told his friend that he was not to be made a fool of *this* time, and would have the lower part. His friend gave him what he wanted.

308. The weaver going to cut grass at sunset.

३०८ कौवा चलल बास के जोलहा चलल घास के

Kauwa chalal bās ke jolha chalal ghās ke.

The weaver went to cut grass (at sunset), when even the crows were going home (Grierson).

309. The weaver tries to swim in a linseed field.

३०९ जोलहा भुतिऐले तोसी खेत

Jolha bhutiaile tīsi khet.

The weaver lost his way in a linseed field.

The allusion is to the following comical exploit of certain *jolhas* (weavers). Once seven of them started on a moonlight journey. They had not gone very far from their home when they lost the road. After trying to find their way, they came to a linseed field, which they took to be a river as the field was in flower, and they fancied the blue colour of the flower to be that of water. They stripped themselves and began swimming. After hard labour they got across. To make certain that no one was drowned, they took the precaution of counting themselves before resuming their journey, but they discovered that one of them was missing as each counter forgot to count himself. Grieved at the loss of one of their company, they had not the heart to pursue their journey, but returned home! The following quotation from C. Kingsley's "The Roman and the Teuton" (1864), p. 184, shows how these stories travel over the world : "A madness from God came over the Herules (the Heruli were a tribe of Huns), and when they came to a field of flax, they took the blue flowers for water and spread out their arms to swim through, and were all slaughtered defencelessly."

310. The weaver's wife.

३१० बहसलि जोलहिनि बापक दाढ़ी नोचे

Bahsali jolhini bāpak dārhi noche.

The wilful weaver's wife will pull her own father's beard.

To pull the beard is to offer the greatest insult to a Mohamedan (Grierson).

311. Weavers' and shoemakers' promises never to be relied on.

३११ जोलहा के आई पाई चमरा के बिहान

Jolha ke āi pāi chamra ke bihān.

When a weaver says the cloth will be soon ready, as he is now brushing it, don't believe him, any more than you believe a shoemaker who says the boots will be ready to-morrow.

आई पाई "*Āi pāi*" means the brushing and the other preparations to which the weaver subjects the thread with which he is going to weave the cloth (Grierson).

312. A weaver as an impressed labourer.

३१२ टँगबह तः टाँगह नहिँ तः नौ नरीक हरकति होएत

Tangbah ta tāngah nahiñ ta nau narik harkati hoet.

If you must load me, load me quickly, otherwise the time of nine shuttles will be wasted.

"A weaver estimates his work by the number of *nari* shuttle-spools which he uses up, as in this proverb, in which he is supposed to address a man who has seized him to carry a load" (Grierson).

313. A fight between a frog and a weaver.

३१३ जोलहा जात नाँव के धीरा रस्ते चलत वेँग से भीरा
पहिल मार वेँग ठेँगक ठेँगा तर भए जोलह उपर भए वेँगा
तव जोलहेँ दरबार पुकारा औ साहेब मोहि वेँगन मारा
ताना तूर नरी ले भागा उलटे मोहि दबावन लागा

रोइ रोइ पूछे जोलह को जोए कैता मनुस वँगैचा होए
लम्बी टँगरी बकुला ठोर तर के मारे उपर के जोर
सूनो भाइ सूनो भतीजा सूनो मेरी माय
अव तो चललौँ बेँग लड़ैया जीव रहै भा जाय

Jolha jāt nāoñ ke dhīra, raste chalat beñg se bhīra.
Pahil mār beñg theñgak theñga, tar bhae jolah upar bhae beñga
Tab jolheñ darbār pukāra, ai, sāheb mohi beñgan māra.
Tāna tar nari le bhāga, ulte mohi dabāban lāga
Roi roi pūchhe jolah ki joe, kaisa manus beñgaicha hoe
Lambi tañgri bakula thor, tar ke māre upar ke jor

> *Sūno bhāi sūno bhatīja, sūno meri māy*
> *Ab to challīñ beñg laraiya, jiu rahe bha jāy.*

Now I am going to the battle of the frogs : it is to be
seen whether I am alive or dead !

This saying is ascribed to the following melodramatic
lines, where the *jolha* (weaver), the usual butt, is represented as waging an unsuccessful combat with a frog,
and then recounting his sad experience to his wondering
wife. The serio-comic description is of course intended
to ridicule the weavers, in the style so common in native
literature. " The *jolha* class are brave (steady) only in
name. Once being on a journey, he met a frog on the
road. The first to strike was the frog with repeated
blows. The *jolha* fell below and the frog was on top
of him (*i.e.* the frog won the fight). Thus defeated, he
appeared in court and cried, ' O, Sir ! the frog has beaten
me. He broke my weaving frame and ran away with my
shuttle, and in addition gave me a thrashing.' The wife of
the weaver, with tears in her eyes, began to inquire, ' What

kind of a being is a froggy?' 'He has long legs, my
dear, and a beak like that of a crane: he hits from above
as well as below' (*lit.* he hits from above and presses
from below), said the weaver, and added : 'Now hear
brother, hear my nephew, and hear my mother dear, I
am now off to do battle with the frogs, whether I live
or die!' "

CLASS IV.

Proverbs relating to Social and Moral Subjects, Religious Customs and Popular Superstitions.

314. Angel of death to be feared.

३१४ बूढ़ के मरले ना डेराईं जम के परिकले डेराईं

Būrh ke marle na derāiñ, jam ke parikle derāiñ.

The death of the old is not to be feared, but lest the Angel of Death should get used (*i.e.* habituated to making constant attacks).

जम "*Jam*" is the Angel of Death.

The idea is that the old are fit victims of the Angel of Death; but when he gets once used to making incursions and seizing the old, he may also begin to prey on the young; therefore his getting habituated to dealing out death is more to be dreaded than the occasional death of an old person. (Applied to deprecate the growth of a pernicious habit.)

315. As the *Debi*, so the offering.

३१५ जैसन बाड़ी देबी वैसन कोदो के अच्छत

Jaisan bāri debi waisan kodo ke achchhat.

As the Goddess, so the offering of *Kodo!*

अच्छत "*Achchhat*" is an offering made of rice to the deity. कोदो *Kodo*, which is a very inferior millet, is never used

for this purpose. Said disparagingly when one has to
be treated according to his deserts; *i.e.* who, though in a
superior position, is not deserving of the consideration
befitting his position. But it is also a fact that each
deity has its peculiar manner of being worshipped, *e.g.* a
she-demon (*Uchchhiṣṭ Chaṇḍālnī*) is worshipped with offerings of refuse and leavings of food.

316. A weak *Debi* and a strong he-goat for sacrifice.

३१६ अब्बर देबी जब्बर बकरा

Abbar debi, Jabbar bakra.

A weak goddess and a strong he-goat (as victim or
offering).

देबी "*Debi*" is a goddess to whom he-goats are sacri-
ficed as offerings. Said when one who ought to be
weaker in the regular order of things is really stronger
than another, *e.g.* when a strong subordinate really rules
his weak superior.

317. A saddening reflection.

३१७ नाँच काछ अिले मोरवा गोड़वा देखि झँवाय

Nāñch kāchh aile morwa, gorwa dekhi jhañwāy.

The peacock having danced (in all its pride) becomes
crest-fallen on seeing its ugly legs!

The popular idea ascribes to the peacock great conceit,
but it is said that in its ostentatious dance it comes to
a dead stop, and becomes crest-fallen on seeing its ugly
legs. Applied to one who, though outwardly jolly, has
some secret cause of unhappiness that acts on him as
a drag.

"A skeleton in the cupboard."

318. A fast woman blames others when she elopes.

३१८ अपना करते उढ़ार लगैली लोग के दोस

Apna karte urhār, lagaili log ke dos.

She was eloped with on account of her own viciousness,
but the people are blamed.

उढ़रब "*Urharab*" (*lit.*) is to cause one to fly or elope
(transitive form). उढ़ारब "*Urhārab*" is to fly or elope
(intransitive form); from this is derived उढ़री "*Urhri,*"
a kept woman, a concubine, *lit.* one who has been made
to fly or elope.

Thrown sarcastically at a woman who has made a false
step, but blames others for it. As if one would say in
irony, "Of course *she* is not to blame, but some one else."

319. A meddlesome woman.

३१९ तेली के बैल ला कुम्हैनि सत्ती

Teli ke bail la, kumhaini satti.

For the sake of the oilman's ox, the potter's wife has
become suttee, *i.e.* she interests herself in other people's
affairs (Grierson).

The meaning of this proverb is not quite clear. Perhaps
it means "To the oilman's ox the potter's wife is as good
as a suttee (*i.e.* perfection)," because she does not harass
him, as the oilman's wife does.

320. A disgraced cat is as humble as a wife of the rat.

३२० कनौड़ी बिल्ली चूहों की जोय

Kanauri billi chūhoñ ki joy.

The disgraced cat is (as humble) as a wife of the rat.

कनौड़ी "*Kanauri.*" This word seems to have two
meanings. In Shāhabad it means "disgraced, ashamed,"

and applied to one who has made a false step. In Maggah it seems to have the meaning of "obligated," and is applied to one who has received a favour from another, and is therefore under an obligation to him. The same idea is expressed in the proverb

पेचाह बिलारि मूसे बाउर "*Pechāh bilāri mūse bāur,*"

i.e. the trampled cat (*lit.* one in a fix or "pressed") is maddened by rats even, *i.e.* she is so weak and heartless that even the rats drive her mad, or is considered stupid by rats even. The meaning is that a disgraced superior is not respected.

321. A forward woman.

३२१   लाजो लाजे मरस ढीठो कहस जे डरे डेरैले
Lājo lāje maras, dhīṭho kahas je dare deraile.

The modest woman is dying from shame, but the impudent says she is frightened!

The forward or over-confident laughed at. Said when any one puts a wrong construction on an act. (The final "*o*" in "*lājo*" and "*dhīṭho*" marks the feminine gender.)

322. Born to labour.

३२२   नैहर जा भा सासुर जा जँगरा चला के कतहूँ खा
Naihar ja, bha sāsur jā, jañgra chala ke kathūñ khā.

Whether you go to your father's or your father-in-law's house, you must labour in order to get your living.

जँगरा "*Jangra*" means thighs.

जँगरा चला के "*Jangra chala ke*" is *lit.* to use one's thighs, *i.e.* to go about and labour. Cast at one who cannot afford to sit at ease, but is born to work for her living wherever she is.

323. Bad lineage.

३२३ चीनाँ का वंश मेँ सपूत जमले मार्हा

Chīnāñ ka bans meñ saput jamle mārha.

In the house of *Chīnāñ* if an excellent son is born, it is only *Mārha*.

चीनाँ *Chīnāñ* (*Panicum frumentosum*) is one of the smaller millets; when boiled and parched, it is called मार्हा *mārha*.

The meaning is that the best of a bad family will after all turn out only a very second-rate fellow. Just as the best thing that can be got from *chīnāñ* is *mārha*, which after all makes a very indifferent kind of food. *Chīnāñ* is despised as a poor man's food.

E.E. Little things are great to little men.

Brother and Sister-in-law.

324. A weak elder brother-in-law is not respected.

३२४ लटल भैंसुर देवर वराबर

Latal bhaiñsur dewar barābar.

A weak elder brother-in-law is like a younger brother-in-law (with whom you may take liberties).

Cast at a weak man who cannot command respect or assert his dignity.

भैंसुर "*Bhaiñsur*" (in relation to the wife) is the elder brother of the husband; देवर "*dewar*" is the younger brother.

A wife is always supposed to pay great respect to her husband's elder brother, whom she must never look full in the face or speak to if possible. If such a necessity should arise, she must speak to him with downcast eyes and in the most abject tone. On the other hand, the elder brother-

10

in-law is enjoined by custom never "to cast eyes" on the wife of his younger brother. The younger brother, on the contrary, is allowed by social etiquette to joke with the wife of his elder brother to any extent.

325. A sister-in-law has a sister-in-law to annoy her.

३२५ ननदो के ननद् होला

Nanado ke nanad hola.

A sister-in-law has a sister-in-law too! (to tyrannize over her). This speech is supposed to be made by the wife, between whom and her sister-in-law (husband's sister) a constant jealousy exists. They can never agree, and are always having "hits at each other," hence the phrase **ननद् डाह** "*nanad dāh*," which means the spite or envy peculiar to the sister-in-law. Here the wife is saying in a sort of self-consoling way, "If she is ill-treating me now, she will also in her turn be ill-treated by her sister-in-law; for she too must have one."

Said by one who is ill-treated, with some satisfaction that his oppressor has also some one to annoy him.

E.E. "Little fleas have lesser fleas upon their backs to bite 'em,
And these again have smaller ones, and so ad infinitum."

Bride and Bridegroom.

326. The bride cannot get rice gruel even, and others get sweets.

३२६ कनेयाँ के माँड़ नाँ लोकदिन के बुँदिया

Kaneyān ke mānr nān, lokdin ke buñdiya.

The bride cannot get rice gruel even, while her servant-maid gets *buñdiya*.

बुँदिया "*Bundiya* is a small round sweetmeat made of gram (बेसन *besan*) fried in *ghi* or oil and covered with sugar" (Grierson). It is dropt into the oil; hence its name, which literally means "drops," or "small drops." Said when favour is shown to the undeserving, while the deserving are left out in the cold.

327. A foolish bride gets no presents.

३२७ बुड़बक कनेयाँ के नव आनाँ खोइँछा

Burbak kaneyāñ ke nao ānāñ khoiñchha.

It is a foolish bride, that only gets nine annas in her pocket (for wedding presents) (Grierson).

खोइँछा "*Khoiñchha*" is the pocket formed in front by loosening the part of the cloth tied round the waist (Grierson). Sometimes villages are given away as wedding presents by राजा *rājas* and rich landed proprietors; and then these villages are known as खोइँछा के गाँव *khoiñchha ke gāoñ*. The way that this is usually done is, the title-deeds transferring the property are put into the front pocket of the bride (*khoiñchha*).

328. The face money to the bride.

३२८ मुँह नीयर मुँह ना रुपैआ मुँह देखौनी

Muñh nīyar muñh na, rupaia muñh dekhauni.

She is nothing to look at, yet "face money" has to be given on seeing her! (*lit.* she has not a face worth looking at).

मुँह देखौनी "*Muñh dekhauni*" is the money usually given on seeing for the first time the face of the daughter-in-law or of a child. "A bridal present."

Said when one undeserving wants you to do him a favour.

329. Crocodile tears of a bride.

३२९ धीया सासुर जाली की मने मने गाजेली

Dhīya sāsur jāli, ki mane mane gājeli.

Is the daughter going to her father-in-law's, or is she rejoicing? (*lit.* laughing inwardly).

A daughter-in-law is expected to weep when going to her father-in-law's house, at least in appearance, if not in reality. That is the native etiquette. That she does not always do it in earnest is shown by the proverb. If one outwardly shows a reluctance or pretends to be sorry, while in reality he or she inwardly rejoices, this saying is used. (Also cast at one whose behaviour is unsuited to the occasion.)

Blind and Deaf.

330. Blind master, deaf pupil.

३३० आँधर गुर बहिर चेला माँगे हरें देला भेला (बहेरा)

Āndhar guru bahir chela, mañge harre dela bhela (bahera).

A blind master and a deaf pupil: he asks for *harre* and is handed *bahera*.

हरें *"Harre"* is black myrobalans.

बहेरा *"Bahera"* is belleric myrobalans.

This describes in a comic way the laugh caused by the mistakes made by the deaf and the blind. Said when two persons misunderstand each other with a ludicrous result. The following story told of a deaf man illustrates this proverb: A deaf Brāhman was once engaged in his homestead garden in breaking brinjals. Some passers-by asked him, "How are you, महाराज *Mahārāj*?" "I am breaking brinjals" answered the Brāhman. "How are your children?" "I am going to make *bharta* of them all ! " (that is, make a mash of them, meaning the brinjals of course).

331. Backbiter.

३३१ मुँह पर तोके गाजी पीठ पीछे के पाजी

Munh par toke gāji, pith pichhe ke pāji.

He who blames one to his face is a hero, but he who backbites is a coward. *Pāji* is a low, mean fellow; a sneak.

गाजी *Gāji*, brave, bold.

332. Charity (sharing the last crust).

३३२ भीक में भीक दे तीनो लोक जीत ले

Bhik men bhik de tinon lok jit le.

He who gives away in alms what he has himself received in charity conquers the three worlds.

तीनो लोक *Tinon lok*, "The three worlds:" they are (1) खरग or अकाश *Swarg or Akāsh*, the Heaven; (2) पताल *Patāl*, or the lower regions ; and (3) मृतु भुअन *Mritu Bhuan*, or the earth of mortals.

i.e. The man who being himself in want is unselfish enough to give away what he has himself received in charity, may be said to have overcome all the three worlds: to have risen above the desires of the three worlds; or, in other words, to have achieved a success which may be envied by the inhabitants of all the three worlds.

333. Dying in Benares is going to Heaven.

३३३ जौं कबीर काशी होय मरे रामें कौन निहोरा

Jaun kabir Kāshi hoy mare, Rāmen kaun nihora.

If the faqir has to go to *Kāshi* (Benares) to die, what

is the use of supplicating *Rām* then? because dying in
Benares is in itself sufficient to take one to Heaven. The
intercession of *Rām*, then, is only necessary if one does
not die there. The meaning is, if one has to get anything
by self-exertion, what is the use of a favour? the obtaining
of it then cannot be called a favour.

Daughter.

334. Beware of overpraising your daughter.

३३४ सराहल बहुरिया डोम घर जाय

Sarāhal bahuriya dom ghar jāy.

The daughter-in-law, so much praised (for her chastity),
goes at last to the *dom's* house (*i.e.* sinks so low as to elope
with a *dom*, who is the lowest of the low).

A caution enjoined on those who boast of and praise too
much a daughter-in-law or any other relative,—a hint that
what is too much valued and lauded might after all turn
out bad. Too lavish a praise of even one's nearest and
dearest is apt to recoil on one's self in the shape of shame.
This proverb shows the common idea that a daughter-in-
law is always to be watched and never to be altogether
trusted.

335. A bad daughter ruins a son-in-law.

३३५ ई धीया मोर दमदो नसलन

Ī dhīya mor damdo naslan.

The daughter is (so bad) that she has even disgraced
the son-in-law. The son-in-law is the one usually found
fault with by the mother-in-law, and not the daughter;
therefore, if the daughter is such a one as would disgrace
a son-in-law, she must be very bad indeed.

Said in joke (as if from the mother), for example, by the husband when playfully blaming his wife.

336. A daughter has three names in succession during her lifetime.

३३६ एके बिटियवा आवे बबुई बझरिया देवानजी कहावे

Eke bitiyawa āwe, babui bahuriya dewānji kahāwe.

The same daughter is successively known by three different names: *babui, bahuriya,* and *dewānji.*

In her father's house, and while still unmarried, she is called बबुई *babui* (an affectionate name given to young girls); in her father-in-law's house she is बझरिया *bahuriya* (*i.e.* daughter-in-law); and when she has a son, and he married, she is addressed by the people of her son's father-in-law as देवानजी *dewānji* (*i.e.* a general manager).

The meaning is, that the same thing has different names under different conditions.

Dependent.

337. A dependent knows no happiness.

३३७ परवस बन्दा सुख का जाने

Parbas banda sukh ka jāne.

He is dependent on another, what does he know of comfort?

बस *"Bas"* is power, authority.

i.e. He who is in the power of another (not independent) can never know what true comfort or joy is.

Dancing.

338. Making absurd conditions for dancing.

३३८ न नव मन काजर होइहैं न राधा नचिहैं

Na nao man kājar hoihen, na Rādha nachihen.

Neither will there be nine maunds of collyrium, nor will Radha (ever dance).

काजर *Kājar* (see note to Proverb 127), a very little of this is necessary. Therefore, when a person makes the doing of a certain act conditional on an impossibility, this saying is aptly applied.

E.E. "I will pay you on the Greek Kalends."

339. False modesty in dancers.

३३९ नचलोँ त घुघुट का
Nachlīñ ta ghughut ka.

She who dances has no need to veil her face!

The dancing women have no character; therefore she who dances publicly has no need to draw a veil over her face from modesty, as **पर्दा** *parda* women do.

Said of those who affect to be modest when they have no need to be so, or are really the opposite.

The following is from Mr. Grierson's "Behar Peasant Life": "In *Manbodh's Haribans*, where the wife of *Akrūr*, although very modest, still wanted to look at Krishna when he came into the house.

बड़ घुँघुट पुनु तकलो चाहिञ
Bar ghūñghut punu taklo chāhia.

"Though always modestly accustomed to hide her face, she still tried to peep at him."

E.E. "Swallowing a camel and straining at a gnat."

Especial haunts or resorts.

340. The blind man's lodging (or resting-place) is at the turner's.

३४० अँधरा के डेरा खरादी घर
Andhra ke dera kharādi ghar.

The blind man's quarters are at the turner's, *i.e.* where he can find just the employment suited to him in turning the turner's lathe.

Said sarcastically of the favourite haunt of any one.

341. A loose horse is sure to stand near the chaff-house.

३४१ छुटल घोड़ी भुसङ्गले ठाढ़

Chhutal ghori bhusahule thārh.

A horse when loose is sure to stand near the chaff-house. Also said in reference to one's haunt, where he is certain to go when he gets an opportunity.

342. Faith makes god of a stone.

३४२ मान तो देव ना तो पत्यर

Mān to deo na to patthar.

If you believe, it is a deity; otherwise a stone, *i.e.* if you have faith, you can believe a common piece of stone to be a god, otherwise it is nothing but a stone.

Fools.

343. A fool's property the prey of all.

३४३ बुड़बक के भैंस लगल साँसे गाँव टहरा ले के दौड़ल

Burbak ke bhaiṉs lagal, saunse gāoṉ tahra le ke daural.

When a fool's buffalo is in milk, every one in the village runs (to him) with milk pails.

A fool's property is always enjoyed by others. This is explained by the next proverb.

344. A fool's property the prey of all.

३४४ बुड़बक के धन होय फहीमाँ मार खाय

Burbak ke dhan hoy, phahīmāṉ mār khāy.

A fool's property is enjoyed by the cunning.

345. A fool thinks of his belly only.

३४५ भाँदू भाव न जाने पेट भरे से काम

Bhoṅdu bhāo na jāne, pet bhare se kām.

The silly (man) knows nothing of etiquette (civility) : his chief business is to fill his belly.

भाव "*Bhāo*" is "rate," "rule," here, rule of society.

346. A fool worries himself with the concern of others.

३४६ बुड़बक मरला बिरानेँ फ़िकिरे

Burbak marla birāneñ phikire.

A fool worries himself (kills himself) with other's concern.

347. A fool went to fish, but lost his fishing basket.

३४७ बुड़बक गेला माँछर मारे टाप ऎलन गँवाय

Burbak gela māṅchhar māre, tāp ailan gaṅwāy.

A fool went to fish, but lost his bamboo basket for catching fish.

टाप "*Tāp*" is a conical bamboo basket for catching fish in shallow water.

i.e. Lost the essential or most material thing.

348. A fool's wife the jest of all.

३४८ बुड़बक (या ऋबरा) के जोरु सब के भौजाई

Burbak (ya abra) ke joru sab ke bhaujāi.

A fool's wife is like an (elder) sister-in-law to everybody, that is, the butt of all.

भौजाई "*Bhaujāi*" is the elder brother's wife, with whom all the younger brothers can joke, while on the other hand the wife of a younger brother is always to be respected by the elder brother (see note to Proverb 324).

349. A fool unable to distinguish the trunk from the tail of an elephant.

३४९ हाथी के आगा पाछा बुझैबे ना करे

Hāthi ke āga pāchha, bujhaibe na kare.

A fool: unable to make out the front from the hind part of an elephant!

Said of a fool who cannot make "head or tail" of any-thing; like the villager who, it is said, on seeing an elephant for the first time, exclaimed, "It has tails on both ends."

350. A simpleton is "cheeked" by a dog even.

३५० सोझ के मूँह कूकुर चाटे

Sojh ke muñh kūkur chāte.

The mouth (face) of the simpleton is licked by a dog, *i.e.* even dogs take a liberty with one who is simple (*lit.* straight).

351. Who are fools according to *Ghāgh* the poet.

३५१ बिन मेहरी ससुरारी जाय साँझ पराते सत्तू खाय
      जेठ मास जे पेन्हे पौआ कहे घाघ ई तीनो कौआ
      काज परे ससुरारी जाय भूख मरत्ते सत्तू खाय
      भगता होय से पेन्हे पौआ कहेँ बहु हाँ घाघे कौआ

Bin mehri sasurāri jāy, sāñjh parāte sattu khāy,
Jeth mās je penhe paua, kahe ghāg ī tino kauwa,
Kāj pare sasurāri jāy, bhukh maratte sattu khāy,
Bhagta hoy se penhe paua, kaheñ bahu hāñ Ghāghe kauwa.

He who goes to his father-in-law's house without his wife; he who eats *sattu* morning and evening (*i.e.* at both

his meals) ; and he who wears sandals in the month of *Jeth*
—are all pronounced fools (*lit.* crows) by *Ghāgh.*

पौआ " *Paua,*" sandals ; कौआ " *kaua,*" the crow,
meaning a stupid fool.

The meaning is, that he who ventures to pay a visit to
his father-in-law's house without his wife, is sure not to
be welcome ; he who eats सत्तू *sattu* (or gram meal) at all
his meals is certain to fall ill; and he who wears sandals
(which are meant for wet weather) in the hot month of
Jeth (May-June) is sure to be looked upon as wanting in
sense.

The above saying is ascribed to the local poet or bard
of Shāhabad called घाघ *Ghāgh*, who, it appears, had an
equally clever daughter-in-law, sharp at repartees, and
who used often to engage with her father-in-law in
wordy wars. The following, for instance, is her reply to
the above dictum : "If there is necessity, a man may go
to his father-in-law's (without his wife) : if a man is
dying of hunger, it is better he should eat *sattu* : and if
a man is a devotee, he can wear sandals always. On
these occasions the daughter-in-law says that *Ghāgh* himself is a fool (crow) ! "

घाघ " *Ghāgh* " *lit.* means sly, shrewd, wily, old, aged.

352. Who are the three greatest fools in this world ?

३५२   घर घोड़ा पैदल चले आछत काढ़े रीन
      थाती धरे दमाद घर जग में बुरबक तीन

Ghar ghora paidal chale, āchhat kārhe rīñ,
Thāti dhare damād ghar, jag meñ burbak tīn.

He who keeps a horse at home and yet goes about on
foot; he who is wealthy and yet borrows ; and he who

keeps anything on trust with a son-in-law—are the three greatest fools in the whole world.

The above are not uncommon practices. The horse is often kept for show, and men well off do take loans, either to make people believe that they are poor or from a false idea that their hoarded wealth if once touched will fly away. The son-in-law according to native etiquette always thinks he has a perfect right to get as much as he possibly can out of his father-in-law's property, and never loses an opportunity to appropriate anything he can get hold of. For this reason a father-in-law (when his son-in-law is on a visit to him) often secretes his valuable belongings; for if the son-in-law gets hold of them, he can't very well ask him to give them up.

Guests and hosts.

353. Unwelcome guests.

३५३ तीन बोलाये तेरह आये देखो घर की रीत
वाहरवाले खा गये घर के गावें गीत

Tīn bolāye terah āye dekho ghar ki rīt,
Bāharwāle kha gaye ghar ke gāweñ gīt.

Three are invited, thirteen intrude: see their manners (*lit.* the rule of their house). The outsiders (guests) eat up everything, while the home people (the hosts) have "to whistle" (*lit.* to sing, to content themselves with singing).

Said when (as usually happens) a host of uninvited guests pounce down (with the invited) upon the host, being generally the friends and relatives of the invited guests. In marriage ceremonies the larger the number of people the bridegroom can bring with him, the more it counts to his credit; though this intrusion can hardly be said to be appreciated by the bride's people, who have to provide for all, on the pain of being thought mean. This rivalry of bringing the largest number of followers the bridegroom can muster, and of entertaining them sumptuously by the bride's father, is the cause of the ruin of many rich houses in Bihar.

The same idea is in the following saying : **बिन बोलाये लड़के बाले साथ आये** *Bin bolāye larke bāle sāth āye* (" Un-invited the whole family have turned up ").

गावैं गीत " *Gāweñ gīt*." To sing is irony for remaining hungry, as in the expression **टप्पर गाना** " *tappar gāna* " is to starve.

354. Guests but in name.

३४४   माँस भात घरैता खाय
हत्या लेले पाहुन जाय

Māns bhāt gharaita khāy,
Hatya lele pāhun jāy.

The hosts (people of the house) eat meat and rice, while the guests have to return home with the sin on their shoulders, *i.e.* the sin of having had the goat killed for their sake, in name only, while others have really enjoyed the feast. Said when any one has to bear the blame without profiting in the least.

355. Assuming the hostess.

३४५   भात दाल केकरो परोसे बैठलन मँगरो

Bhāt dāl kekro, parose baithlan Mangro.

The feast (*lit.* dall and rice) is given by another ; but *Mangaro* (unasked) does the hostess !

परोसब "*Parosab*" is to serve up dinner, to place food before guests.

मँगरो "*Mangaro*" is an assumed name.
Said of one who officiously puts herself forward.

356. Assuming a leading part in a marriage ceremony.

३५६ बेटा बेटी केकरो गुरहथे बैठलन मँगरो

Beta beti kekro, gurhathe baithlan Mangro.

The son and daughter of others (are being married), but *Mangro*, a stranger, (officiously) comes forward to perform the ceremony of *Gurhathe*.

मँगरो "*Mangro*" is the feminine of *Mangar*; also "*Mangri*." The terminal "*o*," besides denoting the feminine gender, implies a familiarity or regard for the person.

The ceremony of गुरहथी *Gurhathi* is thus described by Mr. Grierson in his book of "Bihar Peasant Life":—"In this ceremony the elder brother of the bridegroom (or in default of him some elder of the bridegroom's family) offers sweetmeats, molasses (गुर *gur*) and ornaments to the bride. He then takes some betel-leaves and tyre in his right hand, and presses it against the bride's forehead, at the same time pressing his left hand against the back of her head. These two ceremonies are together called बन्दन *bandan*, गुरहत्थी *gurhatthi* or गुरहत्यन *gurhatthan*, and signify that he has touched her once for all, and that if he touches her again, he will be guilty of a sin."

357. The host and he to get broken bits of cake.

३५७ जेकरे भोज तेकरे खाँड़ा बारा

Jekre bhoj tekre khāñra bāra.

It is his feast, and he gets broken bits of cake!

भोज *"Bhoj"* is food, feast. बरा *" Bara"* or बारा *"bāra"* cakes of " Urid " pulse fried in *ghi* or oil.

खाँड़ा *" Khānra "* is broken, a corruption of खण्ड *"khanda,"* a piece.

Said when a man who has a right to receive or who ought to receive the best (of things) gets inferior things instead.

358. Grandfather's funeral ceremony.

३५८   हलुआई के दुकान दादा जी के फतेहा

Haluāi ke dukān, dāda ji ke phateha.

A confectioner's shop: it is easy to say, "I give the whole of it away in my grandfather's funeral feast ! "

फतेहा *" Phateha "* or फातेहा *phateha* is a feast in honour of the dead at which sweetmeats, etc., are first offered to the saints, and then given away for nothing. It is a Persian word.

Said when one makes free with another's things to which he has no right, just as the man who has not paid for the sweets (but wants to make a show of observing his ancestors' death ceremonies) can easily say, "Here is a whole shop: I give it away in honour of my dead ancestors' funeral feast." Also said when one wastes recklessly another man's things or makes a vain boast.

Habit, Second Nature and Unchangeable.   The Leopard cannot change his spots.

359. Notwithstanding all charms and incantations, the boy will not change his habit.

३५९   केतनो करह जोगा टोनाँ बबुआ बैठिहैँ उहे कोनाँ

Ketno karah joga tonāñ, babua baithiheñ uhe konāñ.

You may practise as many spells and charms as you like, the dear boy will still sit in the same corner! *i.e.* will never leave his way.

A man who, in spite of all persuasions and urgings, still adopts the same course as a force of habit, may be said to go to his usual corner "charm they never so wisely."

A satirical way of condemning a reprehensible force of habit.

360. The rope burns, but not the twist.

३६० जेँवर जरेला ऐँठन ना जरे

Jeṅwar jarela ainthan na jare.

The rope will burn, but not the twist.

This is a fact: the rope will burn into loose ashes where it has not a twist; but where there is one, the impression of it will remain even in the ashes.

Said in reference to an inveterate habit which always sticks to one.

361. A dog's tail can never be straightened.

३६१ कूकुर के पोँछ बारह बरिस गाड़ौँ तब हु टेढ़ के टेढ़

Kūkur ke poṅchh bārah baris gārīṅ, tab hu terh ke terh.

The dog's tail, even if buried for twelve years, will remain as crooked as ever.

Same application as the last proverb (360).

362. Half dead, but still he shakes his head.

३६२ सगरे घर सियारन खाइल
मूँड़ी के झाँटल कत हूँ ना गैल

Sagre dhar siyāran khāil,
Mūñri ke jhāṅtal kat hūñ na gail.

11

His whole body has been devoured by jackals, still he will not leave off shaking his head.

An exaggerated way of saying that one will not give up his vicious habits though reduced to the last extremities.

363. Can the crow become white by eating camphor?

३६३ कौश्रा कपूर खिले उजर होला

Kaua kapūr khaile ujar hola ?

Can the crow become white by eating camphor?
E.E. "Can the leopard change its spots?"

364. Heart's dearest wish—what does a blind man want but his two eyes?

३६४ ऄंधरा चाहि दू ऑंख

Andhra chāhe du ānkh.

What does a blind man want but his two eyes?
Used to express the greatest wish of one's heart.

Husband and Wife.

365. The husband claiming unmerited service from the wife.

३६५ किस विरते पर तत्ता पानी

Kis birte par tatta pānīñ.

For what action (do you expect your feet to be washed in) lukewarm water?

On the return home of the husband, the wife is expected to wash his feet in lukewarm water: if he has returned empty-handed, with nothing to show for his absence, his wife might satirically ask, "for what service or token of love do you expect this warm reception?" Said to an undeserving man who expects a favour, or to one who has no grounds or no claims for asking a favour.

The origin of this saying is ascribed to the following lines, where it comes out with telling effect :

वारः वरस पर पिउ मोर आए ऊँचे महलन सेज बिछाए
जेनाँ एक न देनाँ दो करवट फेर के रह गए सो
भोर भए जब पिरतम जागे तातल पानी माँगन लागे
मुख अञ्चल दे तिरिया मुस्कानी कौन बिरते पर तत्ता पानी

Bārah baras par piu mor āe, ūṅche mahlan sej bichhāe.
Lenāñ ek na denāñ do, karwat pher ke rah gae so.
Bhor bhae jab pirtam jāge, tātal pāni māṅgan lāge.
Mukh aṅchal de tiriya muskāni, kaun birte par tatta pāni.

After twelve long years the husband returned home; but (forgetful of his wife) he placed his couch on the top-storey. He neither took anything (*lit.* one thing) nor gave anything (*lit.* two things), but turned off to sleep. In the morning, when he awoke, he wanted warm water for ablution. Upon which the wife coquettishly smiled and asked, "For what service done is this warm water required?"

366. The diffidence of the husband in making presents to his wife in his father's house.

३६६ सैयाँ के अर्जन भैया के नाँव चूरा पहिर मैं सांसुर जाँव

Saiyāñ ke arjan bhaiya ke nāoñ chūra pahir maiñ sāsur jāoñ.

The wife decked in the anklets bought out of the earnings of the husband, but put down to the brother, goes to her father-in-law's. That is to say, she goes to her father-in-law's house decked in the ornaments purchased from the husband's hard earnings; but she pretends that it has been given to her by her brother. This speech is aimed at the wife by some one of the father-in-law's house (probably the sister-in-law, who is always at daggers drawn with her brother's wife) with the object of running her down for making a boast of her brother's generosity, when it is really to the husband that her thanks are due. It is usual for the father and brother to make presents to the bride when she is returning to her husband's home. The shaft is therefore really aimed at their poverty in being unable to make her a present when returning; while she, to conceal this fact, puts on the ornaments given to her by her husband, so that it may be concluded that she has received them at her father's house.

Among respectable natives of Bihār a husband, out of respect, avoids giving presents to his wife in his father's house or in his presence, as behaviour likely to hurt his father's feelings by showing his independence. While in his father's house, he still maintains the appearance of being dependent on him; and therefore leaves the support and care of his wife to his parents. If he should make any present to his wife, he does so stealthily, so as not to injure the feeling of dependence. In a well-regulated family this feeling of filial reverence is carried so far that it is considered highly disrespectful for a son even to speak to his wife in the presence of his father. A respectable native gentleman, in Government service, told the writer that during his father's lifetime, he never attempted to send anything directly to his family, who were living in his father's house. All or the greater part of his earnings he would remit regularly to his father, and even looked to him for his winter clothes, which he rarely bought himself. One year the cold weather clothes were late in reaching him, but still he never bought any himself: lest he should give his old father an idea that he was becoming less dutiful.

Another explanation of this proverb is:—The anklets have been purchased from the earnings of her lover (*i.e.* she pretends they are a present to her from her brother). She wears them and goes to her father-in-law's house !

This is a taunting speech made by some enemy of the wife, charging her with infidelity. The meaning is, that the anklets she has got on have been really given to her by her paramour while she was on a visit to her father's house (नैहर *naihar*). But she has given out that they are a present to her from her brother ; and decked in these she now goes back shamelessly (with this price of her unchastity) to her father-in-law's house, *i.e.* to her husband ! Said when the credit for anything is given to one who does not deserve it.

367. When the cat is away, the mice do play.

३६७   राजा गैले अँटक रानीँ पौलन छटक

Rāja gaile antak rānīn paulan chhatak.

When the king is away, the queen is free to act as she likes !

छटकब "*Chhatkab*" is to get free from restraint; to dart off, to rebound, to be scattered, and *antak* is *lit.* "to get entangled or to get captured."

E.E. "When the cat is away, the mice will play."

368. Husband unsuited to the wife.

३६८   हम तैसन ऊ न: भैसुर तैसन दिदिया न:

Ham taisan ū nah, bhaisur taisan didiya nah.

He is not suited to me, and my sister-in-law is not suited to my (elder) brother-in-law.

" *U*," "he," is the husband. It is never the custom in Indian domestic life for the wife to call her husband by his name, or even to repeat his name to another person. He is always spoken of as " he," or, if he is a father, he is spoken of as " the father of so and so." The same rule is also observed by the husband when speaking of his wife.

भैसुर " *Bhaisur* " is the elder brother-in-law and दिदिया " *didiya* " is his wife ; the elder sister is addressed as " *didiya*." गोतनी " *Gotni* " are sisters-in-law.

This proverb is supposed to be said by the younger sister-in-law in self-praise. The meaning is, that my husband is not suited to me (*i.e.* is not so good as I am) ; while my sister-in-law is not suited to my elder brother-in-law, *i.e.* he deserves a better wife. Said sarcastically when people think they are wrongly " mated."

369. A greedy wife.

३६९ जेकर माँगी दँतुली ओकर बड़ भाग
दाँत से हँड़िया खखोर के खा गैल
बसिया के कौन काम (बसिया कहाँ से आवो)

Jekar maugi dantuli, okar bar bhāg,
Dānt se hañriya khakhor ke kha gail,
Basiya ke kaun kām (or Basiya kahāñ se āo).

Whoever has a wife with her front teeth protruding is very lucky, for with them she can scrape up the cooking pot (of all its contents) : as for anything being left, that is out of the question ! This is of course said in irony.

A husband is lucky to possess such a wife, who will allow nothing to be wasted, not even the scrapings !

370. The paragon of a wife gives a pommelling to her husband.

३७० हिँस के बनली पतिवरता मूसर खैलन भरता

Hiñs ke banli patibarta músar khailan bharta.

From a desire to imitate another she pretended to become a paragon of a wife: but the end of it was that her poor husband got a pommelling.

पतिवरता "*Patibarta*" is a wife devoted to her husband, *i.e.* a dutiful and faithful wife, who is entirely subservient to her husband's commands.

This proverb is ascribed to the following story : A wife, by her constant dutiful conduct towards her husband, had attained that perfection which devoted and dutiful wives are said to attain, namely, superhuman powers. On one occasion a friend (who was the reverse of dutiful), being on a visit to her, observed that this pattern of a wife, on being called by her husband, had left the pestle, with which she was engaged at the time in pounding rice, as she had lifted it in the act of pounding, lest delay might occur in bringing it down to the mortar; but, strange to say, the pestle, instead of coming down, remained suspended in mid-air. When she returned, her astonished friend asked her how she was able to perform such a miracle. "My friend," said the good wife, "this is the result of being dutiful and obedient to your husband." The scold of a wife, who had a henpecked husband, resolved to try the experiment. Thinking that she had at last attained the perfection she had observed in her friend, she wanted to make a display of it, and invited a few neighbours. The friends came according to invitation, and the pounding of rice went on; but the unfortunate husband, who took little interest in the experiment, had gone to sleep inside the house, and failed to call out to his wife at the right moment, as had been previously arranged. At last, tired of waiting for her husband's call, she threw the pestle up; but, instead of its hanging in mid-air, as she had expected, it came down on her, to the great amusement of her visitors, not to say anything of the hurt she received. Enraged at her failure, which she ascribed to her husband, she rushed in and belaboured him with the pestle.

371. Hard won prize.

३७१   दिहिन खोदा पै रकती हगा

Dihin khoda pai rakti haga.

God has given, but after the greatest hardship.

This proverb is in the language peculiar to the Mohamedan weavers.

Said when one obtains anything after the greatest trouble—after he is made to sweat for it.

Helplessness.

372. He only joins bread who can't make them.

३७२   पकवल रोटी से जुरियावे जेकरा अपना बेले नाँ आवे

Pakwal roti se juriyâwe jekra apna bele nâñ âwe.

He joins hand-made bread (cooked by another) who cannot make them himself.

जुरियाएब "*Juriyaeb*" is to join hand-made bread in couples as they are cooked, and fold them two by two (the usual way they are served up). बेलना "*Belna*" is a wooden rolling-pin with which the dough is rolled out into thin circular sheets.

i.e. He who can make bread himself will not need the help of another to arrange them.

It is only those who do not know the art of making hand-bread, who employ themselves in the ornamental duty of putting them two by two (as is the practice) when they are made by another. Those who know it will of course take a more active and useful part. It means that he who can do anything himself will never wait for the help of another to finish up. To the same effect is the saying पकवल रोटी जोरिआवे अइलन "*Pakwal roti joriāwe ailan.*" He has come to arrange bread already cooked by another, *i.e.* after the real hard work has been done by others, he has come to take the credit of it by doing something which is superfluous.

373. If every one takes to becoming pilgrims, who is to do the worldly work?

३७३ सब कूकुर काश्री जैहें त हाँड़ी कौन ढुढिहें

Sab kūkur kāshi jaiheṅ ta hāṅri kaun dhurhiheṅ.

If all the dogs will go on a pilgrimage to Benares, who will search the pots and pans (for food)? *i.e.* if every one will become pious, who will do the worldly work? Said when all take to a fancied work, leaving their legitimate calling, *e.g.* it might be said with reference to the general seeking after Government appointments and high education, "If everybody will take to the learned professions, who will attend to the agriculture of the country?"

374. Ignorant villagers.

३७४ उजरा गाँविं ऊँट आएल लोग कहल जे दुदे अइलन

Ujra gaṅweṅ ūṅt āel log kahal je dade ailan.

If a camel comes to the village of ignorant people, they all declare that their ancestor has risen from the dead!

उजरा गाँविं *Ujra gaṅweṅ, lit.* means in a desolate village,

in a village which has been forsaken by all the better class
of people.   Hence a village inhabited by low castes only,
who are usually ignorant and easy dupes.

Said in ridicule of the ignorance of the low-class villagers,
who are always ready to worship any strange sight.

375. Ignorant villager mulcted on going to complain.

३७५   लाल.बही में निकलायों तेली खल्ली खिलाइस क्यों
खाइस खल्ली ह्आ साँढ बैल का बैल डाँड़ का डाँड़

Lāl bahi men niklāyoñ, teli khalli khilāis kyoñ.
Khāis khalli hua sāñrh, bail ka bail dāñr ka dāñr.

It is thus recorded in the red book (of laws and regula-
tions) : " Why did the oilman feed his bullock on oilcakes ?
as a consequence the bullock became as unmanageable as a
Brahmini bull" (and ceased to work from being over-fed).
(The order) " He loses his bullock as well as pays a fine!"

This proverb illustrates beautifully the fleecing to which
an ignorant villager is subjected when he goes to complain.
Whatever the nature of his complaint, the tables are turned
upon him, and on one plea or another he has to pay.
Here a rude ignorant rustic is represented as relating his
sad experience to his brother villagers on his return from
a more than bootless complaint, probably to the police
daroga. He quotes, as he thinks, the chaste Urdu language
of the court, quite unmindful that in his attempt he is
doing real violence to the language.   The story is that a
village *Teli*, or oilman, who has lost his bullock, goes to complain to the police, fondly hoping that he will be helped to
find it.   The "Red Book" (on which he looks as the
source of all justice) is brought out.   The daroga gravely
turns leaf after leaf, and then pronounces judgment in the

following words : "Hear you *Teli*, it is thus found in the Red Book : You are really in fault, why did you feed your bullock on oilcakes ? Of course as a consequence he became unmanageable and ran away. You are therefore clearly to blame, and you have to pay a fine." He has lost his bullock, and, far from getting any help, he has to pay a fine. It is a case of "the wolf and the lamb"!

This proverb illustrates the language a rustic (*gaoñwār*) uses when he attempts to speak Urdu.

Jewels.

376. Ornaments as well as means of livelihood.

३७६ सम्पत के सिंगार बीपत के त्रहार

Sampat ke singār bīpat ke ahār.

In easy circumstances jewels are ornaments, in adversity they are a means of livelihood, *i.e.* when in good circumstances, they act as ornaments, but when want overtakes the wearer, they can be turned into money.

The heavy ornaments worn as anklets and armlets by the poorer classes are therefore prized more on account of their weight than on account of their appearance.

377. Job's comforter.

३७७ भल भेल सैयाँ के वाघें धैल कि वेगारी से वचलन

Bhal bhel saiyāñ ke bāghcñ dhail ki begāri se bachlan.

It is just as well that (my) husband has been carried away by a tiger ; for he is saved from much "forced" labour.

This would be said by a third party (as if coming from the aggrieved) in mock-congratulation for a gain totally inadequate to the loss incurred, or said sarcastically to one who foolishly makes a heavy sacrifice and gains a trifling advantage.

378. Love defies law.

३७८ मरदा मौगी राजी का करे गाँव के काजी

Marda maugi rāji, ka kare gāoñ ke kāji.

(When both) man and woman are willing (satisfied consenting parties), what is the village *Kāzi* to do?

Even the conservative mind of the primitive villagers could see the unreasonableness of parting asunder two hearts that naturally drew towards each other: in such a case, what real power had the village magistrate? None at all.

Mischief-makers.

379. Quarrels between relatives are always made up: mischief-makers return home disappointed.

३७९ सास पुतोहिया एके होइहैं भाभा कुटन घर चल जैहैं

Sās putohiya eke hoiheñ bhābha kutan ghar chal jaiheñ.

The mother-in-law and the daughter-in-law will after all make up their quarrels (*lit.* will be one), the respective (opposite) mischief-makers will have to return home (discomfited).

The proverbial quarrels and disagreements of the mother-in-law and the daughter-in-law are not confined to Bihār only. Those who interfere are certain not to be thanked for their pains in the end.

भाभा कुटन "*Bhābha kutan*" are the mischief-makers of the opposite sides. कुटन "*Kutan*" or कुटनी "*kutni*" is a mischief-maker, one who seduces a woman, a procuress, "a go-between." *Bhābha* means of the opposite side, respective.

380. He tells the thief to steal and the wealthy to keep awake.

३८० चोर के कहे चोरी करः साहु के कहे जागल रहः

Chor ke kahe chori karah, sāhu ke kahe jāgal rahah.

He tells the thief to steal and the wealthy to keep awake,
i e. causes mischief by carrying tales to the opposite
sides ; in other words, by informing each rival side the
intentions of the other. A mischief-maker.

The allusion here to **नारद मुनी** "*Nārad Muni*," a sage
(*rishi*) who took a strange delight in communicating secrets
to the opposite sides and bringing about a quarrel. But
his object was, they say, to humiliate those who were proud
of their strength and certain of success.

E.E. "Runs with the hare and hunts with the hounds."

Mother-in-law and Sister-in-law.

381. The happiness of one who has neither mother-in-
law nor sister-in-law.

३८१ सास न ननन्द घर अपने अनन्द

Sās na nanand, ghar apne anand.

Having neither mother-in-law nor sister-in-law (to
tyrannize over her), she is happy in her own house.

The mother-in-law and sister-in-law (husband's sister)
are thorns in the side of the wife, who has scarcely any
voice in household matters so long as these, her opposers,
are present. She cannot assert her authority, and is, in
fact, a nonentity during the lifetime of the husband's
mother. Therefore a wife who has not these causes of
unhappiness by her side may be said to be contented and
happy.

382. Music is charming at a distance.

३८२ दुर के ढोल सोहावन

Dur ke dhol sohāwan.

Distant music is pleasant.

दुर "*Dur*" is distance.

सोहावन "*Sohāwan*" is pleasant, agreeable.

A native's idea of music is usually banging a drum
(*dhol*).

One blamed for another's fault, made a scapegoat.

383. *Chamru* enjoys, while *Deyāl* gets whipped for it.

३८३ सुख पुन करथ चमरू कोड़ा खाथ देयाल

Sukh pun karath Chamru kora khāth Deyāl.

Chamru enjoys ease and comfort (reaps the advantage),
while *Deyāl* gets whipped, *i.e.* is made a scapegoat of.
Said when one suffers for the fault of another or is blamed
though innocent. Usually said when one has illicit connection with another's wife while another man gets blamed
for it.

Hence it is commonly said, "I am a '*Deyāl*,'" meaning
I am a mere tool, or merely the screen.

384. For the sake of one all are disliked.

३८४ एक के तीते तीनो तीत

Ek ke tite tino tit.

Owing to one being bitter all three are bitter, *i.e.* disliked.

For the sake of one of a company, the others, who are in
any way connected, get to be disliked and shunned.

E.E. 1. "A little leaven leaveneth the whole lump."
    2. "One black sheep affects the whole flock."

385. The man with a moustache is blamed for the thieving of the moustacheless.

३८५ चोरी करे निमोछिया लग जाय मोछगरहा के

Chori kare nimochhiya, lag jay mochhgarha ke.

The stealing is done by the moustacheless, but the man with a moustache is blamed for it.

Said when one is blamed for the fault of another. The idea is, that the moustache tells a tale when the thieving has been done in the eating line.

The same idea is expressed in the following proverb common in the Shāhabad district :

सिधरिया चाल पारे भोथवा का कपारे बीते

Sidhriya chāl pāre, bhothwa ka kapāre bite.

"The small fish do the skipping, but it comes down on the head of the big fish," that is to say, the small fry by jumping about afford a sign where the net ought to be cast; and thus the big fish are caught while the little ones escape through the meshes. The meaning is that when the time of reckoning comes the "small" men, who have really done the mischief, escape, while the "big" are caught and suffer.

386. She in tatters is blamed for the one who wears ornaments.

३८६ काम करे नथवाली लग जाय चिरकुटही के

Kām kare nathwāli lag jay chirkutahi ke.

The mischief is done by the woman wearing the nose-ring, but she in tatters is blamed for it, *i.e.* the poor woman is blamed for the fault of the well-to-do.

387. Priest and musician in one.

३८७   गुरु के गुरु बजनियाँ के बजनियाँ

Guru ke guru bajaniyāñ ke bajaniyāñ.

A holy father as well as a fiddler.

Said when one man unites in him two opposite functions.

In the east of Gaya a class of Brāhmans who actually combine the two functions are satirized here. They play on the drum while performing the religious ceremony; and it is said that to ridicule this absurd practice this saying is used.

388. Physician prescribing according to the patient's wish.

३८८   जे रोगिया का भावे सेही बैदा फुरमावे

Je rogiya ka bhāwe, sehi baida phurmāwe.

Whatever the patient likes the doctor prescribes, that is, a sick man does not usually get what he wants to eat, the doctor prescribes a regimen which is distasteful: so when one finds that things are taking place after his heart, exactly as he wishes, this saying is used.

Quarrelsome Women, Firebrands, etc.

389. Quarrelsome women recommended to quarrel with decency.

३८९   लड़ परोसिन दीद रख

Lar parosin did rakh.

Quarrel you (women) neighbours, but be not unmindful of shame.

Those who have any experience of Indian villages will readily and vividly recall the common sight of an altercation between two viragoes, gesticulating and screaming with all their might regardless of shame, and bent on pouring out on each other without delay the full vials of their wrath. On such an occasion a ready by-stander would, half in derision, half in earnest, recommend them "to keep some breath to cool their porridge."

दोद "*Did*," literally "eye"—hence shame.

Fight, but please preserve a little shame in your eyes.

390. A fire-brand, wherever she goes she sets people by the ears.

३९० जेने गेली खेरो रानी ले ले गेली आग पानी

Jene geli khero rāni, le le geli āy pāni.

Wherever went Queen Grass, she took with her fire and water.

Applied usually to "a fire-brand," "a mischief-maker."

A woman with mischief-making propensities strongly developed would take with her wherever she went her unhappy facility of setting by the ears all her neighbours: she would thus carry with her fire and water—the two elements at war with each other.

खेर "*Kher*" is coarse grass, and easily takes fire when dry.

391. The misfortunes of a husband who has a scold of a wife.

३९१ सात सेर के सात पकौलूँ चौदह सेर के एके

तूँ दहिजरू सातो खैल: मैँ कुलवन्ती एके

Sāt ser ke sāt pakaulūñ, chaudah ser ke eke,
Tūñ dahijaru sāto khailah, maiñ kulwanti eke.

I made (cooked) seven cakes of a seer each, and one of fourteen seers: You "burnt beard!" ate up all the seven, while I of high lineage ate the one only! This is cast at a wife who is a scold, but who professes to be innocent

and content with little, while in reality she greedily
eats up even her husband's share. It is supposed to be
innocently spoken by the wife, while in fact she is be-
traying her own failings in the speech.

दहिजरू "*Dahijaru*" is a contraction of दाढ़ी जारा "*dārhi
jāra*," *i.e.* one whose beard has been burnt, a term of
feminine abuse. To burn a man's beard or moustache is
to disgrace him by casting a slur on his manhood. This
is one of the many quaint abuses peculiar to the women
of the low class in Bihār. They are far from being held
in such abject subjection (in domestic matters) as is
commonly supposed, and often make it uncommonly "hot"
for their husbands with their sharp tongue (if not with
their fists), whenever they happen to incur their displeasure.
Their slang vocabulary is very copious indeed. Here
are a few:— मुहजरा "*Muhjara*," one with a burnt face ;
पगरी जरौना "*Pagri jarauna*," one with a burnt headdress ; जुआन ढहा "*Juān dhaha*," one whose youth is
on the decline, or, rather may your youth or manhood
fail you ; निगोड़ा "*Nigora*," one so unfortunate as not
to possess a son (*lit.* one without legs) ; खकमूहाँ "*Khak-
mūhāṅ*," one whose face is smeared with ashes, hence one
disgraced, or one who ought to be ashamed of himself, etc.

This proverb is a verse (the 2nd) out of the following
bitter lampoon styled " The misfortunes of a husband who
has a shrew at home." In this lampoon is adopted the
style so common in Indian sarcasm and pasquinades of
putting the ridiculing speech in the mouth of the object
to be ridiculed, and thus by irony making him or her
appear self-convicted. Here this speech, which really
ridicules her, is made to appear as though uttered by
the wife, although it is evident that nobody in her

senses would make such a confession. The implied
meaning is that this is how a scold is supposed to treat
her husband. Some guests having casually dropt in, she,
instead of taking it in good part, at once turns round
and accuses her husband of having invited them, which
is not a fact, because their coming was quite accidental,
and foretold by the crows (an omen always relied on).
Having falsely accused him of being greedy and of
inviting these guests, she next taunts him with his
poverty; and in her endeavours to show what a good
housewife she is in trying to make both ends meet, she
betrays her own niggardliness by the confession that
she has poured a lot of water into the rice to increase
its quantity. She further adds to her guilt and makes
her case very much worse by confessing that she (being
really a witch at heart) has caused the death of (*lit.* has
eaten up) her friends and relatives both at her father's
and father-in-law's houses, and is now going to supplicate
the gods in the most solemn manner for the death of her
husband. It shows that the saying, " Every man can
tame a shrew, but he that hath her," is universally true.

ताही रे पुरुख के अभाग करकसा जाहि रे घरे

छप्पर पर जे कौआ वैसज पाहुन आैले तीन

तूँ दहिजरू पाहुन टेकल: गोइँठा लाव नाहीँ बीन

सात सेर के सात पकौलूँ चौदह सेर के एक

तूँ दहिजरू सातो खैल: मैँ कुलवन्ती एक

खुदी चूनौँ के भात पकौलूँ अदहन देलूँ वहुत

भर कठौता माँड़ पसौलूँ पीआ ना दहिजरू के पूत

नैहर खैलूँ सासुर खैलूँ खैलूँ कुल परिवार

गंगा पैस के आँचर विनवौँ कव मुईहेँ भतार

Tāhi re purukh ke abhāg, karkasa jāhi re ghare.
Chhappar par je kaua baisal, pāhun aile tīn
Tūñ, dahijaru, pāhun teklah, goiñtha lāo nāhīñ bīn
Sāt ser ke sāt pakaulūñ, chaudah ser ke ek.
Tūñ, dahijaru, sāto khailah, maiñ kulwanti ek.
Khudi chūnīñ ke bhāt pakaulūñ, adahan delūñ bahūt.
Bhar kathauta māñr pasaulūñ pia na dahijaru ke pūt
Naihar khailūñ sāsur khailūñ, khailūn kul pariwār
Ganya pais ke āñchar binwoñ, kab muiheñ bhatār.

The misfortunes of a husband who has a shrew at home.
Although the sitting of the crow upon the roof foretold
the coming of the three guests (still the quarrelsome wife
reproaches her husband thus :) " It is you ' burnt-beard ! '
who have detained these guests : why don't you go and
pick up *goiñtha* ? " (*i.e.* cowdung fuel, to prepare food for
them).

(Then comes the above proverb, 2nd verse, in the above
lampoon.)

" I cooked rice out of *khudi chūni* and put plenty of
water in it. I have poured it out in the wooden platter :
go and have your ' fill,' you son of a burnt-beard ! "

I have eaten (*i e.* caused the death of) those at my
father's house and those at my father-in-law's, and all
my relations, and now I will get into the Ganges and
pray for the death of my husband.

काँआ बैसल *Kaua baisal,* "Augury by crows " ("*Augu-
rium ex avibus*"), is a common mode of ascertaining about
the coming of friends and good news. If, on being
questioned, it should fly away cawing, it is a certain sign
that guests will come, or good news reach the person who
asks. In the text it means that the arrival or visit of the
guests was signified by a crow alighting on the roof, *i.e.*

the husband had nothing to do with inviting them. A crow is supposed to know where anybody is because its cry is *thāṃ, thāṃ,* "place, place."

Different auguries are drawn from the crow alighting on the edge, the middle, or the ridge of a roof of a thatched house, as in a Sanskrit verse of which the following is a translation : if on the edge and it utter a caw and fly away, it means the approach of misfortune ; if on the middle of the roof, it signifies the advent of good news, or a meeting with a dear friend ; if on the ridge, it forebodes a death in the family, loss of property, or a difference between friends.

The following minute instructions are given for interpreting the cawing of a crow. "As soon as you hear a crow, pick up a long straw or grass and measure its shadow by finger-lengths. Add 13 to it. Divide the total by six. The remainder will tell you the news the crow brings. If *one,* then be sure of gain ; if *two,* expect guests ; if *three,* an immediate quarrel in the house ; if *four,* a death ; if *five,* a theft. If there is no remainder, then the crow is simply calling out to its mate" (*i.e.* the cawing has no meaning).

खुदी चूनी "*Khudi chūni*" are grains of rice broken in husking, and used by the poorer class of people : here meant to indicate their poverty and inability to entertain guests.

अदहन "*Adahan,*" is hot water in which rice is boiled. A large quantity of water is put to increase the *māṅr* or gruel, which is drained off and drunk by the poor.

आँचर बिनवब "*Añchar binwab*" means to hold the hem of the sheet to the sun in the act of praying for any wish. To get into the Ganges and supplicate in this

manner is the most solemn way of praying for any wish to
be granted.

392. A shrew strikes terror into a demon even.

३९२   जे जगदीपेँ नगर उजारल राकस छोड़ल पीपर
      से जगदीपा आवत बाड़ी हाथे ले ले मूसर

Je jagdīpeñ nagar ujāral, rākas chhoral pīpar.
Se jagdīpa āwat bāri, hāthe le le mūsar.

That Jagdīpa, who desolated the town (and on whose
account) the demon even left his habitation of the Pīpal,
is now coming with a pestle in her hand.

जगदीपा " *Jagdīpa* " was a village termagant, who by
her constant brawling made it so unpleasant for her fellow-
villagers that they finally quitted the village.   When
there was no one left to quarrel with, she, it is said, used
to vent her rage on a *pīpal* tree.   Every morning armed
with her broom she would attack the tree and vociferate.
A demon, who dwelt on this tree, unable any longer to
stand this daily invasion, also left his abode and sought
refuge elsewhere.

This saying is used as an invocation to exorcise evil
spirits.   Her name is sufficient to make any demon flee.
Also said in joke when one noted for her temper is coming
to a place.

Quarrels and Jokes.

393. The root of quarrels is practical jokes, as the root
of disease is cough.

३९३   झगरा के जर हाँसी रोग के जर खाँसी

Jhagra ke jar hāñsi, rog ke jar khāñsi.

The root of quarrels is practical jokes, just as the root
of all sickness is cough.

i.e. Practical jokes invariably lead to quarrels, just as cough, if not taken care of in proper time, leads to other diseases.

Sisters.

394. Envious tears of an elder sister.

३९४ क्होटकी के होय गवनवाँ बड़की वैठल रोवे अँगनवाँ

Chhotki ke hoy gawanwāṅ barki baithal rowe añganwāṅ.

The younger sister is being married, the elder sits weeping at home.

It is seldom that an elder sister is not married before the younger. If this happens, it is probably due to some defect in her, and therefore a cause of grief.

गवनवाँ "*Gawanwāṅ,*" is the ceremony of going to the bride and bringing her home to her husband's house for the consummation of the marriage" (Grierson).

Sympathy and want of it.

395. Pains of a chapped foot.

३९५ जेकरा गोड़े फाटे वेवाय से जाने दरद पराय

Jekra gore phāte bewāy se jāne darad parāy.

A variation is:

जा के पाँव न फटे वेवाई सो का जाने पीर पराई

Jā ke pāoṅ na phate bewāi, so ka jāne pīr parāi.

One who has suffered from a chapped foot knows the pain of another (suffering similarly).

396. Does a barren woman know the pain of childbirth?

३९६ वाँझ कि जान परसौत की पीरा

Bānjh ki jāne parsaut ki pīra.

How can a barren woman know the pain of childbirth?

वाँझ "*Bānjh*" is a barren woman.

परसौंतो " *Parsauti* " is a woman after childbirth.

परसूत " *Parsūt* " is the pain attending childbirth.

E.E. He jests at scars who never felt a wound.   (To express want of sympathy or feeling.)

397. To cry before a blind man is to waste tears.

३९७   अँधरा के आगे रोइँ आपन दीदा खोइँ

Andhra ke āge roiñ, āpan dīda khoiñ.

To cry before a blind man is to injure (lose) your own sight, (because he can't see and feel); useless supplication before one who cannot feel and appreciate.

Cast at one who does not feel.

398. Single-handed.

३९८   एके पूता दर दरबार से बैठलन चूल्ही के देहार

Eke pūta dar darbār, se baithlan chūlhi ke dehār.

An only son, he has to attend court as well as to sit before the fire-place, *i.e.* single-handed he has to perform both domestic and outdoor work.

Said of one who has nobody to help him.

Son.

399. An unworthy son.

३९९   बूड़ल बंश कबीर के जब जमले पूत कमाल

Būral bans kabīr ke jab jamle pūt kamāl.

The house (race) of *Kabīr* will be extinct now that (a son called) " Perfection " is born.

कबीर " *Kabīr*," name of a faqīr, great senior.

कमाल " *Kamāl* " (Persian), is a name meaning " Perfection."

The meaning is, that a faqīr is always humble, never assuming.   If therefore a son is born to him who prides

himself on being perfect, who fancies that he excels in
worldly matters, then surely the venerable family of the
faqīr will no longer continue to be venerated. "*Kamāl*"
in common parlance also means "an acute fellow," "a
sharper," "a fop." Kamāl was the son of the famous
Kabīr, and spent his time inventing proverbs in refutation
of those invented by his father. Hence the proverb has
two meanings: "Even if your son is named *Kamāl* (perfection), if he is a bad son, your race is ruined."

400. The brave, the *sati*, and the enterprizing son avoid
the beaten track.

৪০০ लीक लीक गाड़ी चले लीके चले कपूत
तीन लीक पर ना चले सुरमा सती सपूत

Līk līk gāri chale līke chale kapūt
Tīn līk par na chale surma, sati, sapūt.

The unenterprizing (bad) son travels on the beaten road
just as a cart moves on the wheel track. But three do not
move on the wonted lines, the bold, the *sati*, and the
enterprizing (good) son.

The meaning is, that those who are not enterprizing
follow the same old course (profession) as their forefathers
did, just like cart wheels which must move on the wheel-
mark. It is only those who are bold, arduous, and enterprizing, that depart from the beaten track and mark out
a course for themselves. These are the सुरमा *surma* "the
hero" (or "picked man"), who, leaving the calling of
his ancestors, becomes a brave warrior; the सती *sati*,
who is so devoted to her husband that at his death she
elects to burn on his funeral pyre; and the सपूत *sapūt*,
the good or worthy son who likes to distinguish himself.
The words *Kapūt* and *Sapūt* are not to be taken too

literally to mean "bad" and good sons, but rather one
who is too "goody, goody," and one who is independent
enough to chalk out a new course for himself.

Singing.

401. Good singers are apt to be bored.

४०१　नाँ नीमन गितिया गाइब नाँ मँड़वा धैल जाइब

Nāñ nīman gitiya gāib, nāñ mañrwa dhail jāib.

Neither shall I sing pretty songs, nor will they compel
me to sing at the wedding feast, *lit.* take me by force to
the wedding house to sing.

Those who sing well are usually asked to entertain the
guests at the marriage house (मँड़वा *mañrwa*).

Therefore any one who is bored on account of displaying
her talents in this way may make a resolution never to
give indication of it, so as to avoid being asked in future
to perform. Would be said by one who felt bored on being
repeatedly asked to lend her services gratuitously in consequence of her excelling in anything.

"Rather keep my light under a bushel, than be asked
frequently to lend it gratuitously!" or it may be cast
ironically at a bad singer.

402. Social aspirant snubbed.

४०२　चाँबे गैले छबे होखे दूबे जी पाँव लागीले

Chaube gaile Chhabe hokhe, Dūbe ji pāoñ lāgile.

The *Chaube* Brāhman went to become *Chhabe* (*i.e.* to get
promoted to a higher status); but on the road was saluted
as *Dūbe* (*i.e.* a lower Brāhman).

दूबे *Dūbe* and *Chaube* are sects of Brāhmans who take
their names from being followers of *two* or *four* Veds.
This is simply a play on the words *Dūbe* and *Chaube*.

Chhabe is a fictitious title. It uniformly with *Chaube* and *Dūbe* means one learned in the six Vedas, which is an impossibility, as there are only four. Really a *Chaube* is not a higher Brāhman than a *Dūbe*, but occasion is taken of the numeral prefixes *two* and *four* to make a joke.

Used in ridiculing one who seeks to be socially raised, but meets with a rebuff.

Troubles increased.

403. She went to ask for a son, but lost her husband.

୪୦୩ पूत माँगे गैलो भतार देलि त्रैलो

Pūt māṅge gailī, bhatār dele aili.

She went to ask for a son, but lost her husband.

When in the attempt to obtain anything one sacrifices something better, the above saying is quoted. It is a common practice for a childless woman to go and supplicate certain gods with votive offerings for a son.

404. He prayed that his troubles may be lessened, but they were doubled.

୪୦୪ देवकुर गेलि दूना दुख

Deokur gele dūna dukh.

He went to the gods (to sue that his affliction may be lessened), but got his troubles doubled.

देवकुर "*Deokur*" is the place where a deity is invoked.

The meaning is, that he went to supplicate the gods that his sufferings might be lessened, but, on the contrary, became burdened with additional troubles.

Said when one endeavours to get any weight removed, but is burdened with more. There is a town of this name too. *Deokur*, or *Deokund*, is the name of a town in Gaya on a bank of a now-deserted bed of the river

Son. It was here that pilgrims crossed the Son on their
way from the north-west provinces to Rajgīr. It is a
holy place. *Deokund* means " well of the gods."

405. The dead boy had fine eyes.

४०५ मूअला पूत के बड़ बड़ आँख

Mūala pūt ke bar bar āṅkh.

The boy when dead is always said to have had fine (big)
eyes, *i.e.* the dead child is always praised for its beauty
by the mother.

" Big eyes " are considered an especial feature of beauty.

Said when one praises anything that does not exist
any longer.

Tobacco.

406. The man who offers you tobacco and lime unasked
is sure to go to heaven.

४०६ चून तमाकू सान के बिन माँगे जे दे
सुरपुर नरपुर नागपुर तीनूँ बस कर ले

Chūn tamāku sān ke, bin māṅge je de
Surpur, Narpur, Nāgpur, tinūñ bas kar le.

The man who mixes tobacco with lime (for chewing)
and offers it without being asked, conquers (by his
virtuous action) heaven, earth, and the lower regions
(Grierson). A common way of praising one who generously
offers another tobacco.

407. Tobacco is necessary for life.

४०७ भोर भए मनुस सभ जागे हुका चिलम बाजन लागे

Bhor bhae manus sabh jāge, huka, chilam bājan lāge.

At daybreak the people awoke and immediately the
hukkas began to gurgle.

"Tobacco is the subject of many proverbs," says Mr. Grierson.

"A folk-tale about tobacco runs that a villager who went to a distant village to visit his friends found them smoking in the morning before they had said prayers, whereupon he said the above lines. To which one of the smoking party replied :

खिनी खाय ना पियनी पिये से नर बतावः कैसे जिये

Khaini khāe, na piyani piye, se nar batāwah kaise jiye.

'Show me the man who can live without either chewing or smoking tobacco.' This verse has passed into a proverb.

"Tobacco is often compared to the River Ganges, which has three streams, one of which flows to heaven, another to hell, and the third to the world of mortals. So also tobacco has three branches, viz. snuff, which by being smelt goes upwards ; smoking tobacco, which by being smoked goes downwards ; and chewing tobacco which goes neither up nor down."

408. The devil even flees from a thrashing.

४०८   मार के डरे भूत भागे

Mār ke dare bhūt bhāge.

Even the devil flees from a thrashing ! *i.e.* every one is afraid of a beating, even the devil. Hence it is often assumed that what nothing will effect a beating will.

This is literally believed by the people, though they may not so frequently now resort to this means of exorcising the evil spirit that may have taken possession of an individual. On one occasion a servant boy, who had unwittingly committed a nuisance under a venerated Pīpal tree, was, as a punishment for the desecration, said to have been seized by the insulted deity who presided over the tree; because shortly after it he was taken ill with fever and ague. He was unmercifully thrashed by his master with the utmost *sang froid*, in the firm conviction that it was the surest way of frightening the devil out of him and saving the boy's life. The boy recovered slowly, and the cure was ascribed to the whipping the poor boy had received. This is a story known to the writer.

Thieves.

409. The thief on the contrary mulcting the police.

४०९   उलटा चोर कोतवाले डंडे

Ulta chor kotwāle dande.

The thief, on the contrary, exacts a penalty from the watchman !

Used when the right order of things is reversed.

410. Thick as thieves.

४१०   चोर चोर मौसियाउत भाई साँझे हँसुवा धैल पजाई

Chor chor mausiāut bhāi, sāñjhe hansuwa dhail pajāi.

Both are thieves: they are like two maternal cousins who keep the sickle ready sharpened in the evening (for operating at night).

मौसियाउत भाई *" Mausiāut bhāi"* are maternal cousins (sons of two sisters), who are said to be more attached to one another than other cousins, probably because they have no property to share, whereas sons of two brothers usually have.

Said of two who are accomplices and help each other in any prearranged wicked act, although outwardly they do not show it.

E.E. "Like two peas in a pod," or " Thick as thieves!"

411. A thief's heart is in the *kakri* field.

४११ चोरवा के मन बसे ककरी के खेत में

Chorwa ke man base kakri ke khet meñ.

The thief's heart is set on the gourd field, *i.e.* a thief sets his heart wherever he can get to steal.

412. With a thief he is a thief, to a watchman he is a servant only.

४१२ चोरक सङ्ग चोर पहरक सङ्ग खवास

Chorak sang chor pahrak sang khawās.

With other thieves he is a thief, but in the presence of the watchman he is simply a servant, *i.e.* who runs with the hare and hunts with the hounds.

खवास " *Khawās*," slave, a male house servant (Grierson).

413. A thief is a thief, whether he steals a diamond or a cucumber.

४१३ चोर जैसने होरा के वैसने खीरा के

Chor jaisne hīra ke, waisne khīra ke.

A thief is a thief, whether he steals a diamond or a cucumber. Cucumber is one of the cheapest vegetables.

414. A thief will not stick at a borrowed plate.

४१४ चोर जाने मँगनी के वासन

Chor jāne mangni ke bāsan.

It does not matter to a thief if it is a borrowed plate, *i.e.* A thief will not hesitate to steal because the plate does not belong to you. It is all the same to him.

415. An impudent thief he warns when he steals.

४१५ वरियार चोर सेंधी मे गावे

Bariyār chor sendhi me gāwe.

A fearless robber : he sings in the breach even!

संधी "*Sendhi*" is the breach or hole made in the wall by thieves.

If a thief sings in the act of stealing, he must indeed be impudent.

Said of one who commits a fault and fearlessly proclaims it, or laughs over it; one who does anything wrong and is shameless enough not to keep quiet over it, but makes it a point to boast over his misdeeds.

416. A thief: and with a face bright as the moon.

४१६　चोर के मुँह चान्द निग्रर

Chor ke muñh chānd niar.

The face of a thief and beaming like the moon! *i.e.* a thief ought to hide his face and be ashamed of showing it, and not "beam" like the moon. If any one commits a fault, and is ready to defend his conduct in a bare-faced manner, this proverb is used.

417. Taking tick *sine die*.

४१७　ले हींग उधारी वैसाख के एक रारी

Le hīng udhāri baisākh ke ek rāri.

Taking assafœtida on tick promising to pay in Baisākh!

Dealers and pedlars in Bihar go round selling their articles of trade, postponing the settlement to Baisākh (April-May) when the *rabbi* (or spring) crop has been harvested. Assafœtida is one of the articles commonly sold in this way. It is used by the Biharis in their food, especially in their *dall*.

Said when one takes tick, thoughtlessly promising to pay, without much prospect of being able to do so.

418. The idler (indolent).

৪१८ काम न धन्धा अढ़ाई रोटी बन्धा

Kām na dhandha, arhāi roti bandha.

Certain of his income (literally of $2\frac{1}{2}$ loaves of bread) he neither works, nor has thoughts.

Aimed at those who have a small fixed income and are idle and thoughtless in consequence.

419. Uncle and nephew always at loggerheads (paying off old scores).

৪१९ चच्चा चोर भतीजा काजी चच्चा के सिर पर पनही बाजी

Chachcha chor bhatīja kāji chachcha ke sir par panhi bāji.

The uncle is the thief and the nephew the magistrate, (it is a foregone conclusion that) the former will receive a shoe-beating on his head.

Among the natives it is a common idea that there is always ill-feeling between the uncle and nephew, owing, perhaps, to the former always chiding the latter to mind his studies or duties, so that, when the nephew gets a chance, he is only too ready to pay off old scores. Said when any result is a foregone conclusion : when any one is sure to come to grief in an encounter.

420. Vicissitudes of life.

৪२० इन नैनों की एही बिसेख वह भी देखा वह भी देख

In nainoñ ki chi bisekh, wah bhi dekha wah bhi dekh.

It is the peculiarity of these eyes : they have witnessed these, now let them witness those.

बिसेख "*Bisekh*," speciality, characteristic, peculiarity.

Said in self-consolation when a complete and un-expected change takes place. It is the peculiarity of the eye to witness all vicissitudes of life.

13

421. Waiting for the auspicious time may bring ruin.

४२१   घरी में घर जरे नव घरी भद्रा

Ghari meñ ghar jare, nau ghari bhadra.

The house is burnt down in an hour: while the unlucky period (during which no attempt must be made to save it) lasts for nine hours.

So long as the **भद्रा** *bhadra* (inauspicious period) lasts, nothing that is to be a success ought to be undertaken. If therefore any one idly waits for the inauspicious hour to pass away, instead of taking time by the forelock, he may fitly be compared to the man who makes no attempt to save his burning house because the inauspicious hour has not yet run out.

Said sarcastically when any one idly waits for an opportunity while it is slipping away.

भद्रा "*Bhadra*," the inauspicious period, comes round every month and on eight certain days (30 dands, or 12 hours, on each day). They are the 3rd, 7th, 10th and 14th of the first or dark half ; and the 4th, 8th, 11th, and 15th of the second or light half of each lunar month. During these periods nothing important is undertaken. Besides these there are the **पचखा** "*pachkha*," or five unlucky days in each month when nothing connected with woodwork is undertaken, *e.g.* houses (*i.e.* thatched houses) are not begun to be built on those days, bamboos are not cut, wells are not constructed, etc. The *pachkha* lasts for about two or three hours on each of the five days.

422. Waverer's repentance.

४२२   घर रहे न वाहर गये मूँड़ मुँड़ा के फजिहत भये

Ghar rahe na bāhar gaye, muñr muñra ke phajihat bhaye.

He is neither a useful domestic man nor a proper faqīr; by having his head shaved he has disgraced himself, that is to say, he is neither fit for attending to domestic duties, nor to worldly business: by shaving his head he has rendered himself (deservedly) an object of ridicule.

This would be said perhaps in self-reproach by one who had placed himself in a fix by his indecision.

"One between two stools." The expression *ghar rahe na bāhar gaye* means "fit for nothing," "of neither side," *lit.* "neither of the house nor of outside."

मूड़ मुंड़ाएव "*Mūṅr muñrāeb*," to shave one's head as a first step towards becoming an ascetic (corresponds to taking the veil by nuns). A man who has taken this step, but has not had the moral courage to leave his home and worldliness, might be said to have disgraced himself.

Widow.

423. A spinster weeping with a widow.

४२३   राँड़ राँड़ एहवाती रोवस संग लागल कुँआरो रोवस

Rāṅr rāṅr ehwāti rowas, sang lāgal kuñāro rowas.

A widow weeps because she is a widow, and perhaps a woman with a husband living (has also cause to weep); but in their company a spinster also weeps!

राँड़ "*Rāṅr*" is a widow, and एहवाती "*ehwāti*" a married woman whose husband is alive; कुँआरो "*kuñāro*" is a spinster, an unmarried girl.

It is the right thing for a widow to weep at all times for her departed husband. Sometimes women whose husbands are alive also join in the wailing.

The meaning is, that it can be understood that a widow weeps because she has lost her husband; and perhaps a woman who has her husband alive also has cause to weep when in company of widows (perhaps she is bewailing her husband's faults); but the marvel is that an unmarried woman also in their company weeps just the same as they do.

Aimed at those who do anything (grieve for example) in imitation of others or who pretend to grieve with others while they have really no cause.

424. Handful of bangles or a widow.

४२४   भर बाँह चूरी (माँग सेंदुर) की पत दे राँड़

Bhar bānh chūri (māng seńdur) ki pat de rānr.

Either have a handful of bangles or at once be a widow, *i.e.* have no ornaments. Variation is, "Either have a head full of vermilion or at once be (*i.e.* behave like) a widow." Widows seldom, or never, adorn themselves: all ornaments and decorations are forbidden. A woman who becomes a widow has to break her lac bangles at once. The idea is perhaps that as suddenly and surely as a woman becomes a widow (*i.e.* from having a handful of ornaments she sinks to one who must henceforth avoid all kinds of ornaments) so should you arrive at a conclusion.

It is a quaint way of urging one to choose one of two courses, and not to vacillate; to come to the point at once; to decide one way or the other.

Wedding.

425. Wedding of the noseless woman and nine hundred obstacles.

४२५   नक्ती के बियाह नव सै भाकठ

Nakti ke biyāh nao sai bhākath.

It is the wedding of the nose-clipt (woman) but there are nine hundred obstacles.

A noseless woman is devoid of beauty, and certainly not likely to be sought after. No objections are likely to be made from her side on the score of the amount to be paid by the bridegroom (as is usually the case about wedding presents). Her marriage therefore ought to be the easiest thing in the world. Hence in the accomplishment of any ordinary duty, if a hundred obstacles are met with, this saying is used. Making too much fuss about a little matter.

E.E. "Much ado about nothing." "Tempest in a teapot."

426. Wedding headdress made of mango leaves even.

४२६ मौर न मिले तः आम के पलवे सही

Maur na mile tah ām ke palwe sahi.

If the (proper) wedding headdress cannot be had, then mango leaves will answer.

मौर "*Maur*" is the headdress worn by Hindu bridegrooms during the marriage ceremony. It is made of talipot leaves, and in some places of date leaves.

Said sarcastically when something else is made to answer for the proper thing in an hour of need.

427. The song ought to be for her whose wedding it is.

४२७ जेकर माँड़ो तेकर गीत

Jekar mānro tekar gīt.

The song should be for her whose wedding it is.

(This proverb is the reverse of Proverb No. 202). The meaning is that we should act in a manner befitting the occasion.

माँड़ो "*Mānro,* the day before the expected arrival of

the marriage procession, the family sets up a bamboo shed in the courtyard over the fireplace.   This shed is called Marhwa, Maurwa, or Manro.   It is the hut in which a marriage ceremony is conducted" (Grierson).

Worshipping.

428. Easy worship of the *pipal* tree.

৪২৮   गोएँड़ा के पीपर दहिनौले जाह

Goeñra ke pipar dahinaule jāh.

The *pipal* tree is in the adjoining (homestead) field; it does not cost anything to keep it to your right in passing it! (and thus do an act of "cheap" worship!)

दहिनौले *"Dahinaule."*   In worshipping, the devotee goes usually five times round the object to be worshipped, keeping it to his right.   If the पीपल *pipal*-tree (which is worshipped in Bihar) is situated right at your door, it is no trouble to keep it to your right in going into your house.   You thus, without any effort, do an act of obeisance as it were, or make a pretence of it.   As a matter of fact, a superstitious Hindu, if he can help it, will always keep a *pipal* tree to his right in passing it.

Said in ridicule of one who tries to get credit without using much exertion, endeavours to satisfy himself that he has done a religious act without going into the trouble and expense of following all the ceremonies and rites.

Also cast in joke at those who make a pretence of observing some religious ceremony.

" Winning cheap the high renown."

429. Making a virtue of necessity in worshipping.

৪২৯   उरल सातू पितरन के पैठ

Ural sātu pitran ke paith.

May the *sattu* wafted by the breeze go to my dead ancestors, *i.e.* a little quantity of the meal he has been carrying in his hand is blown off by the wind and scattered, and this he piously gives as an offering to the souls of his ancestors, saying, "May this be accepted as an offering from me by the ghosts of my ancestors!"

Said to laugh at one who makes a virtue of necessity.

CLASS V.

PROVERBS RELATING TO AGRICULTURE AND SEASONS.

430. Distant farming ruinous.

४३० वण्डा वैल वेलाँजा पाही एक जन मरजन आवे जाही

Banda bail belaunja pāhi, ek jan marlan āwe jāhi.

(A possessor of) a useless (tailless) bullock who cultivates in Belaunja (*i.e.* a distant village) is killed simply
in going and coming, *i.e.* with an inferior bullock it is
simply death for a single man to have a distant cultivation, because he wastes his time in going to and fro.

वण्डा " *Banda* " is without a tail or with a docked tail.
A bullock without a tail is proverbially weak, and therefore useless. (The word is also pronounced *bāñrā* or *bāñr.*)

पाही " *Pāhi* " is a non-resident cultivator. A raiyat
who lives in one village and cultivates in another is a
" pāhi " (or " foreign ") cultivator of the latter village.
To be a " pāhi," one must necessarily possess the means.

वेलाँजा " *Belaunja* " is a pargana in Palāmau. Stands
here for a remote village.

A man who without sufficient means at his command
ventures to cultivate in a distant village is sure to suffer
for his imprudence; for one single man with an indifferent
bullock would simply waste his and his bullock's life in
the journey to and fro, and really be able to do no
cultivation.

Usually said to laugh at a distant *pāhi jot* or remote
cultivation.

431. The closer the field, the easier the culture.

४३१ अरिया के गरिया भला पाही के ना डुब

Ariya ke gariya bhala pāhi ke na dūb.

A field that is contiguous but inferior is to be preferred to one distant and superior (literally one under water, but in another village).

अरिया के गरिया *"Ariya ke gariya."* गरिया *"gariya"* is a field in which a little rain causes puddle : it is unproductive, and *ariya* is adjoining your boundary. The expression therefore means a *" gariya "* field that is adjoining your boundary, *i.e.* near your cultivation. These soils (*gariya*) are difficult to cultivate. In showery weather they cannot be ploughed because the action of the plough and the treading of the plough cattle work the soil into a puddle; while in dry weather these soils become so hard and compact that no ordinary plough will penetrate them.

डुब *Dūb* or द्राव *Dhāb* is land that is for a part of the year under water, and for a part of it dry; it is very productive.

The meaning is, that it is better to possess an inferior field adjoining your boundary (because it can be easily looked after) than a superior one in a distant village where it cannot be attended to so easily.

432. Selling bullocks for seed.

४३२ खेती कैलीँ जीये ला बैल बिकैले बीये ला

Kheti kailiñ jiye la, bail bikaile biye la.

I took to husbandry to gain a livelihood, but the bullocks were sold for seed!

Said when one exhausts his means in gaining an end, a misfortune which literally happens in seasons of drought.

433. A farmer is known when at his field.

৪৩৩ खेत चढ़े किसान

Khet charhe kisān.

When one engages himself in husbandry, then only can it be said whether he is a farmer.

(खेत चढ़े *Khet charhe* is an idiomatic phrase meaning to take action or to go to action; *e.g.* when an army has taken the field it is said, फौज खेत चढ़ले *phauj khet charhale.*)

A true or experienced husbandman can only be known when he begins farming, and not from his talk.

434. Anxieties of agriculture unknown to the lazy lubber.

৪৩৪ करैं न खेती परैं न फन्द पर घर नाँचें मूसर चन्द

Karaiñ na kheti paraiñ na phand,
Par ghar nāñcheñ mūsar chand.

He does not cultivate (and consequently) meets with no difficulty (*i.e.* meets with no failures): thus free from care Mūsar Chand spunges on another (*lit.* dances in another's house).

फन्द "*Phand*" from फन्दा *phanda,* a noose, a net, a difficulty, a scrape.

मूसर चन्द "*Mūsar Chand,*" a metaphorical name borrowed from the word मूसर *Mūsar,* a stout wooden pestle used in cleaning rice from husk. The wooden vessel in which grain is pounded is called ओखरी *okhri,* also उखली *ukhli.*

Mūsar Chand is applied to a fat, well-fed, lazy lout. An able-bodied man who will not work from laziness.

" Fat as a Mūsar " is a common expression. (The nasal *n* at the end of " *Karaiñ,*" " *paraiñ,*" and " *nāñcheñ* " marks the tone of contempt. It is used to denote respect towards the person spoken of, but here used in irony.)

435. If goats and sheep answer for ploughing, why purchase bullocks ?

४३५ छेरी भेड़ी हल चले बरध बेसाहीँ काहे

Chheri bhenri hal chale baradh besāhīñ kāhe.

If goats and sheep can be used for the purpose of ploughing, why buy oxen !

Said ironically when inferior men are expected to perform duties above their capacity. (Compare Proverb No. 151.)

436. Impertinent request to lend a bullock.

४३६ आपन वरधा हमरा के दह तोहरा अँगवार सहेला

Āpan bardha hamra ke dah tohra añgwār sahela.

Pray give me your bullock, for a borrowed bullock (in exchange for your labour) befits you better !

अँगवार "*Angwār*" is one who does not possess any bullock of his own, but gets the loan of a yoke of oxen and plough in exchange for his manual labour (*ang*—"limb"). Thus, for instance, *A* has no bullock; *B* has (say) a yoke. *A* will work as a ploughman in *B's* field for two days, and get the use of *B's* plough and oxen for one day. It is therefore the height of impertinence for a man to ask the owner for his plough and suggest his working as a labourer (in order to get his own field ploughed), because labour befits him better !

The above is the practice when a man has no ox of his own. When he has one, he usually borrows another from a neighbour to complete the yoke for ploughing his field, returning the accommodation by lending his own in return. This is called the *pariha* system, or taking it in turns when both are labourers. But it often happens that one of a respectable caste (say a Brāhman), who is reluctant to

work as a labourer, possesses a plough of oxen. He lends
them to a labourer (who has a field) for one day, and gets
his services to plough his land for two days. The principle is that the labourer and two oxen make three factors :
whichever side owns two of these gets the service of the
yoke for two days, and the other party for one day. If
the ploughman owns one bullock, he gets the use of the
plough for two days.

437. The meaning of a speckled cloud and a widow
applying scented oil.

४३७ तीतर पंखी बदरी राँड फुलेल लगाय
कह भडुर सुन भडुरी वह आबे यह जाय

Titar pankhi badri, rānr phulel lagāy,
Kah bhaddar sun bhaddari wah āwe yah jāy.

"When you see a cloud speckled like the wing of the
partridge, and a widow applying scented oil to her hair,"
saith Bhaddar, "Hear, O Bhaddari, the former will rain
and the latter will elope."

तीतर पंखी *" Titar pankhi,"* spotted or speckled like the
wing of the partridge.

राँड़ *Rānr.* A widow is never supposed to apply scented
oil or adorn herself in any way.

भडुर *"Bhaddar"* was a local poet and of some fame.
He has interpreted the signs of the seasons in rhymes
which have passed into proverbs. Some of his descendants
(an inferior class of Brāhmans) are still supposed to reside
in a village of the Shāhabad district. The following story
is told of Bhaddar :—When very young he was stolen
from his home in Shāhabad by a famous magician or
astrologer, who carried him away to his country and

adopted him. Bhaddar became so thoroughly proficient
in astrology and all the mystic arts, that his patron gave
him his daughter in marriage. Desirous of seeing his
early home, he found out by astrology in what direction
it lay; and then, having ascertained by his science the
exact auspicious hour and day of his departure, he secretly
awaited them, as he knew his wife would be against his
leaving her. Unfortunately the exact auspicious hour
came round when he was at his meals, his wife being
present in attendance. Being well up in *jotish* laws of
astrology, he made a move with his foot (as a beginning
of his journey), which was all that was needed to
make his journey a success. His wife, who was
herself an adept in *jotish*, observed this action of her
husband's, and at once understood what it meant, but
pretended ignorance. In order, however, to frustrate his
intention, she cast a spell over a river which he had to
cross ; and in consequence of this the ferry-boat in
which Bhaddar was crossing upset when in mid-stream.
But as Bhaddar had started in a propitious hour nothing
could effectually stop him. He was therefore borne to the
other side on the back of a fish. This convinced his wife
that her husband was a superior magician and astrologer,
and that nothing that she could do would prevent
him from carrying out his wish. So she gave up the
idea, and followed him to his original home (in Shāhabad),
where they settled for good.

438. The meaning of beginning to rain on Saturday,
Tuesday, Thursday, and Sunday respectively.

शनि अढ़ाई मङ्गल तीन रवि गुर बरसे आठो दीन

Shani arhāi, mangal tīn, Rabi gur barse ātho din.

If it begins to rain on Saturday, it will continue to rain for two days and a half; if on Tuesday, for three days; if on Sunday or Thursday, it will rain for the next eight days.

439. The meaning of the rainbow at the beginning and end of rain.

(इन्द्र धनुष)

४३९ जगत ऊगे मही भरे विसवत ऊगे जाय

(*Indra dhanukh*)

Ūgat ūge mahi bhare, biswat ūge jāy.

If the (rainbow) appears when the rain has just begun, the earth will be filled (*i.e.* there will be a very heavy fall of rain); if at the end, it is a sign that the rain will stop.

440. The meaning of the halo round the moon on Sunday, Tuesday, and Thursday respectively.

४४० रवि गुर मङ्गल जौँ चन्द्रा परिवेष
दिन चौथे अट्टे महि भरन विषेष

Rabi gur mangal jauñ chanda paribekh,
Din chauthe, atthe mahi bharan bishekh.

If the halo is seen round the moon on Sunday (night), it will positively rain the day following; if on Thursday, on the fourth day; and if on Tuesday, on the eighth day.

441. The rain of the beginning of Aradra and end of Hathiya.

४४१ आवत आदर नाँ दिये जात नाँ दिये हस्त
कहेँ भड्डुर दोऊ गये बनिता औ गिरहस्त

Āwat ādar nāñ diye, jāt nāñ diye hast,
Kaheñ bhaddar dou gaye, banita au girhast.

This proverb is a *double entendre* : it may mean the " wife " or the rainy season.

On coming home (to her father-in-law's house), if a wife is not received with due ceremony and regard; and if on going she is not given any present in her hand (the usual etiquette of native domestic life), says Bhaddar, she will go, *i.e.* she will elope. Or,

If at the commencement of the monsoons there is no rain in Adra, and if, at their close, there is none in Hathiya, then says Bhaddar, it is a bad look-out for the farmer as well as the labourer (*i.e.* the farmer is sure to be ruined and the labourers are sure to get no work and will starve).

आदर *Adar* is a colloquial form of अद्रा *Adra*, or अर्द्रा नक्षत्र *Ardra Nachhattra*. It also means "civility." "*Ādar karna*" is to treat one with due civility and ceremony, and हस्त *Hast* is "hand," or the हथिया नक्षत्र *Hathiya Nachhattra*. The *Adra* or *Aradra* and *Hathiya* or *Hast* are two out of twenty-seven *Nachhattras* or lunar asterisms into which the Hindu year is divided. The former embraces parts of June and July; and the latter parts of September and October. They are the beginning and end of the rainy seasons; and are the principal periods of rain, on which chiefly depends the success of agricultural operations. The following extract from Mr. Grierson's " Bihār Peasant Life " (Division VI., par. 1082) shows these divisions clearly :—

" There are 27 of these (*Nachhattras* or lunar asterisms) in each year, and consequently $2\frac{1}{4}$ in each month. Each asterism is not of equal length. The longest is *hathiya*, with 16 lunar days. Every agricultural operation commences in a certain asterism."

442.[1] The asterisms of Maggha, Swāti and Hathiya.

४४२ मगघा लगावे घग्घा सिवाती लावस टाटी
कहतारी हाथी रानी हम हूँ आवत वाटी

Maggha lagāwe ghaggha, Swāti lāwas tāti,
Kahtāri Hāthi rāni, ham hūñ āwat bāti.

Maggha (latter part of August) brings rain-storms;
Swāti (latter part of October) brings a screen (*i.e.* rain
stops); and Queen *Hathiya* (September-October) tells
(by her thunder) that she is coming.

443. The effects of the several rains on the different
crops.

४४३ फागु कराई चैत चुक किर्त्तिक नट्ठहि तार
खाती नट्ठहि माख तिल कहि गए डाक गोआर

Phāgu karāi, chait chuk, kirttik natthahi tār,
Swāti natthahi mākh til, kahi gae Dāk Goār.

If it rains in the month of *Phāgun* (February-March)
urid is spoilt; if in the month of *Chait* (March-April)
lemons; if in the asterism of *Krittika* (about middle of
May) the toddy palms; and if in that of *Swāti* (latter part
of October) beans and sesasum; saith *Dāk* the *Gowāla*.

444. The effect of rain in *Baisākh* (April-May) on
paddy; it is doubled.

४४४ जाँ वरसे बैसक्खा राऊ एक धान मेँ दोबर चाऊ

Jauñ barse Baisakkha rāu, ek dhān meñ dobar chāu.

If King *Baisākh* (April-May) rain, every grain of
paddy will produce two of rice.

---

[1] Proverbs 442 to 491 are taken from Mr. Grierson's "Bihār Peasant Life,"
with the author's kind permission.

445. If there is rain in *Krittika* (middle of May), there
will be no rain for the six following asterisms.

४४५ क्रत्तिका चूए चौ ले मूए जाँ रोहिनी नहीँ कादो करे

Krittika chue chhau le mue, jauñ Rohini nahiñ kādo kare.

If it rains in *Krittika* (middle of May), there will be no
rain for the six following asterisms, provided *Rohini*
(beginning of June) makes no mud. A variation is

क्रत्तिका चूए तीन ले मूए राहर रेँड कपास
जाँ रोहिन दधि कादो करे हरे दोष उञ्चास

Krittika chue tin le mue rāhar renr kapās,
Jauñ rohin dadhi kādo kare hare dokh unchās.

446. When to sow *china*.

४४६ जब जनिहः खरचा के हीन क्रित्तिका मेँ तूँ बोइहः चीन

Jab janihah karchā ke hin, krittika meñ tūñ boihah chin.

Krittika (latter part of May) is the best asterism for
sowing *china* (*Panicum frumentosum*); hence they say in
Tirhut: If you find your stock of food becoming exhausted,
sow *china* in *Krittika* (*i.e.* about middle of May).

447. When rice will be plentiful.

४४७ मिरगसिरा तवय रोहिनी लवय अरदरा जाय बुदबुदाय
कहे डाक सुनु भिझरि कुत्ता भात न खाय

Mirgsira tabay Rohini labay Aradra jāy budbudāy,
Kahe Dāk sunu Bhillari, kutta bhāt na khāy.

If *Mirgsira* (in June) is hot, *Rohini* (about beginning of
June) rains, and *Aradra* (middle of June) gives a few
drops. Saith *Dāk*, hear, O *Bhillari*, (rice will be so
plentiful that) even dogs will turn up their noses at it.

The following notes on the Proverbs 442 to 447 from
Mr. Grierson's book are useful:—

" Cultivation commences in *Jeth* in the asterism of *Rohini*, when ploughing and sowing begin. The rain of *Mirgsira* is not good, and hence no sowing is done in that asterism. In *Aradra* sowing is recommenced and transplanting is done for the winter (*Aghani*) crop. This goes on into *Punarbas* and *Pukh* if the rains are late. In *Magha* and *Purba Phāguni* the *urid, kurthi,* and other pulses are sown. In *Hathiya* rain is very important, both for the winter crops and for sowing of the spring (*rabbi*) crops. In former days (say cultivators) the rains used to stop in *Swāti*, which was very good for the crops, but now they end in *Hathiya*. So valuable is the rain of *Swāti* that any drop which falls during that asterism into a pearl-oyster becomes a pearl: that is how pearls are made. The rain in *Chitra* on the contrary is very bad."

448 to 453. The rain of *Aradra* (middle of June) is of considerable importance to the future crop.

448. The rain of *Aradra* (middle of June) does away with distress.

४४८   अदरा माँस जे बोये साठी दुख के मार निकाल: लाठी

Adra māns je boe sāthi, Dukh ke mār nikālah lāthi.

If you sow sixty day rice in *Aradra*, you strike distress with a club and drive it away.

449. If it does not rain at the commencement of *Aradra* and end of *Hathiya* the cultivator gets ruined.

४४९   आदि न बरसे अरदरा हस्त न बरसे निदान
         कहहीं डाक सुनु भिल्लरि भये किसान पिसान

Ādi na barse aradra, hast na barse nidān,
Kahahīñ Dāk sunu Bhillari bhae kisān pisān.

If *Aradra* does not rain at the commencement, and *Hathiya* at its end, saith Dak, hear, O Bhillari, the cultivator is crushed (see Proverb No. 441).

450. If it rains at the commencement of *Aradra* and end of *Hathiya*, the cultivator can stand any increase to his rent.

४५० चढ़त बरसे अरदरा उतरत बरसे हस्त
कतेक राजा दाँड़े रहे अनन्द गिरहस्त

Charhat barse aradra, utrat barse hast,
Katek rāja dāṅre, rahe anand girhast.

If it rains when *Aradra* commences and when *Hathiya* is ending, no matter how much rent may be demanded, the householder is still happy.

451. The rain of *Aradra* injures *jawās* only.

४५१ अरदरा बरसे सभ किछु हाँ एक जवास पतर बिन भाँ

Aradra barse sabh kichhu hāṅ, ek jawās patar bin bhāṅ.

If *Aradra* rains, everything grows (*lit.* "is"), only one, the *jawās* (*Hedysarum Alhagi*), loses its leaves.

(जवास *Jawās* is a kind of grass.)

452. When to prepare the fields, and when to sow paddy.

४५२ पुख पुनरबस बोये धान मग्घा असलेखा कादो सान

Pukh Punarbas boe dhān, Maggha Aslekha kādo sān.

Sow paddy in *Pukh* and *Punarbas*, and in *Maggha* and *Aslekha* mix thoroughly the mud (*i.e.* prepare the fields).

Aradra and *Punarbas* are the two main asterisms of the month of *Akhārh* (June-July). This is the great month of the year for finishing the preparations of the fields, as the proverb says :—

जेकर बनल अखड़वा रे तेकर बारहो मास

Jekar banal akharwa re tekar bārho mās.

i.e. He whose fields are ready in *Akhārh*, is ready also all the year round.

If the rains are late, paddy sowing goes on as late as *Punarbas* or even *Pukh*, but this is rarely successful. These last two asterisms are usually devoted to transplanting and not sowing. (Paragraph 1086, Grierson.)

453. The effect of paddy being sown in *Aradra, Punarbas,* or *Pukh*.

४५३ अरदरा धान पुनरबस पैया गेल किसान जे बोए चिरैया

Aradra dhān, Punarbas paiya, gel kisān, je boe Chiraiya.

Paddy sown in *Aradra* turns to plenty, in *Punarbas* it has empty ears, and sown in *Pukh* it turns to nothing.

454 to 464. [After *Akhārh* (June-July) comes *Sāwan* or *Sāon* (July-August); to which the following rhymes apply.]

454. The meaning of a cloudy sunrise on the seventh day of the bright half in *Sāwan*.

४५४ सावन सुकला सप्तमी छपि कै ऊगहिँ भान
तौँ लगि मेघा बरसे जौँ लगि देब उठान

Sāon sukla saptami chhapi kai ūgahiñ bhān,
Tauñ lagi megha barse jauñ lagi deb uthān.

If on the morning of the seventh of the bright half of *Sāwan* the sun rises obscured by clouds, it will rain up to the festival of the *Deb Uthān* (11th of the light half of *Kātik, i.e.* early in November).

455. The meaning of a clear sunrise on the same day.

४५५ सावन सुर्कला सप्तमी ऊग के लूकहिँ सूर

हाँको पिया हर बरद बरखा गेल वड़ि दूर

Sāon sukla saptami, ug ke lūkahiñ sūr,

Hāñko piya har barad, barkha gel bari dūr.

If on the same day as that above mentioned (in Proverb 454) the sun rises (clear) and afterwards hides itself behind clouds, drive away, my dear, your plough and bullocks, for the rain is very far off.

456. The meaning of a cloudless morning on the same day.

४५६ सावन सुकला सप्तमी उदै जो देखे भान

तुम जाव पिया मालवा हम जैवोँ मुलतान

Sāon sukla saptami, udai jo dekhe bhān,

Tum jāo piya Mālwa, ham jaiboñ Multān.

A cloudless morning on the same day (is a sure sign of drought). My dear, (let us leave the country); I am going to Multān, and you go to Mālwa.

457. The meaning of a dark night on the same date.

४५७ सावन सुकला सप्तमी रैन हाँहि मसियार

कह भद्दर सुन भद्दरी परवत उपजय सार

Sāon sukla saptami, rain hoñhi masiyār,

Kah Bhaddar sunu Bhaddari, parbat upjay sār.

If on the same date the night is dark, says *Bhaddar,* hear, O *Bhaddari,* excellent crops will grow even on a mountain.

458. The meaning of thunder at midnight on the same date.

४५८ सावन सुकला सप्तमी जौं गरजे आधि रात

तुम जाव पिया मालवा हम जैबौं गुजरात

Sāon sukla saptami, joñ garje ādhi rāt,

Tum jāo piya Mālwa, ham jaiboñ Gujrāt.

If on the same date it thunders at midnight (there will be a drought). You must go to Mūlwa, and I to Gujrāt.

459. The effect of rain in *Sāwan* (July-August), and thunder in *Bhādoñ* (August-September).

४५९ करके भौंजे कंकरी सिंघ गरजै जाय

कह भद्दद सुन भद्दुरी कुत्ता भात न खाय

Karke bhīnjai Kankri, Singh garjai jāy,

Kah Bhaddar sunu Bhaddari, kutta bhāt na khāy.

" If in Cancer (*Sāwan*, July-August) the gravel is wet, and Leo (*Bhādoñ*, August-September) passes by with thunder," saith Bhaddar, " hear, O Bhaddari, rice will be so plentiful that even dogs will refuse it."

460. The meaning of west wind in *Sāwan*, and east in *Bhādoñ*.

४६० सावन पछवा भादव पुरवा आसिन बहै ईशान

कातिक कन्ता सिकियो न डोलि कतै के रखबह धान

Sāon pachhwa, Bhādab purwa, Āsin bahe īsān,

Kātik, Kanta, sikio na dole katai ke rakhbah dhān.

If the west wind blows in *Sāwan*, the east in *Bhādoñ*, and the north-east in *Āsin*, and if there is so little wind in *Kātik* that even the reeds do not shake, where, my dear, will you have room to keep your rice ? (*i.e.* You will have a bumper crop.)

461. The effect of east wind in *Sāwan*.

४६१ सावन मास बहे पुरवैया बेचँह बरद कीनह गैया

Sāon mās bahe purwaiya, beṅchah barad kīnah gaiya.

If the east wind blows in *Sāwan*, sell your bullocks and buy cows (it will be no use trying to plough).

462. The effect of west wind in *Sāwan*.

४६२ सावनक पछवा दीन दुइ चारी चूल्हि के पाछी उपजै सारी

Sāonak pachhwa din dui chāri, chūlhi ke pāchhi upjai sāri.

If the west wind blow in *Sāwan* for only two or three days, rice will grow even behind your hearth.

463. The effect of west and east wind in *Sāwan* and *Bhādoñ*.

४६३ सावन पचेत्रा महि भरे भादोँ पुरवा पत्थल सड़े

Sāon pachea mahi bhare, bhādoñ purwa patthal sare.

If the west wind blow in *Sāwan*, the land will be flooded; and if the east wind blow in *Bhādoñ*, (it will rain so that) the very stones will melt.

464. Heaviest rain in *Asres* and *Maggha*.

४६४ जे ना भरे असरेसा मगघा फेर भरे असरेसा मगघा

Je na bhare Asresa Maggha, pher bhare Asresa Maggha.

That which is not filled up with water in *Asres* and *Maggha* has no chance of being filled up till they come again next year.

465 to 474. To *Bhādoñ* (August-September) the following apply :—

465. Loss to cultivator if he does not finish transplanting rice before *Purwa*.

४६५ पुरवा रोपे पूर किसान आधा खखरी आधा धान

Purwa rope pūr kisān, ādha khakhri ādha dhān.

If a cultivator does not finish transplanting before *Purwa* (*i.e. Purba Phāguni*), half his crop will be paddy and half chaff.

466. The effect of east wind in *Purwa*.

४६६ जौं पुरवा पुरवैया आवे सुखले नदिया नाव चलावे

Jauñ Purwa purwaiya āwe, sukhle nadiya nāo chalāwe.

If the east wind blows in the asterism of *Purwa* (*i.e. Purba Phāguni*), there will be so much rain that ships will float in the dried-up beds of rivers.

Closely connected with this is the following :—

467. The effect of west wind in *Purwa*.

४६७ पुरवा पर जौं पछवा बहैं बिहँसि राँड़ वात करै
    एह दोनों के इहै बिचार ऊ बरसै इ करै भतार

Purwa par jauñ pachhwa bahai, bihañsi rāñr bāt karai,
Eh donoñ ke ihai bichār ū barsai i karai bhatār.

If the west wind blows during *Purwa*, and if a widow chats and smiles, from these facts you may judge that in the first case it will rain, and in the second case she is going to marry a second time.

468. The meaning of clouds flitting like the wings of a partridge.

४६८ तीतिर पख मेघा उड़े ओ बिधवा मुसुकाए
    कहे डाक सुनु डाकिनी ऊ बरसै इ जाए

Tītir pakh megha ure, o bidhwa musukāe.
Kahe Dāk sunu Dākini, ū barse i jāe.

" When the clouds fly like the wings of the partridge and when a widow smiles," saith *Dāk*, "hear, O *Dākni*, the one is going to rain and the other to marry." (Compare Proverb 379.)

469. The meaning of a cloudy sky on Friday and Saturday.

४६९ सुक करे बदरी सनीचर रहे छाए
ऐसन बोले भड्डरी बिन बरसे नहोँ जाय

Sūk kare badri sanīchar rahe chhāy,
Aisan bole Bhaddari bin barse nahīñ jāy.

"A cloudy sky on Friday and Saturday," says *Bhaddari*, "is a sure precursor of rain."

470. The effect of east wind in *Sāon* and west wind in *Bhādoñ*.

४७० सावन के पुरवा भादो पछिमा जोर
बरधा बेँचः सामी चलः देस का ओर

Saon ke purwa, Bhādoñ pachhima jor,
Bardha beñchah Sāmi, chalah des ka or.

My husband let us sell our bullocks and leave the country if there is east wind in *Sāon*, and a strong west one in *Bhādoñ*.

471. When to cease planting paddy.

४७१ कुसी अमावस चौठी चान अब की रोपवः धान किसान

Kusi amāwas chauthi chān, ab ki ropbah dhān kisān.

After the *Kusi Amāwas* (the festival of the 15th *Bhādoñ*, on which Brāhmans dig *kūs* grass), and the *Chauk Chanda* (the moon of the 19th of *Bhādoñ*), O cultivator ! You need not plant out paddy.

472. Not to transplant in *Utra Phaguni*.

४७२ उतरा मेँ जनि रोपहु भैया तीन धान होए तेरह पैया

Utra meñ jani ropahu bhaiya, tin dhān hoe terah paiya.

Do not transplant in *Utra Phaguni* (about the latter half of September); for you will only get three grains to thirteen empty husks.

473. The meaning of a crow speaking by night and a jackal by day.

৪৩৩ রাতক কাগা দীনক সিয়ার কী झরি বাদর কী উপতার

Rātak kāga dinak siyār, ki jhari bādar ki uptār.

If the crow speak by night and the jackal by day, there will be either a rain-storm or an inundation.

474. The meaning of wind blowing from four quarters.

৪৩৪ আऔআ বौআ বহে বতাস তব হোলা বরখা কে আস

Aua baua bahe batās, tab hola barkha ke ās.

When the wind blows from all four quarters, there is hope of rain.

475–479. To *Āsin* (September-October) the following apply :—

475. *Hathiya* rain produces three things and destroys three things.

৪৩৫ হথিয়া বরসে তীন হোতবা সক্কর সালী মাস
হথিয়া বরসে তীন জতব তীল কোদো কপাস

Hathiya barse tin hot-ba, sakkar, sāli, mās,
Hathiya barse tin jat-wa, til, kodo, kapās.

Rain in *Hathiya* produces three things, sugar-cane, rice, and pulse; and destroys three things, sesamum, *kodo*, and cotton. With this may be compared the following.

476. Rainless *Aradra* destroys three crops only, but a rainless *Hathiya* destroys everything.

४७६ अदरा गेल तीनो गेल सन साठी कपास
हथिया गेल सभ गेल आगिल पाछिल चास

Adra gel tīnoñ gel, san, sāthi, kapās,
Hathiya gel sabh gel, āgil, pāchhil chās.

Want of rain in *Aradra* destroys three crops, hemp, sixty-day rice, and cotton. But by want of rain in *Hathiya* everything is ruined, both what has been sown and what will be sown.

477. The effect of rain in *Hathiya* and clouds only in *Chitra*.

४७७ हथिया बरिसे चितरा मेँड़राए
घर बैसे धनहा रिरियाए

Hathiya barise, chitra meñrrāy,
Ghar baise dhanha ririyāy (or agrāy).

If *Hathiya* rains and (the clouds of) *Chitra* hover about, the paddy cultivator sits at home and utters cries of joy.

478. The effect of rain in *Chitra*.

४७८ चितरा वरसे माटी मारे आगे भाइ गेरुई के कारे

Chitra barse māti māre āge bhāi gerui ke kāre.

Rain in *Chitra* (in October) destroys the fertility of the soil and is likely to produce blight.

479. What to sow in *Chitra*.

४७९ आधा चितरा राई मुराई आधा चितरा जव केराई

Ādha chitra rāi murāi, ādha chitra jao kerāi.

In one half of *Chitra* sow mustard and radishes, and in the other half barley and peas.

480–481. To *Kātik* (October-November) the following apply :—

480. The effect of a shower in *Swāti*.

ঃ৪৮০ एको पानो जो वरसे खाती कुरमिन पहिरे सोना पाती

Eko pāni jo barse swāti kurmin pahire sona pāti.

If a single shower come in *Swāti*, it enriches people so much that even *Kurmi* women get golden earrings to wear.

481. Instructions about harvesting rice.

৪৮৭ वेद विदित ना होखे आन विना तुला नहिं फूटे धान
मुख मुखराती देव उठान तकरै वरहै कर: नेमान
तकरै वरहै खेत खरिहान तकरै वरहै कोठिये धान

Bed bidit na hokhe ān, bina Tula nahiñ phūte dhān,
Sukh sukhrāti deb uthān, takrai barhai karah nemān,
Takrai barhai khet kharihān, takrai barhai kothie dhān.

What has been written in the Vedas cannot happen otherwise, and paddy cannot ripen before the balance (*i.e. Libra, Kātik*, October-November). From the festival of the *Sukhrāti* (*i.e.* the *Diwāli*) to the *Deb Uthān* (11th of the light half of *Kātik*) there will be happiness. On the 12th day after that, hold the festival of eating the new grain ; on the 12th after that, heap up the corn on the field and threshing-floor ; and on the 12th after that, put the grain in the store-house.

482–486. The following are the signs of the stoppage of the rains :—

482. Clear nights indicate breaking of the rains.

৪৮২ छप के उगै तो क्या भये निर्मल रैनि करन्त
कीय जल देखिहः सगरा कामिन कूप भरन्त

Chhap ke ugai to kya bhaye nirmal raini karant,
Kiy jal dekhihah sagra, kāmin kūp bharant.

It matters little if the sun rises obscured by clouds,
because when the nights are clear (the rain will stop).
You will only find water in the sea, and women will
have to go to the wells for water.

483. A cloudless night and a cloudy day show that the
rains are at an end.

৪৮৩ रात निवद्दर दिन कें छाया
कहैँ घाघ जे वरखा गया

Rāt nibaddar (or *rātuk chakmuk*) *din keṅ chhāya,*
Kaheṅ Ghāgh je barkha gaya.

If you see a cloudless night and a cloudy day, be sure,
says *Ghāgh*, that the rains are at an end.

484. The barking of the fox and the flowering of the
kās grass are signs of the end of the rains.

৪৮৪ बोली लुखरी फूले कास अव नाहीँ वरखा के आस

Boli lukhri, phūle kās, ab nāhīṅ barkha ke ās.

The barking of the fox and the flowering of the *kās*
grass are signs of the end of the rains.

485. Appearance of the star Canopus indicates the end
of the rains.

৪৮৫ उगे अगस्त वन फूले कास अव नाहीँ वरखा के आस

Ūge agast ban phūle kās, ab nāhīṅ barkha ke ās.

The appearance of the star Canopus and the flowering of
the *kās* grass in the forests are signs of the end of the rains.

486. The meaning of the flowering of the *kās* and *kus*
grass.

৪৮৬ कासी कूसी चौठ के चान अव का रोपव धान किसान

Kāsi kūsi chauth ke chān, ab ka ropba dhān kisān.

If the *kās* grass and the *kus* grass flower on the 4th of the light half of *Bhadoñ*, why do you plant out, O cultivator (for the rains are stopped) ?

487–491. The following refer to the dry seasons :—

487. Respective effects of rain in *Aghan*, *Pūs*, *Māgh*, and *Phāgun*.

४८७ अगहन दोवर पूस डेश्रौढ़ा माघ सवाई
फागुन वरसे घरहूँ के जाइ

Aghan dobar, Pūs dyaurha, Māgh sawāi,
Phāgun barse gharhūñ ke jāi.

If it rains in *Aghan* (November-December), you will get double an average crop; if in *Pūs* (December-January), one and a half; if in *Māgh* (January-February), one and a quarter; but if in *Phāgun* (February-March), then even (the seedlings which you brought from) your house will be lost.

488. The effect of rain in *Aghan*.

४८८ अगहन में जे वरसे मेघ धन ओ राजा धन ओ देस

Aghan meñ je barse megh dhan o rāja dhan o des.

Happy are the king and people when it rains in *Aghan*.

489. The effect of rain in *Pūs*.

४८९ पानी वरसे आधा पूस आधा गेहूँ आधा भूस

Pāni barse ādha Pūs, ādha gehūñ ādha bhūs.

Rain in the middle of the month of *Pūs*, *i.e.* early in January, will give you half wheat and half chaff.

490. Signs of drought.

४९० माघ के गरमी जेठ के जाड़ पहिला पानी भर गैल ताड़
घाघ कहे हम होवाँ जोगी कूआँ का पानी धोइहैँ धोवो

Māgh ke garmi, Jeth ke jār, pahila pāni bhar gail tār,
Ghāgh kahe ham hobauñ jogi, kūāñ ka pāni dhoiheñ dhobi.

Heat in *Māgh* (January-February), cold in *Jeth* (May-June), and the tanks filled with the first fall of rain (are signs of a drought). I'll become a beggar, says *Ghāgh*, and the washerman will wash with well water.

491. The meaning of west wind respectively in *Chait* (March-April) and *Bhādoñ* (August-September).

४९१ चैत के पछेया भादों के जल्ला
भादों के पछेया माघ के पल्ला

Chait ke pachheya, Bhādoñ ke jalla,
Bhādoñ ke pachheya, Māgh ke pālla.

The west wind in *Chait* (March-April) means rain in *Bhādoñ* (August-September), and the west wind in *Bhādoñ* means frost in *Māgh* (January-February).

CLASS VI.

Proverbs Relating to Cattle and Animals in General.

492. A calf takes after its mother, and a foal after its father.

४९२ माँ गुन वाछ पीता गुन घोर
नाहीँ कुछ तो थोरो थोर

Māñ gun bāchh pīta gun ghor,
Nāhīñ kuchh to thoro thor.

A calf takes after its mother, and a foal after its sire : if not in all points, still in a few (*i.e.* to some extent).

493. Can an ass be lean in the month of *Sāwan* ?

४९३ गदहा दूवर सावन माँस

Gadha dūbar Sāwan māñs.

Is it possible for the ass to be thin in the month of *Sāwan* ? *i.e.* when there is abundance of grazing to be had. Said when any one complains or pretends to be in want in the midst of plenty.

A weary Bullock.

494. To a weary bullock its girth even is heavy.

४९४ थाकल वरद के पेटार भारी

Thākal barad ke petār bhāri.

To a weary bullock even his girths are heavy.

पेटार *"Petār"* is the girth of a pack-bullock. It is usually made of निवार *newār*, with a piece of bamboo catch tied to one end of it, and is passed round the bullock.

495. To a weary bullock his empty panniers are even heavy.

४९५ थाके वैल गोन भै भारी
तब अव का लादे वैपारी

Thāke bail gon bhai bhāri,
Tab ab ka lāde baipāri.

To the weary bullock even his empty pack is heavy (to carry): then, why are you going to load more on him, Pedlar?

"*Gon*" also "*gond*," and "*gūnd*," are grain bags for pack bullocks.

वैपारी "*Baipāri*" is a petty trader who deals in grain, and conveys it from market to market on pack bullocks, buying and selling.

E.E. Last straw breaks the camel's back.

496. A separate house for a blind cow.

४९६ कानीँ गैया के अलगे बथान
Kānīñ gaiya ke alge bathān.

A blind cow requires a separate cattle-yard.

बथान "*Bathān*" is a cattle-yard or inclosure where the cattle rest.

i.e. One with a peculiarity, idiosyncracy or crotchet, one who wants everything his own way, *i.e.* is not satisfied with what answers for everybody else.

497. Driving away a grazing cow a sin.

४९७ केकर खेती केकर गाय पापी होए जेहाँ के जाए
Kekar kheti kekar gāi, pāpi hoe jehāñ ke jāe.

It is neither your field nor your cow; you only make yourself a sinner if you drive it away.

A safe but selfish dictum to prevent any harm coming

from interfering in what does not actually concern you. "It does not concern you if another's field is being grazed by somebody else's cow; if you drive it away, you only incur the sin of keeping a cow hungry." This idea underlies and explains the apathetic attitude and total want of public spirit in the mass of the people towards any reform or public measure, because "it is safer not to interfere in what does not concern them." Mill ascribes this feeling in a people to the previous bad Government under which they have suffered, and which has taught them to regard the law as made for other ends than their good, and its administrators as worse enemies than those who openly violate it. He goes on to say, that while this feeling exists, "a people so disposed cannot be governed with as little power exercised over them as a people whose sympathies are on the side of the law, and who are willing to give active assistance in its enforcement."

The death of a cow, no matter how it occurs, is held a sin, and has to be expiated by feeding Brāhmans and other acts of piety. If a cow dies with a halter round its neck, the person who tied the cow last has to expiate its death. For this reason a cow about to die is unloosed from its halter. If a man kills a cow by accident, he has to undergo severe penalties in the way of feasting Brāhmans and doing other expiatory acts. The man (or woman) through whose fault the cow dies, if poor, goes a-begging with a piece of the cow's tether-rope; and with the alms he thus obtains he feeds Brāhmans. Until this is done the sin is not expiated, and the person remains an outcaste. During this interval the sinning person is not supposed to speak. A good Hindu will never sell his bullock or cow to a butcher; but this rule is hardly adhered to now-a-days.

498. God takes care of a blind cow.

४९८ अँधरी गाय धरम रखवार

Andhri gāi dharam rakhwār.

God provides for a helpless (blind) cow.

A blind cow is supposed to be treated kindly from religious feelings, *i.e.* God takes care of the helpless.

E.E. "The wind is tempered to the shorn lamb."

499. In the prancing of the pack bullock his master is visible.

४९९ बैल न कूदे कूदे गोन ई तमाशा देखे कौन
(या) बैल न कूदे कूदे तङ्गी

Bail na kūde kūde gon, ī tamāsha dekhe kaun.
(or *bail na kūde kūde tangi.*)

A bullock does not leap, but his load does : who ever saw such a sight? (Grierson).

गोन *Gon*, Grain bags and panniers for loaded cattle, here by metonymy for the possessor of the *gon*.

It is not really the bullock that leaps, but his master or supporter (*gon*), *i.e.* his master causes him to jump and prance. Said when one is a mere puppet in the hands of another, at whose instance he is acting—when one is outwardly the actor or doer, but is really put up by another who pulls the wire.

500. The calf leaps presuming on the strength of the tethering peg.

५०० खूँटा का बले बछवो कूदेला

Khūñta ka bale bachhwo kūdela.

The young bull jumps according to the strength of the

post or peg to which it is tied. That is to say, relying
on the strength of its supporter. One is strong or weak (or
exerts his strength) in accordance with the support he gets.

Said when one presumes on another's support or pro-
tection.

501. Rules for selecting cattle.

५०१ वैल वेसाहे चललह कन्त वैल वेसहिहः दू दू दन्त
काछ कसौटी सावर वान ई छाड़ि किनिह मति आन
जबि देखिह रूपा धौर टका चारि दीह उपरौर
ओह पार जब देखिह मैना एही पार से दीह वैना
जब देखिह वैरिया गोल उठ वैठ के करिह मोल
जब देखिह करियवा कन्त कैल गोला देखः जनु दन्त
सरग पताली भाँआँ टेर अपन खाए परोसिये हेर
कैला काबर गोल टिकार ईहो हरिहें दाम तोहार

Bail besāhe chalalah kant, bail besahiha du du dant,
Kāchh kasauti sāwar bān, i chhāri kiniha mati ān,
Jabai dekhiha rūpa dhaur, taka chāri dīha upraur,
Oh pār jab dekhiha maina, chi pār se dīha baina.
Jab dekhiha bairiya gol, uth baith ke kariha mol,
Jab dekhiha kariyawa kant, kail gola dekhah janu dant,
Sarag patāli bhaunāñ ter, apan khāe parosiye her,
Kaila kābar gol tikār, iho harihẽ dām tohār.

(1). My dear, you have started to buy a bullock : be
sure and buy one with only two teeth. Do not buy any
which is not some shade of grey; but if you see a pure
white one, you may advance your price four rupees. If
you see one with loose horns, give handsel without crossing
the road (to look at it more carefully, *i.e.* it is sure to be a
good one). If you see one with a red head and a light
red body, don't buy till you have had a good look at it.

But, my dear, if you see a black or a yellow grey or a red one, don't take the trouble to look at its teeth.

(2). The following is a warning against two kinds of bullocks :—A bullock with horns pointing up and down, or one with crooked eyebrows, injures its master and the neighbours as well.—(Grierson).

(3). A yellow grey, or a speckled, or a red one, or one with a spot on its forehead, will make you lose the price you pay for them.

502. The bullock toils, but the bay horse is pampered.

५०२ पीस कूट मरे बैला बैठल खाय सुरंग

Pis kūt mare baila baithal khāy surang.

The ox wastes himself in labour, while the bay horse gets his grain in ease.

पीस कूट *Pis kūt* is to grind and pound, *i.e.* to labour. Said when any one labours, while another reaps the benefit without exerting himself at all.

सुरंग *Surang* is a light bay horse. The valuable horse is seldom used. He is kept more for show in the stables of the rich.

503. The camel is blamed in the whole army.

५०३ सगरे फौद में ऊँट बदनाम

Sagare phaud men ūñt badnām.

In the whole army the camel is most blamed, because it has such a long neck and exposes the position of the army.

504. You can endure kicks from a milch cow.

५०४ जाहि तें किछु पाइए सहिए कड़ुई बैन
लात खात चुचुकार तें सहत दुधारी धेन

Jāhi teñ kichhu pāie, sahie karui bain,
Lāt khāt chuchukār teñ sahat dudhāri dhen.

From whomsoever you expect to receive benefits, you
must bear abusive words; even while being kicked by a
milch cow, a man will endure its action and pat it
(Grierson).

505. You can endure kicks from a milch cow.

४०५ दुधारि गाय के दू लातो भला

Dudhāri gāe ke du lāto bhala.

Even two kicks from a good milker are to be valued
(Grierson).

A man can bear up without grumbling harsh treatment
from whom he expects some benefit, just as one does not
mind a kick or two from a good milch cow.

506. Points of a milch cow.

४०६ अच्छी गाय बेसाहिये जिसकी कज्जल वान
सोलह सिंघ बत्तीस खुरी नव थन तेरः कान
आँगन बरसे घर भरे बाछा घास न खाय
पहिले दही जमाइ के पीछे कीने गाय

Achchhi gāy besāhiye jiski kajjal bān,
Solah singh, battīs khuri, nao than, terah kān,
Āṅgan barse ghar bhare bāchha ghās na khāy,
Pahile dahi jamāi ke pīchhe kīne gāy.

While you are buying a cow, buy a good one with clear
eyes, and horns 16 fingers (inches) long, hoofs 32, udder
9, and ears 13, and you will then have milk pouring in
your yard and your house full: the calf will also have so
much of it that it will not graze. But remember first to
try the milk for tyre before you buy the cow.

APPENDIX.

POPULAR SUPERSTITIONS AND ERRORS.

INTRODUCTORY NOTES.

It would be a hopeless task to attempt to give a full account of the popular superstitions and errors that encompass the natives of Bihār. Their lives are made up of them. From their birth to their death they afford the guiding clue, and furnish the food on which their hopes and fears are fed. When a child is born, it has to be carefully guarded from the evil spirits that usually hover about the house of its birth. If it gets over the early ailments to which all infants are subject, the cure is ascribed to the charms of some respected old woman of the village who possesses the secret. If it dies, some malignant demon, who has not been propitiated, has carried it away; or some supposed village witch, who has long borne a grudge against the family, has gratified her greed for infant life by causing its death.[1]

---

[1] In cases of difficult labour a gun is fired near the lying-in room, ostensibly to scare away the hobgoblins and evil spirits who delay the birth; but probably with a more practical view to help the birth. As often happens a supposed popular error may really rest on sound practical grounds, which experience has shown to be necessary and is followed empirically. Sir A. Lyall, commenting on this practical feature of superstitious observances, remarks, " Many practices, ascertained empirically to be fit and expedient, have become in course of time so overgrown and concealed by the religious

If any one is unsuccessful in an undertaking, he has failed to propitiate his presiding deity; if successful, his deity has favoured him. At birth, death, marriage, and every important event of life, the gods are consulted; and if their warnings and wishes (now very often interpreted according to the circumstance of the consulter) are not implicitly followed, it is rather from his inability to carry them out in their integrity than from a want of faith in their efficacy.

In Bihār, side by side with signs of civilization, will be found ideas and beliefs which have long ago been eradicated from other more advanced provinces. Lingering and interweaving themselves with the daily thoughts and doings of the people are superstitions such as are to be looked for in vain elsewhere. The civilization as yet is only a thin veneer which has hardly permeated the upper crust. The beliefs and mainsprings of action yet remain the same in the mass of people as they were centuries ago. A thin coating of western varnish gives a specious appearance to the culture which is only skin deep, customs and observances aboriginal and Aryan commingle in one confused jumble, and Muhammadan ceremonies and Hindu rituals are mutually interchanged among the lower order of both classes with a most accommodating and tolerant spirit. There are as many Hindus who zealously keep up the *Muharram tamāsha* in Bihār, as Muhammadans who annually celebrate the *Chhat* and *Holi*. A Hindu woman as piously places her

observances in which they were originally wrapped up, that it is now very difficult to extract the original kernel of utility, and one only hits upon it by accident, when in trying to abolish what looks like a ridiculous and useless superstition, the real object and reason are disinterred, and sometimes proves worth knowing.

votive offering on the grave of the Muhammadan Saint, when her child recovers from illness, as a Musalmān woman propitiates the Hindu demon with a black goat when he has devoured her husband's second love, who had weaned his affection from her. The same rites and ceremonies and observances connected with the daily life of the Bihār peasant are practised in the villages now as they were probably centuries ago, the only difference being that they are adapted to suit the altered circumstances. These would sadly be misplaced in the heart of a great city amid the din and bustle of fashionable civilization, but are not out of keeping with the simple peasantry and the retired scenery of Bihār villages. Of such a vast subject, with so many ramifications, all that can be endeavoured is to give a few instances of the popular superstitions and errors that form the warp and the woof of the Bihār peasant life, principally those which bear on some of the proverbs and illustrate them. The same remarks apply to the other subjects which form the Appendix. The notes under each are far from being complete. They give a few only of the prevailing customs, more as illustrations, than as an exhaustive treatment of the subject.

1. *Names of certain individuals and animals not to be taken.*

There is a popular and widely prevailing idea that the names of certain opprobrious individuals and animals ought not to be uttered in the morning from a superstitious feeling that the utterer is sure to meet with some misfortune during the day; *e.g.* (*a*) The name of any well-known miser is never pronounced in the morning, from an idea that he who takes his name will not get his meals till late in the day, or some misfortune will befall him.[1]

This feeling is sometimes carried to such an extent that some places which are named after a known miser are not pronounced in the morning. For example, a well-known village in Champāran known as Munshi ka bazār (on the Sugau-li Gobindganj road) is never named in the morning, because the man after whom it is named—one Munshi Lāl—was a notorious miser; similarly a village in the Betiya Subdivision, called Bhaluāh, is not pronounced, because its name is akin to that of a bear. (b.) The following animals are not readily named in the morning : Owl, monkey, ass, snake, bear, etc., from an idea that some misfortune is sure to befall the person who names them. (c.) Similarly it is considered unfortunate to meet any of these animals in the morning when one is starting on a journey. To see the face of any of a low caste the first thing in the morning is also considered inauspicious. A *Dhobi*, a *Dom*, and a *Chamār* are especially avoided early in the morning.

2. *Jātra or journey. The superstitions connected with a journey. How augured to be auspicious or not.*

No journey is ever undertaken, in fact nothing of importance is begun, without first consulting the Brāhman as to the best hour for commencing it. The propitious hour having been ascertained, the man who is going on a journey starts at that hour. If, on account of some pressing business or some other cause, he cannot conveniently pursue his journey at that exact hour (as

---

[1] The name of Mīr Gadhaiū, in Patna, is an example of this.

it often happens), still, in order to comply with the requirements of the omen, he makes a show start at the exact auspicious time, and halts a few steps from his house. For this purpose Rajas and well-to-do personages have what are called *jâtra* houses, where (after having left at the exact auspicious hour) they halt and finish their urgent business before finally proceeding on their journey. People who cannot afford to have a *jâtra* house send out some of their wearing apparel with money or grain tied to it in advance, and this is kept in a friend's house on the road till they come up. The grain or money (as the case may be) is afterwards distributed amongst beggars. When starting on a journey, the following are considered good omens to see : —

(*a*) Any one carrying a full chattie of water.

(*b*) A pot of tyre or curd.

(*c*) Fish.

(*d*) A *dhobi* carrying a bundle of clean washed clothes, etc.

The following are considered unlucky omens :—

(*a*) Meeting a *Teli*, or oilman, is considered especially unlucky. (The traveller invariably returns home, postponing his journey.)

(*b*) Meeting a jackal crossing from the right side of the road to the left.

(*c*) If any one should call out to the traveller or put any question to him when he is about to begin his journey it is considered unlucky; also if any one should sneeze or cough at such a time.

3. *Marriages of Tanks and Wells.*

When a tank or well is dug and completed, it is emblematically married to a tree or wooden image, which is planted in the middle in the case of tanks, and alongside in the case of wells. A summary marriage (called *jalotsarg*) is gone through, after which the tank or well is declared to be open for use. This superstitious ceremony is probably gone through with the idea that unless these sources of water are married, the yield will be less plentiful. Mango groves on being planted are also married to a *bar* tree (Indian Ficus), which is planted in the north-east corner (called *Īsān Kōn*) of the tope. A thread is passed round the whole grove, or sometimes only round the first planted tree and the "husband" *bar* tree, and a summary marriage ceremony is gone through: after which the mango grove is declared to be married. Mr. Grierson, in his "Bihār Peasant Life," notes that an emblematical marriage of a grove to a well is also gone through, without which preliminary observance it is unlawful to partake of the fruit.

4. *Divination, and charms, incantations and amulets to cure maladies and keep off or exorcise evil spirits, etc.*

There are various means adopted for foretelling events and of finding out whether an undertaking will succeed or fail. The principal way of course is to consult Brāhmans, who are supposed, from a knowledge of astrology and other sources, to possess the power of foretelling events. But other summary ways are resorted to by the common people to ascertain in a rude and ready manner if what they are about to undertake will prove successful or not; *e.g.* a handful of corn is taken and the grains are divided into pairs: if they come out even, the undertaking will succeed; if odd, it will fail. A sneeze from any one present is considered especially an evil omen when anything is about to be begun, while the "tic-ticking" of the lizard under the same circumstances is considered a favourable omen, because it is supposed to say "right" (*thik*). To find out whether an undertaking will succeed, the women commonly wrap the ends of two pieces of stick with cotton : the sticks are then laid down on a plastered floor, and after a time the wraps are examined. If the cotton has unwound itself in both, the action will meet with complete success; if only in one, a partial success. One way to insure success in an undertaking is to lift that foot first which corresponds to the nostril through which one is breathing harder at the time.

There are numberless charms and spells for curing ailments. From a simple headache to the severest malady, from an ant bite to a snake bite, all are supposed to be curable by means of *mantra* or enchantment and incantations. The marvellous efficacy of spells and charms is ingrained in the native mind ; and though he may resort to medicine, he does it more as an auxiliary remedy than in implicit reliance on its healing powers. If a villager is bit by a mad dog or jackal, he betakes himself to the *Ojha*, or wizard, for the purpose of "extracting" the poison (*jhārab*, literally "to cleanse" or "dust"). The wizard repeats some mystic words over a bowl of water held under the wound, and this water the patient has to drink. After awhile he vomits the water, and along with it the hair of the mad animal that has bit him : this is supposed to effect the cure. They believe implicitly in these enchantments and charms.

Amulets are commonly given when any one suffers from a chronic malady or is liable to certain diseases, and also as phylacteries to preserve the wearer from danger or disease. Of all the grotesque superstitions about the curing of diseases not the least ludicrous is the belief in the healing powers possessed by one born with "feet presentation." A kick from him, or even a touch with his toe, is supposed to effect a ready cure in certain diseases, such as sudden rheumatic pains, etc. And, strange to say, the repeated disappointments which they must have met with have not proved sufficient to disabuse the rustic mind of this love of veneration for natural events which happen to be out of the ordinary. They still cling to a belief in their mysterious healing efficacy.

5. *Superstitious ceremonies and observances connected with birth and death.*

On the birth of a child the following ceremonies and observances are gone through:—All ingress to outsiders is forbidden into the lying-in room. Should any of the inmates have occasion to go out, on returning she has to dust her clothes, and warm her feet and hands over a constant fire that is kept up in the doorway. A torn shoe or the neck of a broken earthen chatty is also hung prominently over the doorway. A scorpion, if found, is also burnt in the fire in the doorway, in the belief that a scorpion sting will have no effect on the child in after-life. A weapon of any kind, such as a sword, a knife, a scythe, or a piece of iron even, is put near the head of the infant to guard it from evil demons. A child born in the month of Bhado (August–September) is especially liable to be attacked by the demon called *Jamhua* (which is really "lockjaw") and is guarded against (or if it has already seized the child it is expelled) by firing off a gun close to the child. In lockjaw the sudden start given to the child often produces a beneficial effect.

On death the following are observed :—The corpse is usually washed in an open spot, and then a bier is made of new bamboos (cut from any one's clump near at hand, an act which is not objected to by the owner), on which the corpse is placed and carried by four men on their shoulders to a place outside the village ; and when all the people who are to accompany the funeral have assembled, they go to the bank of a river. A man is usually shrouded in white, a woman whose husband is living is usually shrouded in coloured clothes. A woman who dies before her husband is considered to be very fortunate. On reaching the bank of the river, a funeral pile is erected, the corpse is placed on it, and, after the chief mourner has anointed its mouth, fire is applied to it by him. He walks round the pile three times and sometimes five times, touches its lips each time with fire, and then sets fire to the pile. The fire is usually bought from a *Dom* (the lowest caste in Bihār), who often sticks out for a fabulous price at this emergency. When the body is nearly burnt, every one present throws five sticks into the fire ; any unburnt portion of the corpse left is thrown into the river, and the spot where the body was cremated is washed and plastered with cowdung, and the chief mourner plants a *tulsi* tree near it. After the corpse has been taken out of the house the latter is washed and plastered over, and the following are placed in the doorway or gate of the house : a stone, cowdung, iron, fire, and water for the people to touch on their return from the cremation. On the tenth day after the corpse has been cremated, all the male relatives of the deceased shave their

heads, and those who are sons of the deceased their
moustaches also.　On this occasion the *Kautāha* Brahman
who performs such obsequies is fed and receives as his fee
the wearing apparel of the deceased.　After this the
Brahmans are fed on the thirteenth day after the death
among Brahmans, on the fourteenth day among Vaisyas,
and on the sixteenth day among Sudras.　On this day the
widow of the deceased is clothed in her widow's garment
and henceforth she has to undergo all the penances of her
sad lot.

6. *Planting trees.*

It is considered an act of virtue to plant groves.　Certain
trees, especially the venerated *Pīpal*, the *Bar*, the *Pankar*,
the *Bel*, are the favourite dwelling-places of the deities,
and the gods are supposed " to delight to sit among its
leaves and listen to the music of their rustling," and to
them votive offerings of flags, etc., are made.　They are
hung from the tree itself, or attached to a bamboo which
is erected close to it.　It is considered unlucky to plant a
plum tree near the entrance door, for its thorny branches
are apt to catch the turban every time the dweller comes
out of his house and thus cover his head, which is considered very unlucky.

7. *Manner of detecting thieves.*

A common practice is to weigh out rice with the
Muhammadan rupee, known as (*chār yāri rupiya*) the four
friends of Muhammad, and to give each one of the persons
suspected the weight of a rupee to swallow.　It is said the
thief finds it difficult to masticate and cannot swallow the
dry rice through fear.　There is much practical shrewdness
and knowledge of the people in this device, as the thief

naturally finds it difficult to bring up a quantity of saliva (through fear) to enable him to swallow the rice, and thus betrays himself. Another test, practised by Mahammadans chiefly, is to write down the names of all who are suspected on slips of paper and throw them one by one, rolled up (as in a lottery), into a small chatty. While this is being done two men hold the chatty (by its neck or brim) on their finger ends, and particular *suras* or passages are read from the Kurān. On the slip containing the thief's name being thrown into the chatty, it turns round immediately, which discloses the thief. There are other tests of boiled *ghi* and oil; but these are never resorted to now.

    8. *Charms, spells, and incantations gone through*

        (*a.*) *To bring on rain.*

        (*b.*) *To stop rain.*

(*a.*) The following are gone through to cause rain to fall:

A number of village boys, with faces blackened and in white *dhotis*, leap on all-fours in the open air, in imitation of frogs, calling out all the time, " *Kāla kaloti ujjar dhoti. Pāni de, pāni de,*" i.e. " We have made ourselves black as soot with white *dhotis*. Pray give us rain, pray give us rain!" This is sometimes varied by a few of the boys turning "frogs," and some others playing with sticks on drums made of old sieves. Thus they go before the doors of the villagers. On their approach, the women throw a *ghaila* of water, in which the frogs wallow, "croaking" all the time:

        Alla mīyāñ pāni da,

        Khapra meñ (or *doki men*) *du dāna da.*

"God give us rain, so that we may have two grains

(*i.e.* even a little food) in our earthen platter." Alms are given by each house, and from the collection thus made a feast is held. Brāhmans are also feasted by the well-to-do, if rain holds off for long.

(*b.*) The following are gone through to cause rain to stop:

If the rain continues too long, (1) weights (used in weighing) are dropped into a well; (2) a *chirāg* (or oil lamp) is lit and put on a *mūsal* (pestle for pounding paddy), which is erected in the compound in the open air; (3) some figures are drawn with chalk on walls by the women and are worshipped; (4) in Shāhabad a piece of stick is dressed up as a doll, with a small bundle of grain in one hand and a lighted torch in the other. This effigy is then put up on a pole in the yard. It is called "Musāfar," or "Wayfarer," "Traveller," and is intended to invoke the pity of the god of rain, who, it is supposed, will relent and cause the rain to stop, and thus enable the benighted traveller to find his way home to his family with what he is carrying for them. The young folks in the meantime keep up a vigorous drumming with sieves and sticks, shouting all the while the following:

Chalni meñ āñta bādar phāta.

(Flour in the sieve, the clouds will disperse now.) (5) Also a *chirāg* is lit inside a *dehri* (a wicker basket for storing away grain in) and kept lighted till the rain stops.

HINDI VERBAL INDEX.

(The Numbers refer to the Proverb.)

॥ ख kh ॥

॥ ग g ॥

‖ ट t ‖

टकही takahi, 79.
टका taka, 37.
टके सेर take ser, 63.
टहरा tahra, 343.
टाटी tāti, 76.
टाप tāp, 347.
टिटही titahi, 108.
टीकर tikar, 501.
टुकुर टुकुर tukur tukur, 186.
टेटर tetar, 96.
टोना tona, 359.

‖ ठ th ‖

ठग thag, 283.
ठठा thatha, 115.
ठाकुर thākur, 262.
ठाढ thārh, 30.
ठाँव thāoṅ, 203, 275.
ठिकरिओ thikrio, 240.
ठुठी thuthi, 126.
ठेंगा theṅga, 313.
ठेस thes, 26.
ठेहुना thehuna, 205.
ठोर thor, 313.

‖ ड d ‖

डन्ड डोर danda dor, 32.
डाक dāk, 447, 449, 468.
डाकिनी dākini, 468.

डाढी darhi, 310.
डाही dāhi, 29.
डेउढी deurhi, 73.
डेयौढा dyaurha, 487.
डोइ doi, 175.
डोम dom, 233.
डोली doli, 243.

‖ ढ dh ‖

ढीठो dhītho, 321.
ढेंढर dheṅrhar, 96.
ढेबुआ dhebua, 221.
ढोल dhol, 382.

‖ त t ‖

तङ्गी tangi, 499.
तता पानोँ tata pāniṅ, 365.
तमाशा tamāsha, 305, 499.
तानी tāni, 55.
ताड़ी tāri, 36.
तारी tāri, 288.
ताल tāl, 164.
तिलक tilak, 19.
तीत tīt, 5, 384.
तीयन tīan, 250.
तील tīl, 475.
तीसी tīsi, 200, 309.
तुलशी दास tulshi dās, 41.
तुरुक turuk, 287, 288.
तेल tel, 200, 229, 239.
तेली teli, 296, 319, 375.

तेवासी tewāsi, 44.
तोता tota, 287.

‖ थ th ‖

थाती thāti, 161.
थूरों thūroñ, 198.

‖ द d ‖

दतुली datuli, 369.
दौतन dataun, 45.
दन्त daut, 501.
दमाद damād, 335, 352.
दरजी darji, 270, 274.
दरबार darbār, 92.
दर दरबार dar darbār, 398.
दरवेश darwesh, 78.
दहिजरू dahijaru, 391.
दही dahi, 205.
दाढी dārhi, 290.
दादा dāda, 91.
दाँत dāñt, 3, 246, 369.
दाल dāl, 205, 355.
दिगम्बर digambar, 94, 275.
दीद dīd, 389.
दीन dīn, 15, 61, 440.
दुआरी duāri, 141.
दुधारी dudhāri, 505.
दुपहरिया dupaharia, 117.
दुम कजा dum kaja, 224.
दुलह dullah, 99.

दूध dūdh, 52.
दूवर dūbar, 493.
देयाल deyāl, 383.
देवकुर deokur, 404.
देवता deota, 283.
देबी Debi, 315, 316.
देवर dewar, 324.
देस des, 165.
दोख dokh, 277.
दोबर dobar, 487.
दौरा daura, 82.

‖ ध dh ‖

धन dhan, 105, 178, 344, 488.
धनहा dhanaha, 477.
धनी dhani, 170.
धान dhān, 64, 261, 444, 486.
धीया dhīya, 329, 335.
धीरा dhīra, 313.
धूप dhūp, 179.
धैल dhail, 401, 410.
धोखा dhokha, 254.
धोती dhoti, 80.
धोबी dhobi, 271, 272, 283, 490.
धोबीन dhobīn, 133.

‖ न n ‖

नकटा nakta, 193.
नकटी nakti, 425.
नखूना nakhūna, 253.

‖ प p ‖

रानीँ rānīn̐, 367.
रिरियाय ririyāy, 477.
रुखान rukhān, 267.
रूपा rūpa, 501.
रूसल rūsal, 185.
रेँड़ reṅr, 184.
रैन rain, 482.
रोइ रोइ roi roi, 158.
रोग rog, 393.
रोगिया rogiya, 388.
रोहु rohu, 196.
रोहन rohan, 445, 447.

॥ ल l ॥

लकड़ी lakari, 38.
लगाम lagām, 300.
लटल latal, 324.
लड़िका larika, 11, 47, 276.
लड्डु laddu, 192, 281.
लबार labār, 43.
लमेरा lamera, 40.
लमैचर lamaichar, 40.
लम्बी lambi, 80, 81, 313.
लरिकन larikan, 119, 154.
लाख lākh, 43.
लाजे lāje, 321.
लाठी lāthi, 195, 257, 448.
लात lāt, 183, 227.
लालबही lāl bahi, 375.
लिलार lilār, 19, 79.
लीक līk, 400.

लुआठ luāth, 210.
लुकवारी lukwari, 146.
लुखरी lukhari, 484.
लुगरी lugari, 136.
लेखे lekhe, 276.
लोक lok, 332.
लोकदिन lokdin, 326.
लोग log, 318.
लोरिक lorik, 256.
लोहार lahār, 254, 295.
लौका lauka, 210.
लौर laur, 33, 186, 188.
लँका lan̐ka, 29.
लँगटा langta, 116.

॥ स s ॥

सगरा sagara, 482.
सगरे sagare, 153.
सँझवत san̐jhwat, 83.
सतो sati, 400.
सत्तू sattu, 351, 429.
सताउन sataun, 45.
सन्तोख santokh, 17, 277.
सनसनाहट sansanāhat, 183.
सँसार san̐sār, 182.
सनीचर sanichar, 469.
सपूत sapūt, 323.
सप्तमी saptmi, 454, 455, 456,
457, 458.
सपहेरो sapaheri, 51.
समधिन samdhin, 103.

हरिवंस haribans, 265.
हरियरे hariyare, 244.
हलुआई haluāi, 358.
हाकिम hākim, 197.
हाट hāt, 164.
हाँड़ी hāṅri, 71.
हाथी hāthi, 3, 246, 349.
हारल hāral, 213.

हाही hāhi, 17.
हींग hiṅg, 417.
हीरा hira, 413.
हुकल hukal, 23.
हुँड़ार hunrār, 130.
हुमना humna, 298.
हुरों hūroṅ, 198.
हंसी hansi, 158.

STEPHEN AUSTIN AND SONS, PRINTERS, HERTFORD.